Liminal High School

Shirley R. Steinberg
Series Editor

Vol. 561

Liminal High School

Life as a Teacher Student

Edited by
David P. Owen, Jr.

New York · Berlin · Bruxelles · Chennai · Lausanne · Oxford

Library of Congress Cataloging-in-Publication Data

Names: Owen, David P., Jr., 1977- editor
Title: Liminal high school : life as a teacher student / edited by David P. Owen, Jr.
Description: New York : Peter Lang, 2025. | Series: Counterpoints, 1058-1634 ; vol. 561 | Includes bibliographical references.
Identifiers: LCCN 2025004136 (print) | LCCN 2025004137 (ebook) | ISBN 9781636676548 paperback | ISBN 9781636676555 pdf | ISBN 9781636676562 epub
Subjects: LCSH: High school teachers—United States. | Teachers—Education (Continuing education) | Teachers—Professional relationships—United States.
Classification: LCC LB1620 .L56 2025 (print) | LCC LB1620 (ebook) | DDC 373.1102—dc23/eng/20250430
LC record available at https://lccn.loc.gov/2025004136
LC ebook record available at https://lccn.loc.gov/2025004137

Bibliographic information published by the Deutsche Nationalbibliothek.
The German National Library lists this publication in the German National Bibliography; detailed bibliographic data is available on the Internet at http://dnb.d-nb.de.

Cover design by Peter Lang Group AG
Cover illustration: © "November", by Courtney Rae Hancock Owen

ISSN 1058-1634 (print)
ISBN 9781636676548 (paperback)
ISBN 9781636676555 (ebook)
ISBN 9781636676562 (epub)
DOI 10.3726/b22802

© 2025 Peter Lang Group AG, Lausanne
Published by Peter Lang Publishing Inc., New York, USA
info@peterlang.com - www.peterlang.com

All rights reserved.
All parts of this publication are protected by copyright.
Any utilization outside the strict limits of the copyright law, without the permission of the publisher, is forbidden and liable to prosecution.
This applies in particular to reproductions, translations, microfilming, and storage and processing in electronic retrieval systems.

This publication has been peer reviewed.

DEDICATION

For Courtney and Patrick, of course.

CONTENTS

Acknowledgments   xi

Inventing Scholarly Lives   xiii
John A. Weaver

Introduction: Inventing Hope   1
David P. Owen, Jr.

Chapter 1. Humble Beginnings   7
Jack D. Arrington

Chapter 2. Conducting the Orchestra   11
Jack D. Arrington

Chapter 3. Trials and Triumphs: A Timeline of My Teaching Journey   23
Kathleen E. Barbara

Chapter 4. Spanish Language Success Stories: Insights from My Most Achieved Learners   31
Kathleen E. Barbara

Chapter 5.	The Space Between the Wall and the Bed *Stacey T. Brown*	55
Chapter 6.	Teacher on Trial: The Case of the Public Intellectual *Stacey T. Brown*	63
Chapter 7.	Seeking the Fundamental, Elegant, and Simple *John H. Cato*	79
Chapter 8.	The High A: Opera's Highest Note Should Be Education's, Too *John H. Cato*	85
Chapter 9.	Never Say Never *Mary K. Davis*	105
Chapter 10.	The Power Struggle in Education *Mary K. Davis*	113
Chapter 11.	Dr. Coach Davis *Thomas J. Davis*	131
Chapter 12.	Athletics and Education: All Men Were Created Equal, Then Some Became Athletes *Thomas J. Davis*	139
Chapter 13.	An Educator's Path: Journey of an Unexpected Teacher *Kay R. Lilly*	157
Chapter 14.	Building Bridges: Ensuring Every Voice Is Heard Within the Social Studies Classroom *Kay R. Lilly*	163
Chapter 15.	Finding Anchorage *Dawn R. May*	179

Chapter 16.	The Ontology of Metamodernism and the Reconstruction of Human Civility *Dawn R. May*	187
Chapter 17.	How Way Leads on to Way *David P. Owen, Jr.*	201
Chapter 18.	Getting the Big Screen Through a Small Door: Film and the High School Classroom *David P. Owen, Jr.*	207
	Notes on Contributors	225

ACKNOWLEDGMENTS

I first want to thank my family for never telling me not to try things, or take chances; liminality has its costs, but they never told me to be anyone or anything else, and for that I am eternally grateful. And speaking of costs, I'd also like to acknowledge how hard this work is for the teachers featured in this book. As I've said in other places, there is very little time or career incentive for teachers to do theoretical work and contribute to fields of research, and so I'm really proud to be a part of this group of authors who do it anyway. I'm also proud to be working again with Shirley Steinberg, John Weaver, and Peter Lang, and I'm thankful for the support they've given my career. Finally, and most importantly, I thank God for another day to do this kind of thing.

INVENTING SCHOLARLY LIVES
John A. Weaver

This is our second go around, David and me. If you count serving as his dissertation chair then it is our third, but it is our second with David editing a book. I decided to do something different for this preface. One of the disturbing trends in education fields like curriculum studies is that few scholars read other scholars' work. Peter Appelbaum and I recently edited a special issue for *The Journal of the American Association for the Advancement of Curriculum Studies* on data and algorithms. A few of the participants posted on Facebook that the issue was published, and numerous colleagues wrote their congratulations and promised to read the essays. To my knowledge, no one has read these articles. These friends and colleagues were not being mean spirited, but sincere. They just were not going to fulfill their promise. This is why I rarely think about my audience when I write. I cannot make someone read, nor do I want to, unless you are my student—then you have no choice. You will read! But even then, there have been students who were faking it and playing a game. So, I am going to do something different in this preface. I am not going to write something pronouncing how this book is important and others should read it. I will not write a lengthy explanation of why you, as a teacher and a scholar, should read this book. I am writing this preface to the chapter writers, most of whom I taught, chaired their dissertations, or served on their committees. I applaud your commitments to reading and writing. You are scholars, and never give that title up. Schooling, as you know, will suck the intellectual soul out of your body and laugh at your lifeless teacher corpse as the administrative, political, and capitalistic buzzards circle around you. Fight back from these political, economic, and (ill)cultural forces by reading more, writing more, and thinking incessantly. We few scholars at the university, and there are only a few of us left, desperately need and crave companionship. We need, like you, people to talk to about books and ideas.

Quickly, what do I mean by inventing a scholar's life? By "inventing" I mean living a scholarly life must be nurtured every day, or it withers away and dies a tragic, lonely death. As scholars we get to invent our work. Please invent; very few get to define our work conditions. To be a scholar you must read almost every day. If you do not crave reading, then you are not a scholar. There is no way around it. Once you have mastered the art of reading, you need to put your thoughts down in some coherent structure so your peers can critique, judge, respect, and, hopefully, honor you. It can be a frustrating and risky endeavor, but there is no better way than peer review from a community of scholars. Sometimes they make good suggestions, but always they know your field of study. Some within the field may let you down or steer you in the wrong direction, but the whole community of scholars never will. Finally, inventing yourself as a scholar means thinking without much pause. Thinking *through* is necessary no matter the topic; thinking intently and letting answers emerge without a time frame in mind is sage advice even for teachers who are required "to think on their feet." Thinking *with* is necessary. With colleagues, ideas, inspiration, dedication, perseverance, and curiosity—these are all essential. Thinking philosophically should be nurtured. This means diving deep into the traditions of Western, Eastern, Latinx, Indigenous, African, Judaic, Aboriginal, Feminist, Queer, and Subcontinental thought and letting those traditions take you on a journey where you do not know where you will end up. It means thinking historically, culturally, sociologically, anthropologically, theologically, artistically, and even economically, too. This is what I mean by inventing a scholarly life.

If by chance you are not one of the contributors of this book, good. Read it. Be a scholar, learn from it, and create something else from it.

My Friend David

Robert Pogue Harrison wrote these words in his book *Forests* (1992, p. 238): "for when a nation loses its poets it loses access to the meaning of dwelling. When it loses the meaning of dwelling, it loses the means to build ... for when a nation ignores its poets it becomes a nation of the homeless."

The United States of America is a mess because of the willful choice they made to shun poets and embrace hucksters. I have said this many times, but I will write it down for the first time. U.S.A.: where the S stands for "suckers." What a delusional people the U.S.A. citizens are. You and I are U.S.A. citizens, yet we are not delusional. It is because we did not, like so many of our peers, reject the path of the poets. We embraced them instead. I think this is why we gravitated towards each other when you were a student. We read different people, but we shared similar ideas about what life is. We learned from our teachers and professors to dwell not in a house filled with possessions and a garage with three cars plus our vacation house at the shore (I am from Eastern Pennsylvania) and in the mountains. We dwell in a well-built home enveloped by the embrace of books. We are dwelling poetically in the madness, figuring out—as you note in your introductory chapter—how to steal time for reading. You are a great thief, and this book shows everyone that. Actually, it does not take much to be a great thief of time for reading. If one wishes to steal time to read, one will find it no matter what. This is why you continue to be a scholar. You have created your own work, live at your own pace, and while so many around you are frazzled and bedazzled by shiny objects on social media, there you are, setting your own path with a poetic goal in mind. You have built your own dwelling.

David—No, the Other David

Hi David. I have never met you, but I have read about you. You mentioned noise in your autobiographical chapter and appropriately defined noise in schools as meetings, duties, emails and the like. Let me add to your idea of noise to include unfunded mandates from state legislatures who purposely add more work to teachers and administrators but no extra funds to hire new teachers, and interference from businesspeople who think they know best and wish to turn every school from kindergarten to graduate school into a technical school so they can find cheap, docile labor. In this noise, the actual purpose of education gets lost. Students and their intellectual development are almost completely lost in educational systems. Students have been reduced to economic entities whose sole purpose in life is to get a job and buy things. That is not life; that is inhumane treatment and soullessness. Teachers are lost, too. They are merely information, not knowledge, conduits which students are to plug into and download information. This too is not life; it is spiritless, mere existence.

I want to share with you a quote from the French philosopher Michel Serres and present to you a modest proposal. In his book *Parasite* (1980/2007, p. 14), Serres writes, "a parasite is responsible for the growth of the system's complexity, such a parasite stops it ... are we in the pathology of systems or in their emergence and evolution?" For Serres a parasite is a source of noise. It can be a disrupting knowledge-less noise, or it can be a productive, meaningful, awe-inspiring noise. What kind of noise is an educational system? Is it one that is pathological, or is it one that creates, invents, emerges with new meaning and purpose every year as the students change? This is your challenge. What kind of noise is your school creating? Is it mind-numbing, standardized, politically-safe and chamber-of-commerce-approved noise which will require more meetings, more classroom time disruption, and more teacher alienation—or is it uncertain, risky, intellectual, creative noise emanating from students and teachers?

My modest proposal for you is this: help your administration do everything to open up your school to new, thoughtful ideas that do not come from sanctioned sources like leadership programs or other outside sources. Instead of latching onto the latest "how to ..." and "the secret to ..." books, return to the classics and share the vision of different educators. Share with your teachers and students Robert Frost's vision of education that he develops in "Education by Poetry" (1931). Yes, poets have long thought about the importance of education, and they have never followed easy steps or passed a standardized test. Then turn to another poet, Audre Lorde, and read her "Poet as Teacher—Human as Poet—Teacher as Human" (2009). She will not let you down. You will see teaching differently. Once you do read these, do not stop. Enter the journey that leads you into areas you never thought existed but now seem essential to your life. Once you do this, then create your orchestra and invite teachers and administrators to join you. When they do, and they will because they will see the positive changes in you, the meetings will diminish, the emails will subside, and the noise will change. Then invite the parents, and once the parents are in your orchestra, then the politicians and businesspeople can be held at bay because their vision of an education is the very essence of pathological noise.

Kathleen: Will's 69.4 and the Many Masks of Utility

Kathleen, I remember "Will" from your dissertation. It is always disconcerting to hear about or see students who value little except that which they think is useful. Then I think of where they got such a notion of life and education. Students who view learning as an economic transaction are only parrots who hear it from adults like their parents, businesspeople, and even sadly their teachers. I want to share a passage from Virginia Woolf's wonderful book, A Room of One's Own (1929/1981, p. 47): "She picked a book up now and again, one of her brother's perhaps, and read a few pages. But then her parents came in and told her to mend the stockings or mind the stew and not moon about with books and papers." Make sure your students moon over books, papers, and ideas in Spanish, English, or another language. Languages are important to master, but it does not matter which ones. Will is at peace with his 69.4 because he lost the ability to moon over. The difference between Woolf's fictional female character and Will is Woolf's character had her mooning privileges taken away from her and Will's were extinguished through the inculcation of wrong values. Both, though, share this in common. Utility, or the vision of what is useful, was the culprit behind their denial of an education. Woolf's character was a woman. She was supposed to darn socks, mind stew, and do useful household chores. Will, as a male, is supposed to get an education so he can get a job. Spanish will not get him a job, he so mistakenly has been told and now assumes to be true, so he can buy things and rev that economic engine that defines so many people's lives. Your task as a teacher is to never use utility as a rationale for why Spanish as a second language or third is so very important. Spanish, like any second or third language, opens up the world to new possibilities and never lets the multi-lingual person down. Every day becomes an adventure when utility is abandoned in education. With utility checked at the schoolhouse door, Will has no more purpose for defining a 69.4 as good enough. 69.4 becomes meaningless, and anything short of fluency is not acceptable, even if he were to turn that 69.4 into a 96.4. Those numbers are the result of a utility-based society; multi-lingual speakers are a result of a better world.

Stacey the Landlubber?

Stacey, your metaphors are strong in this book. You have always coveted solitude, and I know why and where that was nurtured. Can one ever read Whitman or Serres and not covet solitude? When you wrote of the seas of solitude, I immediately thought of Serres's imagery of how the learner must leave the embankment, cross the waters, and return to another embankment, forever changing those waters and themselves. You are not the same person you were when you entered the Curriculum Studies program at Georgia Southern University. Any educational experience that does not transform a person is not an educational experience. It is indoctrination. It is time, though, for you to enter those seas again and say goodbye to a land you have moored yourself to. I noticed you referred to Sabrina and me as "Drs." Of course we are. We earned that title and most importantly the degree. This earning of a terminal degree means we earned the right to educate ourselves, and that is what we did and continue to do. It is your turn. We are not "Doctors" to you anymore. We are passing islands of solitude on your seaward journey searching for your own island. It is time to depart again, this time leaving behind old formalities and texts you read while a student. These texts shaped who you are, and they are old friends you can always count on. But it is time to leave the friendly confines of your formal educational neighborhoods and find new companions, new ideas, and new forms of solitude. Alfred Whitehead (1929/1967, p. 39), whom you cite and understand, also wrote these words that I share with you:

> Education is the guidance of the individual towards a comprehension of the art of life; and by the art of life I mean the most complete achievement of varied activity expressing the potentialities of that living creature in the face of its actual environment.

Your actual environment can be all that you dread—meetings, standardized testing, homogeneous thought, and isolation, but that is not what Whitehead meant by life or actual environment. Your life and environment are for you to create. What will you read to create your environment? What thoughts will emerge? What will you write that is free from your intellectual past and part of your new, emerging future? Once you figure this out, place a message in a bottle and send it adrift. It will reach my island eventually, and in my solitude, I will read it with joy. I will reminisce of the times we spent with common books and ideas, and I will revel in what you created on your own.

The Simple Eloquence of John Cato

I am sure you remember, John, that in *Field Theory* (Owen, 2019) I called you a liar. You may think I have changed my opinion of you, since now I am suggesting you are simply eloquent. No, I still think you are a liar—a really good liar—and I still think that paper you wrote for me in our ethics class is one the best papers I have read. Calling you a liar and eloquent is just my way of saying I like your style. I want to share with you a thought from Michel Serres's (1995/2017, pp. 172–173) book *Geometry: The Third Book of Foundations*:

> Observe with what precision all the elements of an algorithm are put in place: the path or method to reach a goal, the practical and simple finality of a mechanism, the exact measurement of the segment traveled, the decomposition of the process into elements, the step-by-step procedure ... the repetition that is repeated in the figure and the form, in the scene and for number, the same action to be done after the same action done, the very probable deviation from a fable.

As you seek out simple eloquence, and there is absolutely no reason to stop searching for it, in your classroom, always remember in spite of all the precision of algorithms, the tight methods, simplicity of a mechanism, the exact measurement, and the step-by-step procedures that make life seemingly easier, predictable, or manageable, there are stories, fables, by which we live. It is the complex eloquence of the stories that we humans tell ourselves that make the search for simply eloquent classrooms possible. Another way to put this is wherever there are eloquent physics classrooms and laboratories, there is messy, necessary, life-affirming art. Physics and art have been separated by our society because it is simpler, which is never simply eloquent, to compartmentalize than to contemplate entanglements, but physics and art go together naturally. It is always your job as an excellent teacher to sort that whole mess out through the stories you tell your students. You already know this and if you told me otherwise you would be lying.

Mary Davis Should Never Say Never

Let me tell you a story about one of my favorite books. Back when I began reading in the history, philosophy, sociology, and anthropology of science in the early 1990s, there were still Borders bookstores. Remember those? There were two in Pittsburgh. I lived in the northeast part of Pittsburgh called Turtle Creek (pronounced in Pittsburgh as "Crick") so the Borders on the Southside was closer. I would drive 45 minutes to get there, winding through dying old steel mill (in Pittsburgh pronounced "still") communities to get there. When I arrived, it was like traveling through purgatory to get to nirvana. Borders was as close as a scholar could get to their kind of bookstore at the national chain level. One day I came across a book edited by Andrew Pickering titled *Science as Practice and Culture* (1992). It was not the first book in my science endeavors that I read, because I already knew most of the chapter writers in the book like Bruno Latour, Karin Knorr, Michel Callon, Steve Fuller, and Steve Woolgar. So when I got my copy, I marked each chapter I was going to read. Then I came across the last chapter, which was on Japanese physicists.

I said to myself and maybe out loud, "Who in the hell is interested in Japanese physicists?" After I read all the chapters I wanted to read, I thought what the heck, let's see what Japanese physicists have to offer me. Would you not know it, Sharon Traweek's anthropological study of these physicists was the most interesting chapter in the whole book, and to this day whatever Traweek writes (now her focus is on astronomy and technology), I make sure to read it. When we never give into the temptation of saying never, we never find ourselves without surprises. There are plenty of Sharon Traweek's in the world, we just have to search for them and always keep our minds open. My "never say never" moment was a book and a now defunct bookstore. Yours was a southern college and teaching. Look what you would be missing if you did say never to both? For the record, you were right to draw the line at the Alabama border.

T.J., What Do You Tell a Pitcher When You Visit the Mound?

I know you are a literature teacher and a baseball coach. I knew this before you wrote these chapters for this book. I also knew about your heart abnormality. I often worried that like so many in the U.S.A., you would reverse the flow of our educational values and pump out vibes to your students that baseball was more important to you than literature. I have a solution to my worries. Did you ever see the movie *Bull Durham* (1988)? It is not my favorite baseball movie; that is reserved for *A Field of Dreams* (1989), *A League of Their Own* (1992), and *Eight Men Out* (1988), but it is a really good movie. There is a scene where Tim Robbins is visibly rattled on the mound by his father's presence at the game, so Kevin Costner as the catcher visits to ask what is going on. Before we know it, the whole infield is on the mound discussing a curse on the first baseman's glove and Jimmy and Millie's upcoming wedding. Robert Wuhl, the pitching coach, visits and asks what is going on. Costner informs the coach of the dilemma, and Wuhl replies that candlesticks always make a nice gift, and that maybe he should find out where she is registered for a nice china set.

It is scenes like this that remind me that Walt Whitman was right when he wrote in the 1880s that "base-ball is our game: the American game: I connect it with our national character" (Folsom, 1994, p. 42). I know football is now more popular than base-ball, but this does not, nor will it ever, change the fact that base-ball is our national pastime. We can lose football from our cultural conscientiousness and everyday reality, but if we were to ever lose base-ball we would lose our national identity. I want your base-ball players to always remember that you are a literature teacher first and base-ball is a luxury, because no matter how important base-ball is to our national identity, if we lose literature and poetry we lose our souls as human beings. No one can recover from such a loss. So next time you visit the mound in a not-so-tight situation, I do not want you to recommend that the players buy candlesticks for a wedding gift. Instead, I want you to go up to the mound and cite from memory a stanza or two from your favorite poet just so those players know what is most important in their lives. I know you will do it, because even though your heart pumps blood in the opposite direction, your heart has always been in the right place, right there with Whitman and the other great literary figures of our nation.

Kay, You Have Chosen Wisely

Like David Arrington, we have not met, but in reality, in the intellectual realm that is, we most certainly have met. When you purposely decided to challenge what was etched in the political sand of sanctioned curriculum, we were on the same path—a path of intellectual curiosity and wonder. It can be a lonely path, because there are few people who choose it. Most are like whitewater rafters. They enter choppy waters with all the other people, hang on for dear life, and just go with the flow. They never think to go down a different river. They are content with what is, and never think to question what is, or imagine that there is a different path to follow. When they come across someone like yourself, they do not curiously ask "what is that person doing different? It seems to be working better." Instead, they form gossip groups and wonder what is wrong with you. They doubt you for questioning the dominant assumptions that dictate the school days. But once you realize the certainty of your path, the loneliness disappears, and the judgment of peers no longer matters. What matters is all the ways you have developed as an intellectual, and that your students appreciate your sincere concerns for their intellectual development.

Selecting a different path and overcoming your doubts does not mean everything will go smoothly. Gossipers will begin to undermine you, and the forces of political power will seek to contain you. When this happens, remember your Nietzsche. If you have never read Nietzsche, he is your friend and can serve as an important guide along your new pathway. In *The Gay Science* (1974, p. 259), Nietzsche shares this aphorism with his readers:

> Living in a constant chase after gain compels people to expend their spirit to the point of exhaustion ... Virtue has come to consist of doing something in less time than someone else. Hours in which honesty is permitted have become rare.

If you have not already found out, your new pathway will feed and sustain you along the way. When others are exhausted because the race for test scores, job satisfaction surveys, countless meetings, and incessant banter over test score points and extra credit will tire them out, their zest for life will diminish while yours will only grow. Yours will grow because you did not take the easy path; you took the one you are still creating. Please do not stop creating. We have enough virtuous teachers who create nothing. We need more hours of honesty from people like you.

What Is Your Business, Dawn May?

I will not ask you what business does a Spanish teacher have philosophizing, because it is everyone's business to be a philosopher. This does not make everyone an entrepreneur, because the business of philosophy is no business at all. This is why businesspeople are so interested in education. They are worried that students will discover the beauty and wonder of life and then not settle for being groomed as cheap labor and righteous consumers of wasteful things. A Spanish teacher turning to philosophy scares them, too. All the more reason to philosophize, Dawn! But putting businesspeople and business-thinking administrators aside, there are more important reasons for you to turn to philosophy. Philosophy requires that you think thoroughly through ideas that matter. I am not talking about your philosophy of teaching and life. When most people talk about a philosophy of teaching or life, it usually is code for not thinking at all. The point of a mere Spanish teacher turning to philosophy is to realize that what we think is the truth is nothing but a mirage of lies. Once the lies are removed, then the real challenge presents itself. We have to create meaning from a meaningless world. Now this is philosophy! As you turn to philosophy more, remember the words of the poet Mark Burkhard (Ruefle, 2017, p. 25): "keep in mind that the very act of writing is an imaginative act, ... Even memory is an act of imagination, you never tell the same story twice, not even to yourself." As you read more philosophy and think more intently, you are recreating yourself and reality. You and reality are never the same twice. It changes with every new thought you shape. This truth is the same for your students. The more they begin to think philosophically, the more they change, and the more the world around them changes. Your classroom and their life are never the same the day after a pedagogical epiphany. This is why a Spanish teacher needs to turn to philosophy.

References

Folsom, E. (1994). *Walt Whitman's native representations*. Cambridge Press.

Frost, R. (1931, February). Education by poetry. *Amherst Graduates' Quarterly*. Amherst College.

Harrison, R. (1992). *Forests: The shadow of civilization*. University of Chicago Press.

Lorde, A. (2009). Poet as teacher—Human as poet—Teacher as human. In R. P. Byrd, J. B. Cole, & B. Guy-Sheftall (Eds.), *I am your sister: Collected and unpublished writings of Audre Lorde* (pp. 182–183). Oxford University Press.

Marshall, P. (Director). (1992). *A league of their own* [Film]. Columbia Pictures; Parkway Productions.

Nietzsche, F. (1974). *The gay science* (Walter Kaufmann Trans.). Vintage Press.

Owen, D. P., Jr. (Ed.). (2019). *Field theory: Curriculum studies at work*. DIO Press.

Pickering, A. (1992). *Science as practice and culture*. University of Chicago Press.

Robinson, P. A. (Director). (1989). *Field of dreams* [Film]. Gordon Company.

Ruefle, M. (2017). *On imagination*. Sarabande Books.

Sayles, J. (Director). (1988). *Eight men out* [Film]. Orion Pictures.

Serres, M. (1980/2007). *The parasite*. University of Minnesota Press.

Serres, M. (1995/2017). *Geometry: The third book of foundations*. Bloomsbury Press.

Shelton, R. (Director). (1988). *Bull Durham* [Film]. The Mount Company.

Whitehead, A. (1929/1967). *The aims of education*. The Free Press.

Woolf, V. (1929/1981). *A room of one's own*. A Harvest Book.

INTRODUCTION: INVENTING HOPE
David P. Owen, Jr.

> Out of some persistent sense of large-scale ruin, we kept inventing hope.
> –Don DeLillo, *White Noise*, 1984, p. 141

Anyone who has read *White Noise* is likely to tell you that it is a "masterpiece of postmodernism," and a "reflection on how alienating modern American life can be" (Kisner, 2023, p. 73), and I am one of those people. Jordan Kisner also claims that the novel manages to "render visible (or audible, if we want to follow DeLillo's metaphor) aspects of social and political life that have been normalized into near invisibility" (p. 75), and I would add that what DeLillo notices about 1984 is also often present in 2025, in ways that are bothersome and profound. Just like the Gladney family in the novel, everyone is obsessed with and worried about TV (p. 50), except now "TV" is everywhere all the time on screens that are evermore magnetic and interactive and exponentially proliferating. And all those screens have found so many ways to flood our senses and sensibilities with ads that when I read Jack Gladney's amazement that his daughter might utter, mystically, "*Toyota Celica*" (p. 148, his italics) in her sleep, it hardly registers with me. Of course she does. Who doesn't, when they're not humming "Nationwide is on your side"? The Gladney family TV moves around the house, from room to room, but now there seems to be no escape at all.

The parts of the book that sting the most, though, are the ones that make me think of school. As I've mentioned (and drawn from) in my previous works, I teach at a high school. It's one of the "good schools," but it's still a high school in America in 2025, and DeLillo seems to have us pegged, too. For example, Covid was everywhere, of course, in everyone's life and workplace, but my experience of working in a school during the pandemic lines up disconcertingly with the novel's fictional catastrophe. During that period, my school seemed to be both hyper aware of (masks of various kinds, altered schedules, constantly shifting protocols, never-enough cleaning with unidentifiable substances) and also ignoring (no real rules about any of those things, and only sporadic compliance) our very own "airborne toxic event" (p. 105), and that befuddling experience haunts me when I read the book now. When the catastrophes we usually just watch for news-entertainment come to our own neighborhoods, what should we do? To whom should we listen? What is actually happening? None of us seemed to know for sure exactly what Covid was or what to do about it, and now that it's over (is it?), what did it all mean? Just like the characters in the novel, we almost seem to have had some collective bad dream. And that dream is recurring, both in and out of *White Noise*; from time to time in episodes throughout the book, it is hard to tell when the catastrophe-obsessed Gladney family is watching fictional disaster, watching real disaster, living through real disaster, or simulating disaster during a disaster in preparation for a real disaster ("we thought we could use it as a model," p. 134)—and all I can think of in those passages is live shooter drills. And when the SIMUVAC official tells Jack "you are the sum total of your data" (p. 136), and Jack later asks himself "would I promote ignorance, prejudice and superstition to protect my family from the world?" I wonder if DeLillo has been sneaking into our faculty meetings. Is he reading my emails, as people are wont to do to teachers these days?

Teaching has probably always been hard, but it feels like it's getting harder, even at "good schools" like mine, and you don't need to read DeLillo to understand why. Just ask any teacher you meet, and five minutes of stories will likely make it easy to see why study after study concludes that fewer people want this job every time anyone checks the numbers (Partelow, 2019). The forces and factors that make teaching such an unattractive job to so many are so numerous, and seem to come from almost every direction these days, that it can feel a bit like DeLillo's world of Blacksmith and College-on-the-Hill; lots of things feel wrong, but you would hardly know where to begin to "fix" anything. But I begin here with *White Noise* because I'd like to get the "white noise" of public education out of the way right at the beginning, if possible, and actually talk about why so many of us are still here. When Jack Gladney talks about "inventing hope" in the statement that begins this introductory chapter, he's talking about tabloid headlines, and seems to be musing on how foolish we all are, looking for—insisting on—signs of positivity in the apocalypse. But I don't hear it that way; to me, it sounds like the way teachers know that their profession has plenty of failure and obstacles in it, but they come to work anyway. They care, and think, and invest in the future anyway. When I meet with young people who are considering teaching, I'm honest and blunt about the job; I think they need to know what they are signing up for, and go into it with eyes open. It is a job absolutely worth doing, but it's not for everyone, and it's certainly not for the faint of heart or short of patience. And it is true that you may have to "invent hope," as Jack puts it—but you *should* invent hope, whenever you can. That's a pretty good living, when you think hard enough about it.

***

I got the idea for this book after hearing that yet another of my colleagues was returning to graduate school, and I began to think about how uncommon that commonality at my school might be. According to the National Center for Education Statistics (updated May 2023), 1.4% of high school teachers held a doctorate degree in the 2020–2021 school year. My own high school runs closer to 15%, and I know that enough of them are curriculum studies scholars for John A. Weaver to joke that I work at "Curriculum Studies High School"; ten people at my school have finished a doctorate through the Curriculum Studies program at Georgia Southern University, or are enrolled in it now, and that runs our current total to fifteen faculty members with doctorates or in doctoral programs. Many others, throughout the building, are working on Master's and Specialist's degrees as well; it might be harder to find someone who *isn't* going back to school. I do think this creates an interesting curricular atmosphere at my school, and what I'm interested in looking at for this book is both why so many of my colleagues have decided to pursue such advanced studies, and also why so many of them have stayed afterwards to continue to teach high school classes.

I want to be clear, again, about something before I go any further: my school is a "good school," but it's not perfect, not some ideal model every school should follow. The goal here is not jealousy, but exploration and celebration of the kind of thing that I think could happen lots of places: people who are committed to teaching and also committed to learning, to approaching life and the world as something to study, to recognizing that being students ourselves is an excellent way to guide the students in our classrooms. I often tell my students that I think the biggest differences between me and them are age and experience, and I mean it.

Though there is nothing especially magical about my school, I do think it's unusual in that we have a kind of *network*, not just a *number*, of people in the building who are pursuing advanced studies, or have completed them. And some of us who have completed those studies have continued to live not just as teachers, but also as scholars and students, contributing published work to our fields. This book is an edited collection of work from my colleagues and me—every chapter has been written by someone at my high school who has completed a doctorate or is enrolled in a program now—about what I think is a pretty unusual educational experience. Each teacher has written two chapters: one autobiographical chapter about their life as a "teacher student" (how and why they've pursued their studies, why they continue to work at a high school, etc.), and one chapter of curriculum theory related to their experiences. This work is similar in some ways to my last book, *Field Theory: Curriculum Studies at Work* (DIO Press, 2019), in that it, sometimes directly and sometimes indirectly, makes the argument that high school teachers can and should be curriculum theorists, but this time the focus is on one high school, and more on the life of a teacher who continues advanced studies, and how those studies have affected them inside and outside the classroom. This project also continues the interest in "liminal scholarship," the academic "life-between," I have pursued in all my work.

In fact, the title of this book comes from my feeling that what we have currently is like a "Liminal High School," full of people who work "in the windows and doorways of the academy, now at the conference table or library, now in the hallways, now in the world" outside (Owen, 2011, p. 2). Many of us seem to exist in a kind of "liminal," or "between" space in the high school—not quite a high school teacher, not quite a professor, but a "liminal scholar" who can participate effectively in multiple curricular spaces, and encourage conversation and understanding across those spaces. Part of the life of a "liminal scholar" is what I am here calling the "teacher student" (as opposed to "student teacher"); these are full-time teaching professionals who have returned to life as a student, and now exist as both, or neither, depending on the day or conversation. I often spend part of my lunch duty talking about curricular theory with any other "teacher student" who might pass by; sometimes our IB faculty meetings are followed by impromptu discussions of the ways IB curriculum intersects with our curriculum studies experiences; plenty of our between-classes hallway discussions (maybe the ideal spot for "liminality"?) are about dissertation or defense strategies; and two teachers talking in any area of the building are as likely to be recommending books to each other as they are to be discussing weekend plans. We coach tennis and baseball, sponsor Science Bowl teams, serve as Department Chairs, and sit through countless meetings—but we also steal away moments to live the "life of the mind," as some of my professors have called it, and do what we can to bring that life to our students as well. I argued in *The Need for Revision: Curriculum, Literature, and the 21st Century* (2011) that some of us should "make a home of our homelessness, and serve as conduits for the open transit of ideas across academy thresholds" (p. 2), and now that our numbers are growing, I think we should explore that experience and curricular environment. This particular exploration has resulted in a book that reads like a collection of discussions of many subjects in many fields from many perspectives, all interested in teaching and learning to the best of our abilities and helping others do the same; in some ways it feels like our hallway and classroom and meeting conversations would if they weren't limited by the bell schedule.

***

This book is intended for current and prospective teachers—scholars, undergraduates, graduates, and high school teachers like us. I'm hoping that such a book will serve as a reminder to all of us—authors of this book included—about why this work (studying and teaching) is still so important and worthwhile. I really did think that writing this book might be good for us as well, in the sense that sometimes we all need to just come out and say why we do what we do; writing these chapters, I hope, will refocus, rededicate us to what we know we ought to be doing. Sometimes the hope we need to invent, as teachers, is our own hope. I also hope that this book will speak to prospective students and teachers out there who are considering this life, and maybe even to current teachers weighed down by an educational climate that sometimes seems to deteriorate each year. Maybe more people will teach, maybe more teachers will stay, and maybe more teachers will continue to be students. I would love for this book to contribute to any of those things. So many people in education talk about "life-long learning," and the people in this book exemplify that idea.

References

DeLillo, D. (1984). *White noise*. Penguin Books.

Kisner, J. (2023, January/February). *White noise* used to be satire: What was once mildly absurd is now funny because it's true. *The Atlantic, 331*(1), 72–76.

National Center for Education Statistics. (2023). Characteristics of public school teachers. NCES. http://www.nces.ed.gov

Owen, D. P., Jr. (2011). *The need for revision: Curriculum, literature, and the 21st century*. Sense Publishers.

Owen, D. P., Jr. (Ed.). (2019). *Field theory: Curriculum studies at work*. DIO Press.

Partelow, L. (2019, December 3). What to make of declining enrollment in teacher preparation programs. *Center for American Progress*. https://www.americanprogress.org/article/make-declining-enrollment-teacher-preparation-programs/

· 1 ·

HUMBLE BEGINNINGS

Jack D. Arrington

I am a science teacher and department chair at a high school that serves around 2,000 students in Georgia. I have taught at my school for the past 24 years. While teaching, I have also served as an instructional coach and tennis coach, and sponsored several different school organizations. While I have taught many science courses over the years, my primary focus lies in chemistry and anatomy. I have taught chemistry for the past 20 or so years and anatomy for about 18 years. I also teach chemistry as part of our International Baccalaureate Programme and really have enjoyed the broad international curriculum that is part of this program. I enjoy teaching and feel that it is my calling in life to educate students in science and prepare them for their futures, whatever they may be.

It is surprising to many that education was not my first choice of careers. I sort of "fell" into education and have not looked back since. My parents were both from relatively poor families, but education was a high priority from the beginning of my life. After many changes in schools, I ended up graduating high school from a school in the Atlanta area. With relatively few choices and no money set aside for college, I attended a small college in south Georgia on an academic scholarship. I graduated from there with a bachelor's degree in biology. The next year I was admitted to medical school in Georgia. After two years of medical school and failing to pass the medical boards, I decided to try something else. I began working in a lab as a technician testing filters all day. Meanwhile, my wife had been teaching for a few years and really seemed to have a rewarding career. Fortunately, in hindsight, the plant laid me off due to the loss of a contract. I decided to give teaching a go. I entered TAPP (Teacher Alternative Preparation Program) in Georgia as a new teacher and earned my certification while teaching. The first few years were tough but rewarding at the same time.

For me, the impetus for returning to school to earn higher degrees was initially to earn a pay increase in order to support my family. With each degree earned, teachers get an automatic pay increase in Georgia. However, what started off as simply a financial push evolved into a craving to learn more and achieve higher and higher goals. When I started my master's degree, I would not have imagined that I would continue on through my doctorate. There is something so rewarding about setting an educational goal and achieving it, and I think this has been contagious in the school in which I serve. I began working on my master's degree as a means of providing for my family, which then consisted of two children. I dove into the master's program and took as many courses as I could in order to finish early. It was difficult, but after a year I had earned the degree. I then saw that the pay increase was fairly substantial, which spurred me on to additional degrees. I completed my specialist's degree in a year as well. My wife already had earned her specialist's degree by this time, and I thought I was finished with my higher educational endeavors. However, in a couple of years I was a little restless to not only earn more money, but also to get back in the classroom as a student myself. At that time there were very few teachers in my building and district who had earned doctoral degrees. My department chair was currently in a doctoral program and highly encouraged me to start one. So, after a little trepidation, I began the journey to earn my degree in educational leadership. Our cohort of fifteen students was told that half of us would either drop out or not complete the program in seven years. I did not believe that so few members of our cohort would stay the course, as we were quite an impressive group of students. The two years of coursework flew by and soon I was spending nights working on my dissertation. I completed my work and degree within the next two years.

According to Brill and McCartney (2008),

> 33 percent of teachers leave their schools in the first three years, 46 percent after five years. These high attrition rates result in inexperienced teachers, high economic costs as teachers must be continually hired and trained, and a lack of continuity that makes institutional development and planning difficult.

In my first few years of teaching, I taught lower-level science classes where discipline was often a problem. Since my background was not in education and I had no teaching experience to draw on from college, I did the best I could. I did not have a very involved assigned mentor; however, another teacher in my department was hired the same year but had many years of experience in teaching. She and my wife were a tremendous help those first few years and assisted me in not only surviving but thriving. Having someone who could act as a mentor teacher was vital not only in helping me have a successful first year, but also in encouraging me to stay in the profession. Brill and McCartney (2008) agree saying, "improving teachers' work environment and professional development are more cost effective and influential in convincing teachers to remain. We conclude, therefore, that well-operated induction and mentoring programs are the best method for increasing teacher retention."

Although I had primarily lower-level courses my first few years of teaching, these were some of the most rewarding experiences of my career so far. I taught students who had no science foundation, who had poor home situations, who struggled with authority, and who had no confidence. I could see that many of them had no one who encouraged them throughout their day. If nothing else, I wanted to be the one who encouraged them and told them that they could do it. They could learn and could master the things I was teaching them. I got through to some of them and failed in others. However, it was the ones who I reached that spurred me on in education. Meeting students where they are and trying my very best to reach and teach them has become my primary focus in education. Ideally, I would like them to not only learn, but to fall in love with learning.

Developing a strong rapport with students is an important facet of my classroom. Mellgren (2020) says of this importance, "Teacher-student relationships affect students academically but also as a whole person." I make a point to greet students every day and get to know them. We become part of each other's worlds, and I feel their elation after a great test performance and despair in failure. It's almost as if I am taking tests with them, and likewise, as if I am getting graded papers back as well. I feel their elation and disappointment, and it affects me. I often ask myself if most teachers feel the same and cannot wait to give a test back to a particular student or dread giving a test back to another. I cannot seem to separate myself from these feelings and do not think that I would want to even if I could. As I have grown as a teacher, I realize that these feelings push me to be a more effective teacher. Mainhard et al. (2018) say "teachers may be even more important for student emotions than previous research has indicated." The relationship between teachers and students is a strong one and pushes me to work harder and harder each day.

Teacher-student experiences are the most important thing in a school building. And it is my firm belief that most teachers will make the most of that time and do as much as possible to meet students where they are and facilitate learning within their classrooms. And if teachers are not doing that, administrators should step in and make sure that they do. I think of my students as an orchestra and I am the conductor. If they have confidence in me, they can play beautiful music with the right instruction. However, all of the extraneous noise (lack of time, meetings, emails, duties) obscures the music and the symphony is not what it could or should be. Both the violinists and the conductor leave with a lesser experience. So, I ask myself, why are we here? Are we here to attend incessant meetings, update Google Classroom constantly, answer emails, and herd students from one class to another? Or are we here to do as much for our students as possible in our classrooms, so that they leave us more educated and more self-confident?

References

Brill, S., & McCartney, A. (2008). Stopping the revolving door: Increasing teacher retention. *Politics & Policy, 36*(5), 750–774. https://doi.org/10.1111/j.1747-1346.2008.00133.x

Mainhard, T., Oudman, S., Hornstra, L., Bosker, R. J., Goetz, T. (2018). Student emotions in class: The relative importance of teachers and their interpersonal relations with students. *Learning and Instruction, 53*, 109–119. https://doi.org/10.1016/j.learninstruc.2017.07.011

Mellgren, A. D. (2020). *How teacher-student rapport impacts student academics and achievement* [Master's thesis, Bethel University]. Spark Repository. https://spark.bethel.edu/etd/436

· 2 ·

CONDUCTING THE ORCHESTRA
Jack D. Arrington

The Early Years Before Teaching

Growing up in rural Alabama, like most children, I viewed school as a fun place to go and have fun with friends. However, my first couple of years of elementary school were strict and very little fun as I had teachers who were stern and didn't allow fun to enter through their classroom doors. Third grade was not a lot different, but fourth grade changed my view of education forever. My fourth-grade teacher infused so much fun and games into our classroom, I oftentimes did not even know we were learning. Even today, I can remember so many activities we did in her classroom which made me love being there and not just loving recess and physical education class. She was an educational genius, and I don't know if other teachers at that time appreciated her style of teaching. In fact, after discussing this with my father who was also in education, I believe she was ostracized for her methods. Even as a fourth grader I already knew my preferred learning style and hoped that my future teachers would be as fun and involved in my education as my current teacher. I viewed teachers as educational experts and the portal through which my education would be delivered.

My early views of school administration mostly had a negative disciplinary connotation. In elementary school, students' only interactions with principals were for disciplinary purposes. Most students feared even going to the office, much less having to talk to the principal. Our principals always seemed stern, with very little time for positive interactions with students. This became my view of school administration throughout my elementary, middle, and high school experiences.

My middle and high school experiences were laden with a variety of teachers. I had strict, unyielding teachers who had a traditional approach to learning and others more like my fourth-grade teacher who infused fun into most activities. I liked the diversity of teachers, but yearned for more fun in education. Still, I viewed administration as having more to do with discipline than learning. Through my college years, my views on education changed very little—until I actually started teaching.

What Academia Says

Once I started coursework for my advanced degrees, I learned what professors and the literature said about teaching and administration. I learned about what great schools do. Langer (2004) says of excellent schools, "More effective schools look and feel different; they are marked by an overriding sense of knowledge, coherence, organization, and caring. Teachers and administration learn what's needed, work toward common goals, get ongoing feedback, and grow professionally." Edward Wynne (1981) in "Looking at Good Schools" agrees with coherence, saying that "coherence was the characteristic most commonly associated with good schools." He defines coherence as being similar to school efficiency.

My advanced degrees are in educational administration, so I spent more of my time learning what administration should be like within a school and school system. Dufour and Mattos (2013) point administration toward learning communities, saying that "instead of micromanaging teachers, principals should lead efforts to collectively monitor student achievement through professional learning communities." Liz Free (2020) agrees that we should start with students in mind, saying that a "good guiding principle for decision making is to focus systematically on how the decisions we make as school leaders will affect our pupils, and work down from there."

The Truth—In My Experience

My views of education quickly started changing once I began teaching in 2001. I quickly had a better understanding of the vast responsibilities of teachers, and even more so of administration. Teachers must balance teaching lessons, discipline, paperwork, meetings, planning, grading, copying, duties, cleaning, and developing rapport with students. Many teachers are also coaching and sponsoring clubs, which are outside work hours, as well. And administration must balance not only discipline, as I once thought, but also daily school activities, teacher issues, parent issues, building issues, phone calls, emails, county expectations, and many others. Both groups have daunting responsibilities that fill their days. I do believe, though, that teacher responsibilities should be trimmed so that we can focus more on our students and our own personal lives. Chase Mielke (2023) says, "For too long we have normalized the pressure to do it all." He goes on to say that teacher workloads are "borrowed investments with high interest rates—taxing an educator's energy levels without translating to higher student performance." Arens and Moren (2016), in a study of 380 teachers and 7899 students, found that teacher exhaustion had a negative impact on student test scores, grades, and school satisfaction. Mielke (2023) identifies the source of teacher stress, saying that "teaching is not the source of excessive workloads. It's the secondary and tertiary responsibilities that put pressure on educators' schedules." He says that grading, planning, professional development, meetings, and duties are the specific sources. Several of these sources are directly impacted by administrative decisions. School administration can reduce mandatory planning, mandatory professional development, many meetings, and duties. This begins at the county or local school system administrative level. Mielke sums it up in one statement: "It's not a question of whether we can reduce workloads for the sake of teacher well-being—it's a question of whether we will reduce workloads for the sake of student learning." They need to make conscientious decisions to reduce teacher workload other than teaching (educational noise) and give more time within the day to focus on teaching.

The Educational Noise

Imagine purchasing tickets to the world's best orchestra a year in advance. The day has arrived, and you are walking into the theater for the performance of a lifetime. You take your seat, the lights dim, and the orchestra starts playing. The sound fills the theater with its beautiful melody. The conductor and orchestra are working in tandem to produce music you have never heard before. Then your seat starts to shake and you realize that there is a construction crew with a jackhammer just outside the exit door beside you. You can still hear the orchestra; however, the jackhammer is just about as loud as the violins. Soon, you are so focused on the jackhammer that you no longer even hear the beautiful music. The once-in-a-lifetime concert is ruined by outside noise. The symphony would be even worse if the conductor could not hear the orchestra due to the jackhammer. Teachers are the conductors and their students the symphony. When "outside educational noise" interferes with the relationships and interactions between teachers and students, there is a problem. According to Valli and Beuse in "The Changing Roles of Teachers in an Era of High-Stakes Accountability,"

> Through a detailed analysis of changes in teacher tasks over a 4-year period, the authors determined that role expectations increased, intensified, and expanded in four areas: instructional, institutional, collaborative, and learning. These changes had unanticipated, and often negative, consequences for teachers' relationships with students, pedagogy, and sense of professional well-being. (2007)

Teachers have limited time with their students each year and must make the most of that time. In a symphony performance it takes the musicians, conductor, and building staff all working together to achieve a great experience. Likewise, in education it takes the students, teachers, and the building staff (administration and others) working together in order to provide an optimal educational experience. We cannot necessarily control student decisions; however, we have complete control over what we do as both administration and teachers. I propose there are a few things that need to change, because many times the educational experience for students is subpar.

What is Creating the Noise?

As previously mentioned, the main sources of "educational noise" are planning, meetings, professional development, and duties. What ultimately pays the price is the student's learning experience. Teachers do not adequately prepare for lessons and the teacher-student experience is not optimal, which decreases learning. Over the years, teaching has become so involved and stressful for teachers. Some frame of reference is necessary here. This was teaching when I started in 2001:

- 5 teaching periods (54 min each)
- 1 planning period (54 min)
- 1–2 different classes to prepare for
- Teaching a maximum of 120 students (including many maximum class-size limitations)
- Lunch duty, morning duty, or afternoon duty (only one)
- Grading platform (for grade entry only)
- Around 5 emails per day
- Few meetings throughout the month (faculty and IEP)

Teaching today:

- 6 teaching periods (47 min each)
- 1 planning period (47 min)
- 2–3 different classes
- Students allowed to retest over all content, every unit (more papers to grade and additional test prep)
- Teaching 150 or more students
- Lunch duty and either a morning or afternoon duty, and constant hall duty
- Google Classroom (all class material and plans posted)
- Online platforms (attendance, IEP, 504, grades, etc.)
- Around 30 emails per day
- Many meetings (faculty meetings, common planning for each prep, county meetings, 504/IEP meetings)

Have you ever wondered what it would be like to have time during school hours to research and prepare for the students you teach, and feel you are completely ready for them to walk into your classroom and have the best experience possible? I, like many others, feel I never have enough time to prepare for these educational experiences. According to a survey reported by Najarro (2022), teachers work on average about 54 hours per week. Preparation time for my classes has increased over the years and the time available has decreased, which forces me and many other teachers to stay after school and/or take work home. According to a study analysis of teacher work compared to other professional work by Krantz-Kent in 2008, "Thirty percent of teachers worked at home on an average day, compared with 20 percent of other full-time professionals." In today's world in which self-care is vitally important, this is unacceptable. Sato (2020) says that long working hours can cause mental health issues and working on weekends can compound this issue. One's time away from the workplace should not be spent grading papers, working on plans, or even researching best practices. This time should be filled with family time, leisure activities, and hobbies. With better work-life balance, teacher job satisfaction would increase, which in turn would increase teacher retention. Teachers would encourage students to go into education, and teachers would not resent their profession after years of being beaten down by its demands.

When districts like mine add an extra teaching period in the workday, that means teachers have more students per day, less time to teach per period, and more papers to grade. A study done by Lin (2024) finds,

> Most teachers (84%) say there's not enough time during their regular work hours to do tasks like grading, lesson planning, paperwork and answering work emails. Among those who feel this way, 81% say simply having too much work is a major reason.

Not only are teachers sometimes forced to teach more classes, with the same curriculum, in a shorter class period, but adding class periods to the day also forces many teachers to take on an extra prep (teach an additional, different course), which means drastically more planning time. And do not forget that the planning period time is cut shorter as well. It is no wonder that teacher burnout and poor retention are huge problems. Garcia and Weiss (2019) say "schools struggle to find and retain highly qualified individuals to teach, low teacher pay is reducing the attractiveness of teaching jobs, and the tough school environment is demoralizing to teachers." When I began teaching, we had around 10 applicants for each science position vacancy at my school. Now we are lucky to have one or two. Over the years, county administrations along with the evolution of technology have continued to add more and more responsibilities to teachers without any respite. Teachers are often forced to make a choice between grading student work and spending time with their families. Lin's study (2024) found that, "A majority of teachers (54%) say it's very or somewhat difficult for them to balance work and their personal life." Those who choose to grade everything spend hours at home grading student work and inputting those grades into a grade platform. Those who choose their families and personal time do not grade all the student work and do not give as much feedback to students.

With online classroom management, more classes, more students, more papers to grade, less prep time, more duty time, and less time per class, one would assume that teacher planning time would be filled with preparing for the time you have with your students. One might also assume that more planning and prep time would be allocated to teachers as well. Unfortunately, planning time is often filled with answering emails, analyzing data, filling out common planning documents, completing discipline referrals, calling parents, copying material, and cleaning. In reality, there is little time remaining to actually grade papers, plan, and research new ideas for teaching and learning.

What Can Educational Administration Do?

I have taught science in a high school classroom for 24 years. All of those years, school systems have pushed for higher test scores and higher ratings/rankings by the state or nation. If they want those results, though, teachers need an administration who will actually be willing to make the changes necessary to increase teacher morale and give teachers what they really need to facilitate learning, which is dedicated time. Johnson (2020) says, "The schools where teachers thrive are actually schools that are very well managed by principals who protect teachers from interruptions and unrealistic demands." One simple question should be asked: "Is it in the best interest of our children, teachers, and schools?" If the answer is no, another option should be found. What should the county and building administration be doing to correctly promote education?

1. **Protect class time**
   Class time should be protected time with few interruptions. As much time as possible should be spent with teachers. Leonard (2008) says,

   > Making less than optimal use of allotted instructional time is likely to make meeting the demands of the heightened federal and state performance and accountability directives even more of a challenge. It may well be time for the kind of leadership that provides strong leadership for time.

2. **Protect planning and expect effective common planning**
   This may include self-planning and common planning with others. Administrators should observe weekly common planning meetings. Handley (2024) says, "The gift of time is not about creating more time, but rather honoring the time teachers already have."

3. **Do not overwhelm teachers with responsibilities**
   Duties need to be limited. Anderson (2019) says, "Reduce administrative tasks that have little or nothing to do with teaching or supporting students. Can someone else supervise bus arrivals, rest rooms, or the cafeteria?" How can teachers be expected to stand in the hall before and after each class, and also have bathroom duty, lunch duty, and before or after school duty? I am so busy before and after each class getting ready for my next class or answering questions from the previous class. Am I to neglect those duties? Many teachers have coaching and club sponsor responsibilities as well. It becomes such an impossible juggling act that leads to teacher burnout or resentment.

4. **Expect effective instruction (hold teachers accountable)**
   Administrators should be in classrooms holding teachers accountable for teaching and students accountable for learning and behavior. Administrator observations can increase student achievement. Hunter and Ege (2021) found that student achievement rose when teachers were observed more frequently throughout the school year. The time we have with students is the most valuable time throughout the day. It is essential that effective instruction is occurring throughout the building. I was our instructional coach for several years and observed a variety of classrooms. Administration cannot be reluctant to get involved when they observe poor teaching and poor test results. Fink and Resnick (2001) say that school administrators should

   > play a substantive role in curriculum choices, in establishing expectations for the quality of student work, in analyzing the form and quality of teaching and in organizing targeted opportunities for teachers in the school to learn the specifics of teaching their subject matters well.

5. **Hold students accountable**
   Gooden (2023) has found that "teacher burnout was higher in schools with high suspension rates, where teachers had issues handling students with disruptive behavior." Students today get so many chances before discipline of any regard is issued. This has been an evolution of discipline which saw a dramatic increase in rate during Covid. Many teachers have so many discipline problems in class that they have little time for instruction. So much time is spent correcting behaviors and then documenting these behaviors. Students are not held accountable

for behavior, getting so many chances before any disciplinary action is implemented. And even then, disciplinary actions begin as mild and become ever so slightly more punitive with each successive infraction. This long trail of discipline is frustrating to many. Rosen (2005) emphasizes the importance of rules and their implementation, saying, "It is important for schools to teach students about the importance of rules." He goes on to say that "it is in schools that students are introduced to the fact that they have rights, privileges, and responsibilities under the law."

I want to be the conductor of a symphony in my classroom. I would like to not have to worry about rushing off to duty or a meeting. I want to have time to answer my students' questions, set up a lab, clean up from a lab, or even catch my breath between the six classes that I teach every day. I am already responsible for conducting a symphony for an entire class period. Is that not enough? The answer today is a resounding NO. It is not enough today, and that is a main reason for the lack of qualified teachers. Intelligent and capable people are not choosing to teach—why would they? No one is advising them to, the pay is low, and the workload is high and stressful. Baker (2021) says in his article, "The Experience of COVID-19 and Its Impact on Teachers' Mental Health, Coping, and Teaching," that

> Teaching has always been a demanding profession, and the demands have only escalated during the COVID-19 pandemic. Around three-fourths of teachers surveyed had considered leaving their positions during the 2022–23 school year, with more than half considering positions outside education. Teachers describe the increased workload, ongoing stress, and lack of support from administrators and parents as factors that led them to consider leaving.

A change of tone is needed and could come at the hands of educational administration. With a few changes in the teaching environment, teaching would be more enjoyable, and more teachers would advise students to join teaching. We would be able to attract some of our students to the profession and retain good teachers. This starts with school administration.

Why Are We Doing This Anyway?

With teachers and administration doing what is best for the students, education can thrive within a school. It is a two-way street, and blame could lie in many places. But instead of assigning blame, we need to recognize what is not working for our teachers and make changes. It will require some acknowledgment of harsh realities. Harrison (2023) showed a strong relationship between teacher satisfaction and effectiveness. He went on to say,

> Our findings suggest that policies and practices which meaningfully focus on teachers' job satisfaction and the quality of their relationships with students should be strategic priorities for school leaders and policymakers, given the strong association between instructional quality and student outcomes.

In an ideal world, I am on the stage conducting the most beautiful piece of music played by the most wonderful musicians. They are giving their all and the audience is absorbing everything in the music hall. The audience is taking it in and are realizing that the money spent on a ticket is the best money they have ever spent. The audience, the conductor, and the musicians will leave this place changed forever. Meanwhile, the building administration and staff have worked in the background to make sure the show runs smoothly and there are no distractions. That is my ideal world, and I can see it every day in my students. They have the ability, but unfortunately many times the outside noise ruins the experience. We do our very best, but the "jackhammer" is there in the background relentlessly pounding the concrete day after day. Will the administration please silence the noise so that the concert can go on?

With teachers and administration working together in a school building, we can improve education and hopefully not only hold onto successful teachers, but also attract people to the profession. I know that no situation is ideal; however, freeing most teachers to perform inside the classroom instead of having to focus so much of their attention elsewhere will lead to boosts in education.

References

Anderson, J. (2019). The gift of teacher time. Harvard Graduate School of Education. https://www.gse.harvard.edu/ideas/usable-knowledge/19/09/gift-teacher-time

Arens, A. K., &, Morin, A. J. S. (2016). Relations between teachers' emotional exhaustion and students' educational outcomes. *Journal of Educational Psychology, 108*(6), 800–813.

Baker C. N., Peele H., Daniels M., Saybe M., Whalen K., Overstreet S., & The New Orleans Trauma-Informed Schools Learning Collaborative. (2021). The experience of COVID-19 and its impact on teachers' mental health, coping, and teaching. *School Psychology Review, 50*(4), 491–504.

DuFour, R., & Mattos, M. (2013). Improve schools. *Educational Leadership, 70*(7), 34–39.

Fink, E., & Resnick, L. B. (2001). Developing principals as instructional leaders. *Phi Delta Kappan, 82*(8), 598–610.

Free, L. (2020, April 29). *Decisions, decisions ... How can school leaders become better decision-makers?* "Great leaders inspire greatness in others." https://lizfree.com/2020/05/12/decisions-decisions-how-can-school-leaders-become-better-decision-makers/

García, E., & Weiss, E. (2019). The teacher shortage is real, large and growing, and worse than we thought. The first report in "the perfect storm in the teacher labor market" series. *Economic Policy Institute*.

Gooden, C., Zelkowski, J., & Smith, F. A. (2023). A systematic literature review on factors of stress, burnout and job satisfaction of secondary grades teachers at time of professional crisis. *Clearing House, 96*(5), 162–171. https://doi.org/10.1080/00098655.2023.2238880

Handley, J., & Donnelly, L. (2024, September 19). *4 ways to give teachers the gift of time*. https://ascd.org/blogs/4-ways-to-give-teachers-the-gift-of-time

Harrison, M. G., King, R. B., & Wang, H. (2023). Satisfied teachers are good teachers: The association between teacher job satisfaction and instructional quality. *British Educational Research Journal, 49*(3), 476–498. https://doi.org/10.1002/berj.3851

Hunter, S. B., & Ege, A. (2021). Linking student outcomes to school administrator discretion in the implementation of teacher observations. *Educational Administration Quarterly, 57*(4), 607–640. https://doi.org/10.1177/0013161X211003134

Johnson, S. M. (2020). *Where teachers thrive: Organizing schools for success*. Harvard Education Press.

Krantz-Kent, R. (2008). Teachers' work patterns: When, where, and how much do U.S. teachers work? *Monthly Labor Review, 131*(3), 52–59.

Langer, J. A. (2004). *Getting to excellent: How to create better schools*. Teachers College Press.

Leonard, L. (2008). Preserving the learning environment: Leadership for time. *International Electronic Journal for Leadership in Learning, 12*(16).

Lin, L. (2024, April 4). *What's it like to be a teacher in America today?* Pew Research Center. https://www.pewresearch.org/social-trends/2024/04/04/whats-it-like-to-be-a-teacher-in-America-today/

Mielke, C. (2023). Reducing teacher workloads: For too long, we've normalized the pressure to "do it all." *Educational Leadership, 81*(1), 42–47.

Najarro, I. (2022). Here's how many hours a week teachers work. *Education Week, 41*(31), 17–18.

Rosen, L. (2005). *School discipline: Best practices for administrators*. Corwin press.

Sato, K., Kuroda, S., & Owan, H. (2020). Mental health effects of long work hours, night and weekend work, and short rest periods. *Social Science & Medicine, 246*, 112774. https://doi.org/10.1016/j.socscimed.2019.112774

Valli, L., & Buese, D. (2007). The changing roles of teachers in an era of high-stakes accountability. *American Educational Research Journal, 44*(3), 519–558. https://doi.org/10.3102/0002831207306859

Wynne, E. A. (1981). Looking at good schools. *The Phi Delta Kappan, 62*(5), 377–381. http://www.jstor.org/stable/20385899

· 3 ·

TRIALS AND TRIUMPHS: A TIMELINE OF MY TEACHING JOURNEY

Kathleen E. Barbara

When I tell people that I am a teacher, I typically get one of two responses. The first one is, "Oh, I could never do that, I don't have the patience." The other is, "You are really making a difference." Reflecting on their comments, I am inspired to review how I selected my career path and why it is right for me. Additionally, how would a young person know whether the field is right for them? I will share my thoughts and my story.

I have been a high school Spanish teacher since my graduation from the University of Georgia over a dozen years ago, and my plans are to continue working in education for the foreseeable future.

A number of factors pointed me toward teaching. It was much more than the logical opportunity presenting itself and the pieces falling into place, although there was some element of that. Growing up, I was introduced to Spanish in elementary and middle school and from there I developed a passion for the language and a desire to learn more. This affinity for the Spanish language and my success with it soon found me exploring career options and ultimately studying to be a teacher. It was my love for the Spanish language and culture that revealed to me that teaching was the right path.

Discovering My Love for Spanish and Teaching

Central to my desire to teach is satisfaction in working with others, sharing my knowledge, and making a difference in my work environment. Although I believe that a direct approach in the classroom is often very effective, I also believe that compassion and seeking to understand my students' varying life experiences and backgrounds can yield notable results. My objective is to form relationships that enable students to reach their goals. When they are successful, it also provides me with job satisfaction. It's a win-win and very fulfilling model.

For me, the importance of empathy was made evident at a young age. People often describe defining moments in their lives, and one such early moment of mine was a mid-year move from Illinois to Georgia during elementary school. It was hard to move, and I had a difficult time adjusting. I learned how important empathy for others is, as I experienced my own culture shock and difficulty adjusting to my new environment. Being told, "you talk funny," and breaking into a new school setting where everyone already knows one another is difficult. My classmates had studied from the same textbooks all year and were synched with each other and with the teacher. I had none of this, and just felt left out. Worse, I was given a terrible short haircut to accommodate the heat in the South, and my new fellow classmates were quick to point out all of my deficiencies, academic and personal. This left a lasting impression.

In retrospect, the silver lining is that I learned how important empathy is to make students comfortable, and how this facilitates learning. Empathy should be interpreted broadly, as it applies not only to individual circumstances, but also to cultural differences. I experienced my own form of culture shock moving from the North to the South. Although this was mild relative to those who move from country to country, the point is now personally obvious to me that I need to be sensitive to individual and cultural differences in my classroom if I want students to be receptive. This sensitivity, or empathy, is an added dimension that affords me greater impact as a teacher.

The Beginning of My Formal Education in Spanish

Piaget (1962) stated, "Play is the work of childhood" (p. 166). In my pre-college years, I learned Spanish early on, taking classes in elementary and middle school, and continuing Spanish each year through high school, gaining college credit. I enjoyed learning Spanish, making connections with other like-minded people and exploring its interesting cultures. I found it so engaging to learn through songs, games, and dramatic play. I can still remember the very first song I learned in elementary school. The lyrics were, "Juanito cuando baila, baila con el dedito," which can be translated as, "Juanito, when he dances, he dances with his little finger." This song had the children up and dancing as they recited different body parts in Spanish. I looked forward daily to being able to dance and sing the body parts in Spanish with the rest of the class. After singing this song, the class would stage a puppet play, with various characters asking and answering questions about our age, what we liked to do, and other information about ourselves. We also discussed the calendar and weather, and then dressed a paper doll in clothing appropriate for the weather and sang the date in Spanish. I enjoyed this so much that I would go home and speak Spanish with myself in the mirror, with my stuffed animals, and any family member who would listen. I ran around the housing dancing and singing in Spanish all day.

I continued my Spanish studies in middle school where I learned the basics of reading, writing, listening, and speaking in Spanish. I enjoyed school and learning so much that I would play school and teach my imaginary students Spanish. Even today, I challenge myself to provide instruction beyond the book with real world scenarios that are fun.

In high school, I enhanced my classroom studies by making connections with native speakers, as well as through community service and work experience. At this point, Spanish became relevant for me. My proficiency in Spanish soared as my outreach experience closely aligned with Vygotsky's Sociocultural Theory (1978) that language acquisition develops through social interactions both inside and outside of the classroom. I find that even today, as a teacher and continuous researcher, the lessons are more meaningful with social and cultural context. In my classroom, I try to simulate these types of interactions and situations with my students. I consistently ask myself how I can make Spanish language and culture relevant and accessible for my students who do not have cultural ties, and this provides the basis for my research in the next chapter.

My Favorite Classroom Experiences When I Was a Student

Ward (1968) stated, "You can teach a student a lesson for a day, but if you can teach to learn by creating curiosity, he will continue the learning process as long as he lives" (p. 64). Acquiring grammar and writing skills through songs, movies, role-play, and dialogues was my favorite way to learn. These types of activities allow students to pursue language through a variety of interesting means. Similarly, connections between language and culture have more depth when proverbs and fiction are used. I have been fortunate to have Spanish teachers that truly inspired me. The common thread was their passion for teaching. As cliché as that sounds, they all provided engaging lessons that centered around real-life scenarios and Spanish culture as just described.

In high school, one assignment that particularly helped me was listening to Spanish music through an educational website. We studied many authentic songs in Spanish that were popular to native speakers of Latin American countries and Spain. One of my favorites was "Fotografía" by artists Juanes and Nelly Furtado that addressed themes presented in real life, such as love and distance. This song meant a lot to me, and I connected to it. It made me remember my distant friends and family left behind when I moved across the country. Listening to songs like this encouraged me and others in the class to explore new music and genres outside of what we would typically choose. It also provided us with the opportunity to reflect on life, realizing a commonality that these themes resonated in the Hispanic community as well.

From a linguistical standpoint, I recall another exercise that was very helpful. It required that we listen to a song, write down the Spanish lyrics, and then translate them to English. We were given multiple chances to listen. After this step was completed, we watched the music video with lyrics in both English and Spanish provided at the bottom of the screen. We checked and revised our work by filling in the segments we did not understand. Exercises like these helped me improve my listening and vocabulary skills in both the formal and informal language, as well as strengthening my grammar and translation skills. These types of hands-on activities piqued my interest and allowed Spanish to come alive and be relevant.

Study Abroad in College

Aristotle is known for saying in *The Nicomachean Ethics* that "Education of the mind without education of the heart is no education at all" (translated by W.D. Ross). Through my study abroad in Mexico, I was able to develop a deeper connection with the local community and culture. As part of the study-abroad group, we traveled to many different parts of Mexico, including Cuernavaca, Puebla, Tepoztlán, Taxco, Mexico City, Miacatlán, and other towns. During all the fun and the sightseeing, I lived with a family and participated in service projects in two orphanages: Nuestros Pequeños Hermanos in Miacatlán, and a local one in Cuernavaca, where we stayed. We attended classes Monday through Friday. I really enjoyed the classes because they were small and individualized, which differed greatly from my usual classes. Through this program, each class had only four people, so students were able to obtain one-on-one instruction and more individualized feedback. I learned so much during that time, because I was fully immersed in the culture and given adequate feedback from my teachers. I would categorize my study abroad trip to Mexico as my best experience regarding language learning. Being able to partake in the daily life of another culture and forming meaningful connections through communication is what language learning is all about. I felt included in a world that was different from my own in the United States. Developing these new friendships and relationships was another defining experience, realizing we are more closely knit and connected by our similarities than we are separated by our cultural differences. This study abroad experience developed my self-awareness and compassion, adding another dimension to my love for Spanish and confirming my desire to become an educator.

Choosing Teaching as My Career

Dewey (1916) stated, "Education is not preparation for life; education is life itself" (p. 239). I was attracted to teaching because of the opportunities to continuously learn. I have always loved to learn, and I try to learn something new every day, whether it be about Spanish, pedagogy, or life in general. I expect this of myself, and I encourage my students to adopt this mindset as well. For example, as an Advanced Placement teacher, new learning occurs daily, even for me. We follow a curriculum guide filled with topics and units of study that encourage us to explore new insights and current events. For instance, climate change and artificial intelligence were topics recently discussed in the Spanish classroom. These topics keep Spanish relevant and engaging and allow me to stretch my mind as well.

Another reason for selecting teaching as a profession is that I am particularly interested in Latin America culture. Throughout high school and college, I was fortunate to spend time with members of the Latin American community, and participate in their cultural events and practices. Because I grew to love and appreciate this culture firsthand, I was inspired to become a Spanish teacher, where I now inspire others on a daily basis.

Finally, teaching provides job satisfaction. I love the metaphor of starting with a student as a blank canvas and adding various colors, styles, and artistic techniques to that canvas throughout the year. The result is a unique composition, perhaps a masterpiece, by the end of the course. I value this ongoing classroom time and contact, where I can have a positive impact on the final result.

Having taught in high school for many years, I often get asked, "Why don't you teach at the college level?" At this stage, I see high school as my best fit. The camaraderie, challenges, and one-on-one experiences with the students are rewarding. Getting to know each student, and encouraging advanced study when appropriate, is important to me, and I would venture that all of this is more obscured at the college level.

My Teaching Experiences

Confucius is widely referenced for the quotation, "Education breeds confidence; confidence breeds hope; hope breeds peace" (translated by Arthur Waley, 1938). Educators no longer teach inside the box. We have to teach outside the box to reach every student. While we can't expect all students to receive the highest scores, every student can show relative improvement. For example, students may struggle, but with encouragement and a variety of learning techniques, students will leave the classroom with the confidence that they know quite a bit more than on their first day. For me, there is always satisfaction when a student masters a difficult task or simply learns a meaningful lesson.

There will always be students that wait until the last minute before grades are due to see if extra credit can save the day. On the other end of the spectrum are the students who give their all, all of the time. These students are not necessarily the smartest, but are generally passionate and hungry to learn. If they are struggling, they come to tutoring at every opportunity. They may not earn the grade they want, but they stay positive and resilient. These students have an innate desire to learn and to do their best, which is all anyone can ask. My job is to encourage them throughout the year. Teaching these students is very rewarding, and I believe they will move to the forefront in the workforce and be quite successful in life.

Staying Positive in Teaching

Thales is known for the wise words, "Happiness consists in a healthy body, a wealthy soul, and a life well-ordered" (translated by C. D. Yonge, 1853). There are certain things that educators simply have to do to survive. In any career, there will be challenges, and no career is perfect. As educators, we must focus on what really matters and be at peace with ourselves first so that we can put our best face forward for the students. I stay positive by staying healthy. If I am in good health, I can give my students the best version of myself.

The biggest challenge I face is the ever-changing workplace and seemingly limitless demands and opportunities. Administratively, teachers take a lot of work home. Lesson plans and grading are a constant, with an endless number of opportunities to do more. It is not a 9-to-5 job easily turned off and on. When working with students, we may also be drawn into their issues if they are manifested in the classroom. They are human beings, and we are not machines, and this may take an emotional toll on teaching. In the teaching profession we really have to learn to be masters of time management and balance, and to make time for ourselves and our personal interests.

Pursuing Advanced Degrees

Aristotle stated, "We are what we repeatedly do. Excellence, then, is not an act but a habit" (translated by W.D. Ross, 1931). Pursuing an advanced degree is time consuming. I have three of them, and they have allowed me to stay current with the best strategies for students, while bolstering my credentials and pay. The opportunities for personal and professional growth keep me fresh, and I am able to refine my classroom practices. Most importantly, I feel challenged and not stagnant. These degrees have laid the pathway for me to continue learning and serving as a constant researcher.

Who Am I as a Teacher and Researcher Now?

Socrates is attributed the well-known saying paraphrased in a passage from Plato's "Meno," "Education is the kindling of a flame, not the filling of a vessel" (Meno, 98B-C, translated by G. Grube, 1991). My goal as a teacher, and researcher in fact, is to continually enhance and refine the curriculum to make it applicable to the everyday lives of my students. I try to develop instructional techniques that keep students motivated and engaged. In my own classroom, I assess what can be done differently to make my students' classroom experiences meaningful to their lives. The objective is to foster an environment of cultural awareness that ultimately inspires the uninterested to be receptive to learning about people who are culturally different from themselves. Lessons reflective of the real world foster compassion, humanity, and awareness of other cultures. This technique is further described in the next chapter.

Also in the next chapter, I explore what educators can learn from the experiences of students who are considered "successful" Spanish learners. I examine what we can take from their experiences so that educators can create a Spanish curriculum that engages students and cultivates their cultural and linguistic empathy and inspires them to make connections with others. This ultimately is why I chose to pursue advanced studies and conduct my own research to further such instruction.

References

Aristotle. (1931). *The Nicomachean ethics* (W. D. Ross, Trans.). Oxford University Press. (Original work written around 350 BCE)

Dewey, J. (1916). *Democracy and education*. Macmillan.

Laertius, D. (1853). *The lives and opinions of eminent philosophers* (C. D. Yonge, Trans.). Henry G. Bohn. (Original work written around 230 CE)

Piaget, J. (1962). *Play, dreams, and imitation in childhood*. W.W. Norton & Company.

Plato. (1991). Meno (G. Grube, Trans.). In E. Hamilton & H. Cairns (Eds.), *The collected dialogues of Plato* (pp. 357–384). Princeton University Press. (Original work published circa 380 BCE)

Waley, A. (1938). *The analects of Confucius*. Vintage Books. (Original work written around 475 BCE)

Ward, W. A. (1968). *Reader's Digest*, 93(557), 64.

Vygotsky. (1978). *Mind in society: The development of higher psychological processes*. Harvard University Press.

· 4 ·

SPANISH LANGUAGE SUCCESS STORIES: INSIGHTS FROM MY MOST ACHIEVED LEARNERS

Kathleen E. Barbara

As I examine my own pedagogy, I often wonder what sets my most successful students apart from the rest. What did they do differently? What educational experiences and attitudes did they have and what were their experiences regarding curriculum in the Spanish classroom that seemed to make a difference? To begin this chapter, I would like to share a personal story from two of my high school classes that displays polar opposite attitudes between a struggling student and a more successful one. This story showcases the varying experiences of two students while learning Spanish–the first is Will, who is struggling and merely wants to obtain course credit, and the other is Carl, who has achieved Advanced Placement Spanish and demonstrated his proficiency with a top score on the national exam.

Will's Story

In my Spanish II class, students were completing the warm-up activity. Tension was in the air because reports cards were coming soon. I was walking the rows and passed by Will's desk:

"Will, turn around. Focus on the warm-up, please."
"But I have a 69.4 with you this year. Why do we even have to learn Spanish anyway? I have got to pass. I can't take Spanish again. Can I do some extra credit?"
"Please see me after class so we can develop a plan to get you back on track. OK class, back to the lesson!"

It was not the time to get into a discussion with teenagers. We were on a pacing guide. We had to master the preterite and imperfect verb conjugations by the end of the year. There were more important things to do at that moment than persuade a student about the importance of learning Spanish. Some students would not go beyond Spanish II. They were just not interested. All they wanted was credit. I had to make sure we met our objectives. Sadly, Will was not the only student that has made comments of this nature. In fact, he was one of a number of students feeling this way. To him, Spanish was just a requirement to complete high school.

Carl's Story

Meanwhile, in my Advanced Placement Spanish class, students were preparing diligently for the AP Exam. That day, they were engaging in a simulated conversation. With the simulated conversation, students would engage with a fictitious new student (the recording) who was asking them about the demographics at school. The prompts for the simulated conversations were a little forced to meet the standards: however, they provided a good venue for learning.

An excerpt of Carl's simulated conversation, beginning with the voice from the recording:

"Are your closest friends from the same social and ethnic group as you?"
"No, I have friends from all ethnicities. My best friend is from Chile and also has Mexican roots. My girlfriend has a diverse cultural background. I have friends who are Asian and Indian. But that is not how I base my friendships and priorities."
"The last question: what have you learned from others about social and cultural diversity? Have you experienced any life lessons?"
"Obviously, I have learned a lot from my diverse friends. They have taught me the importance of being open-minded and not closed off to ideas that differ from ours."

Carl's experience illustrates how personal attitudes affected his motivation to learn another language, Spanish. Carl was open-minded and willing to learn about other cultures and ideas even if they differed from his own. He was motivated to learn Spanish and form relationships with people of different backgrounds. Will, on the other hand, based on his comments, did not see the value of learning Spanish and had trouble justifying the significance of learning Spanish beyond the college credit. Instantly, I began to question what kind of experiences engage learners and encourage them to value other cultures.

Speaking from the Heart: My Reasons for Examining the Experiences of My Most Successful Learners

As a passionate teacher, I deeply desire to understand the stark differences in attitudes toward learning exhibited by Will and Carl and improve the situation. These are not uncommon attitudes, and it is important to foster an environment that inspires students like Will to want to learn Spanish beyond the course credit.

To achieve this, I collected stories from four graduated students who finished the Spanish pathway in high school. In this chapter, I have included precise transcriptions of conversations and interactions with these students as a point of reference for the discussion. Previously, I had taught all of the students in my Advanced Placement Spanish course. Due to the small class size, the students and I developed a family-like relationship throughout the course of the year. The small class size allows for more opportunities for each student to participate in class, ultimately allowing me to get to know each student on a personal level. Unfortunately, after the students graduate, I do not talk to them on a regular basis. However, before Winter Break and Summer Break, some of my former Advanced Placement students return to visit since their college classes are often released for vacation earlier than ours. Through these yearly visits, I have been able to keep in touch with my former Advanced Placement students to follow up.

It was a goal of mine to find out what my most successful students did differently. What motivated them to finish the Spanish pathway? What was the root cause for the difference of experiences between Will and Carl?

One of the students, Kimberly, scored a five, the highest score on the National Spanish Advanced Placement Exam. Taylor, another participant, scored a four, a very respectable score. The other two students scored a three, meaning they were proficient in Spanish. Obtaining any of these scores is an accomplishment, for all the scores represent a level of proficiency that allows students to communicate with Spanish speakers.

As students reflected upon their own experiences, they shared how they learned Spanish and what made a difference for them. In turn, educators can use this type of feedback to improve instruction so that students are able to learn the language, communicate with a fast-growing Hispanic population, and ultimately become more open-minded and engaged citizens in an increasingly diversified world.

I. What My Most Successful Students Did Differently: Real Life Connections

My most successful students have made Spanish relevant through their connection of educational material to real-life situations. They explored their own interests, passions, and hobbies in Spanish; they used technology as a tool for language skill development; and they fostered connections with native speakers. Through these avenues, students have developed cultural awareness and empathy.

Krashen (1982) stated, "In the real world, conversations with sympathetic native speakers who are willing to help the acquirer understand are very helpful" (p. 32). Real-life connections make Spanish relevant for someone who does not have cultural ties. Similarly, communicating in Spanish with others in real-life situations enhances Spanish proficiency through "comprehensible input" (Krashen, 1982). Much like Krashen's notion of learning a language through relevant and real experiences, Cutshall (2012) highlighted the importance of creating real-life situations for learning when he stated, "Language learning activities in the classroom need to mirror real-world, authentic communication as much as possible" (p. 35). In accordance with the respected World-Readiness Standards for Learning Languages (2012), learning experiences are more beneficial when the emphasis is placed on acquiring the language for communication rather than accuracy in grammar, and I have found that my former AP students used their Spanish in real-life experiences beyond the textbook. Their focus was not placed on solely learning the information to pass the test. All of the more successful students saw learning Spanish as relevant to their own lives, whether for traveling, friendships, or other real-life situations. These situations included serving as an interpreter at a local health clinic and simply initiating conversations with friends and acquaintances that spoke Spanish. Some of these interactions are digital friendships developed through technological means like Instagram and other social apps. In all cases, whether real life or digital, it was apparent that when Spanish was viewed as a useful skill, it was learned for its practicality, and the focus was on communication, rather than drilling verb conjugations.

Approaching Learning with the Mindset of Developing a Skill for Connections

Lightbown and Spada (2013) stated, "[Motivation] has been defined in terms of two factors: on the one hand, learners' communicative needs, and on the other, their attitudes towards the second language" (p. 87). When there is an authentic need to use the language in a particular context, the students are motivated by the need to communicate. Likewise, if students have positive attitudes toward the target language and culture, they will be more willing to learn. One of the reasons that I examined Kimberly's experiences was that she was very successful with Spanish, as well as with her other classes. She was awarded the title of high school class valedictorian, and I wanted to examine her Spanish experiences in order to improve Spanish instruction for all my students, especially students like Will. In a conversation Kimberly, she explained her attitude to learning Spanish:

> I think that what helped me a lot in learning a foreign language was going into it with the mindset that you want to learn a new skill as opposed to just checking off a requirement that you need in terms of classes. When sitting in class, I would think about how learning Spanish would open many doors in the future, allowing me to travel and to communicate with those who have Spanish as their first language. In the future, I am considering participating in programs that involve teaching in foreign countries. If I were to teach in Spain or Mexico, two of the most popular countries, my past experience in learning Spanish would be undoubtedly useful. (Interview with Kimberly, May 10, 2019)

Kimberly recognized that Spanish is used to create connections with real-life benefits for travel and career. She saw learning Spanish as a means to develop a skill for her personal asset base and something she could draw on in the future. It made her a better person. From the educator's point of view, students should be made aware that they are not merely acquiring facts or information, but rather developing a useful skill that can provide opportunities in the future. When Spanish information is seen as useful, one is more likely to remember and recall it.

Using Spanish for Service

Correspondingly, another former student, Chandler, found his language skills useful as he applied them to real-life situations. He used his Spanish skills by volunteering at the health clinic as an interpreter. Apart from developing compassion for the patients, he refined his Spanish skills. Chandler described how he acquired vocabulary in this authentic setting:

I took advantage of opportunities to take and really enrich my knowledge. One of those opportunities for me was a clinic downtown and, honestly, thinking back I don't know how I did it, but I was a Spanish interpreter for the patients in the clinic—one of the Spanish interpreters. I would be the middleman for the patient and the doctor or nurse, in which the patient didn't speak much English and sometimes no English at all and the doctor or nurse maybe only spoke a little Spanish, but not enough to carry on a professional conversation. So, in that environment—that was a huge positive experience because I learned so many new, enriching words for my vocabulary that brought me to understand a lot about medicine, and also just helped me interact with people in their native language, and not feel ashamed to express the knowledge I knew. I learned a lot of words in the clinic for working, for example *cicatriz*, scar, *pastilla*, pill, I'm sure we learned that word in school too, but when I had to use it, I remembered it. Oh! *Propina*! I remembered that *propina* was tip after looking it up because I didn't know how to say it at Poblano's [a local Mexican restaurant]. (Interview with Chandler, July 6, 2019)

Krashen's (1982) The Acquisition-Learning Hypothesis breaks learning languages into two strains: acquisition and formal learning. With this hypothesis, *acquisition* occurs when the context and the language are used in meaningful and natural contexts, where messages are conveyed with importance, such as with Chandler's experiences. On the other hand, *learning* occurs through formal settings, such as the classroom, where grammatical rules are the focus for creating a strong foundation. In such settings where this is the main method, the content may not seem transferable to real-life situations, which in turn makes learning a struggle for students. Krashen (1982) has made two controversial claims: (1) learning cannot turn into acquisition, and (2) only acquired language cultivates natural and fluent communication (Krashen, 1982). Therefore, the sole use of grammar-based instruction to teach a second language will not allow for natural acquisition of language. This was substantiated with Chandler's reflections. His authentic Spanish interactions made it easier to recall vocabulary words later. Chandler also noted that by interacting with the patients in Spanish, he worked through personal fears about his Spanish speaking abilities. Chandler's experiences demonstrated that when words appear in authentic settings, the learner witnesses the practical application of Spanish and is more likely to remember the words in the future.

Using Spanish with Other Learners

Similar to Chandler, Kimberly used Spanish in real-life situations too, as well as with her friends who were also Spanish learners. Kimberly described how she used Spanish:

Some friends and I just found it fun to casually talk in Spanish outside of class and stuff to practice. While we might not be learning new skills per se, I think it kind of helped to become accustomed to the language. And also you inadvertently become accustomed to the different tenses and things as you are talking. When I was younger in high school, I remember my friends and I used to talk to each other in Spanish so that our parents wouldn't understand what we were saying, not that we were saying anything bad, but the idea of being top secret was always fun. So, I thought that was pretty helpful. (Interview with Kimberly, May 10, 2019)

Kimberly found a creative and fun way to use her Spanish skills in real-life situations even though she described having minimal opportunities to speak in Spanish outside of school. Kimberly and her friends would speak in Spanish for privacy and entertainment. While Kimberly recognized that she did not acquire new knowledge from engaging in these dialogues with her Spanish-learning peers, the exercise was fun and it kept Spanish fresh in her mind and gave her practice speaking in a nonthreatening setting.

Spanish for Friendships and Connections with People of Other Cultures

Correspondingly, Amelia was fortunate enough to develop friendships with Spanish speakers. These friendships allowed her to practice her Spanish in real-life situations as well. Amelia sent me a video of one of her interactions with a Spanish-speaking friend, Isabella. In this video, it became apparent that Amelia used her language skills to engage in conversations about topics of personal interest, such as shopping. In the video, the two girls are sitting at the table at a Mexican restaurant with a very colorful, vibrant background of the booth. Isabella asked Amelia how her summer had been going. Amelia answered by saying that it was going well. The girls were smiling and giggling. Amelia then said that she went shopping earlier that day with her mother. As she spoke, one could see that she was thinking and recalling information. At this point, speaking Spanish was still a cognitive process because at times she had to think before producing language. Isabella continued the conversation asking about what Amelia bought. Amelia replied by saying that she would show her the dresses later because they were in her car. Amelia then changed the subject, using an impressive transitional phrase, drawing attention to how good the food tastes. Both the girls agreed. Then, the video cut to the next scene where the girls were in the back seat of the car. Amelia pulled out a dress from the bag and showed her. Isabella grabbed the dress and said, "Wow! How beautiful! I love the design!" Amelia continued showing and passing the items she purchased to Isabella. Isabella commented on them by saying, "I like the colors" or "I think it is going to look very pretty on you." In Amelia's video, I was able to see how she used her Spanish skills to discuss shopping experiences with a Spanish-speaking friend. Amelia continued to maintain her language skills by practicing on occasion with a few friends that are native speakers of Spanish, although she admitted that she did not practice as much as she should. Regardless, she took advantage of opportunities to speak Spanish on occasion, which allowed her to see the relevancy of learning Spanish. Additionally, making connections with Spanish speakers in real-life situations, such as eating out and discussing shopping purchases, allowed her to improve her language skills.

All of these experiences allowed students to improve Spanish because they were using the language, not just acquiring knowledge about it. Students continue to learn when they find opportunities to use their classroom knowledge in real-life situations.

Application to the Classroom: Creating Real-Life Connections Through the Exchange of Personal Stories

In the classroom we can try to simulate these types of real-life situations though creating a caring environment where students can share personal stories about their own lives and experiences. Krashen (1982) stated, "The effective language teacher is someone who can provide input and help make it comprehensible in a low anxiety situation" (p. 32). When a teacher connects with students, the Affective Filter is lowered, students feel comfortable, and students can focus on acquiring the language. In turn, students are motivated to learn because they are interested in learning about each other.

Creating a space for students to share personal stories about themselves in Spanish is another important strategy for fostering learning in the Spanish curriculum. Likewise, personal connections with the teacher plays a key role in fostering positive classroom experiences. Creating an environment where students feel comfortable is ideal for learning and the exchange of such stories.

Taylor explained how some of his other teachers had made a connection with him and ultimately how that inspired him to learn:

> My favorite days are when a teacher says *I have a story to tell you about my life*. When a teacher can pull a story that relates to the lesson, it makes me want to learn so much more. It makes me like that teacher and when you like the teacher it makes me feel

like I want to hear what they have to say. The game is that you want to make your students want to listen to you. A lot of them don't want to, you have to win them over. (Interview with Taylor, July 6, 2019)

Taylor highlighted the importance of being candid and forthcoming about personal experiences. When teachers shared personal stories that related to Spanish, this allowed the teachers to connect with their students on an emotional level, often inspiring them. The teacher can share their travel experiences or how they keep in contact with people they have met. It is not just about the language, but also about the personal connection. Knowing someone else's language is showing compassion and an interest in others, which is exactly what educators strive to do.

Likewise, Amelia added to Taylor's discussion of sharing stories by highlighting the importance of providing a varied curriculum, especially one that leaves room for the exchange of information about oneself. After all, many people enjoy talking about themselves. Amelia discussed how she enjoyed sharing her personal experiences with her teacher during a Spanish vlog assignment:

Blogging is essentially talking about a specific topic either through text or by video. In class, I always did video blogs, or vlogs, and I talked about whatever activities I was doing at the time. For example, I made video blogs about what I do at home in my free time or hanging out with friends outside of school. I had never blogged before Spanish class, so this was a new experience for me that I ended up really liking. I would blog in the future probably more in English than in Spanish until I get more comfortable with it, but I would vlog about college life, maybe hanging out with friends, or anything else about my personal life that I would be excited to share with people. Blogging is a fun way to show other people what you like to do and what you get to experience. (Interview with Amelia, July 20, 2019)

When Amelia was given the opportunity to discuss her own opinions and interests in the vlog assignment, Spanish became interesting to her. She created a connection with the teacher because she knew the teacher would grade the assignment and listen to her personal experiences. It is not hard to figure out that people enjoy talking about topics that interest them. Therefore, it makes sense that Amelia preferred activities and assignments where she was able to express her own interests and experiences, which ultimately opened the door for her second-language learning development. Thus, sharing interests, even through technology, can promote real-life language experiences, one of the main reasons for learning a second language.

Taylor and Amelia both expressed the importance of sharing personal stories to foster a teacher-student relationship. When the teacher shared stories with students, such as sharing an experience about traveling to another part of the world, for example, students saw the teacher as a human being, not just a dispenser of knowledge. In turn, when teachers provided ways for the students to share about themselves, students were engaged and happy that their teacher would learn about them. Amelia and Taylor showed that when students view the teacher as human and are given opportunities to share about themselves through the exchange of stories, they were motivated to listen and learn from the teacher, which ultimately contributed to creating positive experiences in the Spanish classroom.

II. What My Most Successful Students Did Differently: Nurturing Open-mindedness and Personal Interest Through the Arts

One of the best and most important ways to create compassionate and worldly Spanish language students is to appeal to their personal interests in the arts using music, theater, poetry, literature, etc. Unfortunately, activities that enrich the curriculum and feed student interest are often the first to be eliminated under time constraints.

Nussbaum (1997) stated, "We must educate people who can operate as world citizens with sensitivity and understanding" (p. 54). We need to see ourselves as a world citizen; however, we often perceive ourselves as members of a local community. We are separated within national and geographic boundaries, which highlights the division between groups. On the other hand, if we see ourselves as part of a world system, we can develop empathy for people who coexist with us in the world.

In order to develop world citizenship, Nussbaum (1997) highlighted the importance of developing a narrative imagination through studying the arts: "The arts cultivate capacities of judgment and sensitivity that can and should be expressing the choices a citizen makes. To some extent this is true of all the arts. Music, dance, painting and sculpture, architecture—all have a role in shaping our understanding of the people around" (p. 86). Learning through the arts is important for understanding other cultures, as well as creating the desire to learn another language. Absent this exposure, interest can wane, resulting in students like Will whose primary objective is gaining academic credit.

In a 2018 discussion with researchers, scholars, and professors Dr. John Weaver and Dr. MiFang He, the idea of language and culture being taught simultaneously was explored. Dr. Weaver (2018) explained, "What is missing from the language curriculum? We can't treat language as an object, we can't learn it without cultural knowledge" (Weaver, personal communication, October 16, 2018). Unfortunately, language is not taught simultaneously with culture in many school systems. The result is a disengaged monocultural mainstream population that does not see the relevance in learning another language. Similarly, Dr. He called for an "intertwined" foreign language curriculum. Dr. He (2018) stated, "We might know another language, but we need to learn about culture as well. They have to be intertwined: bicultural, bilingual, and biliterate" (He). Dr. He, who grew up in China and currently lives in the United States, narrated her experiences of learning English as a foreign language in China. He (2018) explained, "In China, there is a culture class to learn philosophy. There is another class for language. I do not understand why we do not have that here." Moreover, He and Phillion (2004) defined Nussbaum's (1997) narrative imagination as "the ability to reflect on experience, question assumptions, and actively empathize with others" (p. 3). In order to empathize, one must be able to listen to others' experiences, especially when they are different from their own. This promotes receptivity and openness, an essential component to language learning.

When learning Spanish, students can benefit from learning through the arts. Outlets such as stories, plays, movies, art, poetry, and music assist in learning about culture and promote open-mindedness. Teaching through the arts allows students to learn about culture and offers educators an effective way to develop, create, and utilize linkages between the lives of their students and those in other cultures, and to foster appreciation.

By separating the arts from the curriculum, we are left with teaching a language in a vacuum and a fragmented view of Spanish culture. Without Nussbaum's "narrative imagination," students do not learn to empathize with others, or to understand other cultures. They are not becoming the well-rounded citizens they aspire to become, thus making it essential to include arts in the curriculum.

One testimony to the importance of fostering culture and open-mindedness in the teaching of language is presented by Dr. Stevenson (2015) who conducted a qualitative sociolinguistic research study that examined Latino students' relationship between language and society, particularly students' language use in a 5th grade science classroom. The findings demonstrated "students' conceptualization of English as the language of academic success [...] resulting in an implicit institutionalized bias against Spanish" (Stevenson, 2015, p. 25). In this study, the implicit bias affected those who speak Spanish and their self-image, reinforced by media and other societal stereotypes. When mainstream culture is perceived as superior to other cultures, it only creates barriers between the dominant group and other cultures; thus, mainstream students may not want to learn Spanish. This highlights the importance of teaching the arts because these perceptions can be addressed to foster cultural appreciation and embrace multiple perspectives.

Fortunately, many students are inquisitive about Hispanic culture. Learning Spanish through study of the arts provides students with the insight to become world citizens by seeing the humanistic side of Spanish language as it relates to members of the Hispanic community. Kimberly, one of my students, described what she liked in her Spanish classrooms:

> I do definitely have an interest in learning Spanish and about Spanish culture. I think teachers can create a genuine interest for students, who don't have one, by showing them how this could be applicable to their lives and also talking more about cultural aspects so that they gain more of an appreciation for the language, like my teachers did. For me, one thing that really helped me appreciate the language was, interestingly enough, just listening to Spanish music. I really liked the sound of it and it became somewhat of an internal game to see how well I could understand what they were saying. (Interview with Kimberly, May 10, 2019)

Kimberly likes music. Music styles vary around the world, but music itself is universal. She does not create music herself, but she enjoys listening to it. She was able to connect with the Spanish language through this interest while learning about the culture. Because of this interest, some of her favorite class activities were listening to songs in Spanish. Through the study of song, she was able to examine Spanish on a personal level through the eyes of the singer, as well as relate to Latino listeners her age.

Creative expression—one's passion for music, songs, poetry, fiction and play—helps students learn Spanish with joy. Morris (2016) called the arts the "heart and soul" of curriculum and claimed that without these elements, students are receiving an "impoverished education" (p. 25). All of my students who finished their Spanish pathway studied their personal interests in Spanish through the arts. For example, students have written songs, performed in plays, created makeup artistry tutorials, and painted works of art, all while doing so in Spanish. They pursued their individual passion and expressed it through a Spanish lens. In turn, they were more engaged in learning. Through the inclusion of the arts such as music, plays, and poetry, these students not only learned the Spanish language with joy, but they also learned about cultures and "the world we live in" (Morris, 2016, p. 25).

My students who finished the Spanish pathway demonstrated that they were motivated and engaged by music, songs, poetry, and plays, which in turn led to Spanish improvement and learning Spanish with joy. As Alipour et al. (2012) specified in their research, many people's first exposure to another language is through popular songs, which in some circumstances fosters interest in that culture and language while increasing the desire to learn, as well as being fun. Correspondingly, music can improve performance and retention, since the second language is stored into long-term memory through repetition, rhyme, and rhythm long after the song has finished.

While these students found creative expression through music, plays, and poetry, it should be noted that a wide array of topics fall under the realm of creative expression, such as science experiments, drawing, painting, digital art, comic strips, comedy, literature, short stories, riddles, music, dance, architecture, theater, etc. Students have multiple talents and interests, and when teachers build on students' talents, rather than their deficits, students are motivated to learn with joy (González, Moll, & Amanti, 2009).

Exploring Individual Interests in Spanish

Two of my more successful students, Chandler and Taylor, explored their personal passion for music performance through a Spanish lens. Both students were part of the music school in college and performed in both Spanish and English.

I observed Taylor sing the song "Donde Voy" by Tish Hinojosa where he had perfected his Spanish musical performance through consistent practice and repetition. Taylor described how singing helped refine his Spanish skills: "I think singing really helped me learn the rhythm of the language . . . I think it really helped me understand how words are said together. For instance, vowels in Spanish . . . They kind of just merge together. It's like a stream of words. It's very fluid" (Interview with Taylor, May 3, 2019). Taylor performed this song for a large audience where he brought tears to the eyes of one of the professors at the school.

Similar to Taylor, I was able to observe Chandler sing while playing piano. He performed Carlos Guastavino's "Pampamapa" at a music festival in California. Chandler stated:

> I have to learn the text of all the art songs that I'm going to play with this singer. With Spanish, because I know the language, I really got to understand what the song was saying, and what the meaning was, and how it related to the music I was playing. So, ultimately once preparing both the written text and memorizing that and then, preparing the piece very well, it was like a transformation happened with my musical playing. I've never enjoyed something musical that much in my whole life. I found this connection between something that I love so much—Spanish language and culture—with piano in my case, and the two blended beautifully, and it really opened my mind to what else is out there in terms of expressing myself and what I love to do. (Interview with Chandler, June 26, 2019)

With song and piano performance, performers were required to learn the song inside and out. It required much dedication and practice. By studying the meaning of the song, Chandler was able to relate to the music, and ultimately better perform. The passion and the emotion shined throughout his performance through his dramatic movements and vocal skills.

Taylor and Chandler combined their passion for music with Spanish by creating performances in Spanish. Preparation required much practice and repetition, allowing them to refine their Spanish skills. Initiating opportunities for students to create a product around their own interests in Spanish is key. Students learn by doing, and when they "do" or "create" around a topic of their interest, the learning effects are magnified. Educators may begin by asking students about their personal experiences and interests, and having them identify a product to create in Spanish. For example, a music student like Taylor or Chandler may pursue their passion for music performance by performing a song in Spanish and explaining the musical elements of the work to the rest of class. This not only allows the learner to develop their passion but provides endless opportunities for improving Spanish speaking and pronunciation. By allowing students to study Spanish limitlessly through their own interests, students are able to learn Spanish with joy.

Application to the Classroom: Creating a Space for the Arts

To this day, I have found it helpful to encourage my students to explore their own interests in Spanish. This has the obvious benefit for language learning because they simply are practicing it more. However, the real benefit is that students are pursuing their own artistic passions through a Spanish lens, which in turn improves their motivation.

It might be countered that although Taylor and Chandler had a unique passion for music and performance, many students do not have this level of passion for any realm of the arts. However, it is important to note that most students do still enjoy music to some extent, and using music is a successful avenue to pique student interest and increase their love for language learning. One of the most relatable forms of art for students is song. Almost everyone loves music and listens to it at some point during the day whether they are in their car, walking in the neighborhood, or just playing it in the background as they do daily tasks. In class, teachers may start off by introducing songs, remembering the trick is not to find a song that everyone likes, but to set the expectation that the course is expanding horizons by introducing different genres of music that would not have been chosen otherwise. There is not only a language benefit, but students broaden their scope and tastes as well. This is part of education—exposing students to new ideas. In Spanish, as many educators know, it is so important to have constant language input to refine listening skills. Listening skills tend to be one of the hardest skills to master because the listener is listening to sounds that pass in real time to construct meaning from messages that are fleeting and usually extemporaneous. On top of this, messages are not always polished like in textual passages, and this challenge comes in addition to whatever challenges exist with foundational vocabulary and grammar acquisition. Giving the students the opportunity to listen to songs is inspirational, but the most rewarding is when they are able to sing the song themselves. I have had students with a range of musical abilities. I have had a few like Taylor and Chandler who are exceptionally talented and pursue it as a serious hobby. However, most students just enjoy music to some extent, and I make space for them to perform as well merely with Karaoke or composing their own verse to a song. I usually start with having them perform the chorus on Friday and add a verse each week until they have learned the whole song. Meanwhile, we examine vocabulary, grammar, and content of the song together as a class. This is one of many ways to provide a venue for the arts to all students no matter their artistic interest and skill level.

III. What My Most Successful Students Did Differently: Using Technology as a Tool for Connections and Pursuing Personal Interests

Krashen's (1982) *Input Hypothesis* involves having input that is able to be understood and meaningful so that the learner can further develop language skills. Language acquisition is a direct result of a learner's understanding of the target language in a variety of situations. Comprehensible input involves a variety of elements, including gestures and drawings that build upon what the learner already knows, which encourages the learner to continue. Acquiring language occurs when messages are understood (Krashen, 1982).

My most successful students have used technology—YouTube, Instagram, Google Home, and language apps—as a tool for Krashen's (1982) *language input*. Using technology as a tool for exposure allows students to learn Spanish more effectively and make connections with people around the world. Taylor became an exception by really integrating Spanish into his daily life through the use of technology. Taylor attributed his success to continually developing the skill of speaking Spanish by taking advantage of opportunities to use it in conjunction with his own activities during his free time. Taylor accomplishes this by using YouTube, Instagram, and Google Home, as well as by chatting with friends on the language apps.

Lazy Learning

Part of our jobs as teachers is creating a love for language learning and appreciation for other cultures. This can be a daunting task, especially when we only see our students for one hour a day. One way to foster a love for learning is to encourage students to explore their own interests within the realm of Spanish—especially if they are taking an advanced level course.

During a conversation about using YouTube to learn Spanish, Taylor stated:

> I like the idea of lazy learning—and what I mean by that is even when you are not sitting down and saying I am going to study and write notes, you can still become acclimated to a language from more than just a studying environment. I learn and obtain knowledge and become familiar with the language through immersion on YouTube. I sit down and watch YouTube videos and learn Spanish and improve upon my listening skills. This is about entertainment. You can learn Spanish while entertaining yourself. (Interview with Taylor on July 7, 2019)

Taylor was able to study Spanish on his own terms, viewing videos that were in line with his personal interests. For example, at one point in other conversations, Taylor mentioned his love for makeup artistry. On YouTube, he learned about that love in Spanish, watching Spanish makeup artists and acquiring vocabulary that was aligned with his interests. As he mentioned above, Taylor did not see this learning process as rigid or exhausting, but rather as entertaining and something he could do while relaxing.

More successful students, like Taylor, who developed a deep love for Spanish, used digital technologies—YouTube, Instagram, Google Home, and language apps and settings—for language and cultural immersion on a daily basis. Taylor also explained how he uses YouTube to improve language skills while learning about culture:

> I also use YouTube for cultural videos. Johanna Haussmann, she is Venezuelan and she makes videos about social topics and also the humorous aspects of different accents—accidental curse words and reasons Venezuela is a total disaster. She talks a lot about the economy there. She talks about global politics and awareness is really important in her videos. Awareness through comedy is what she really likes to do. And I love watching this. She has a very, very thick Venezuelan accent, which is interesting. (Interview with Taylor, June 12, 2019)

Using technology, Taylor enjoyed engaging with a variety of topics. Some topics related to his personal interests, such as makeup artistry, while others related to culture, politics, and traveling. Through viewing cultural videos, such as the aforementioned YouTube video by Johanna Haussmann, he furthered his learning of the Spanish language and cultures.

Language Apps for Friendships

Similarly, Taylor had found ways to connect with Spanish speakers via apps such as HiNative. HiNative is described as a Q&A community for language learners. On this app, learners can post questions and get answers while connecting with native speakers from over 170 different countries. Native speakers of different languages help each other learn a second language. The HiNative app has multiple features for communication, primarily by exchanging text messages, voice recordings, pictures, or videos. Taylor used this app two ways: he offered help to others who are learning English, and he sought help with Spanish. Taylor shared two experiences: one where he helped a nursing student refine her English skills and another with an older woman where they helped each other improve their proficiency in both English and Spanish.

Taylor further describes how he used the language app to interact with Spanish speakers:

> I signed up for this language-sharing app where people can post questions about a language, and you can find someone who speaks that language to answer the question

for you and then if you find someone who is learning the mutual language—or like the opposite language—you can help each other. There was this one time on HiNative, I helped this girl with her pronunciation in English. There's this function where people can dictate a sentence and native speakers can hear it and offer criticism. She said, "I study nursing in the university in Chile," and so I told her that she could just say "at the university" or that it might be more common to say "I'm studying to be a nurse in college." She also dropped the g at the end of nursing, and I told her about that. Oh yeah. Once I was talking to an older woman for a long time in English and Spanish. We helped each other. We were talking and I tried to explain what a cognate was to her. She had never heard of the term .... Also, I have talked to a few guys on Instagram, I have the app on my phone. They are usually really excited once I tell them I am learning Spanish. (Interview with Taylor, June 21, 2019)

In summary, Taylor used language apps such as HiNative to communicate with Spanish speakers. He used the technology as a way to immerse himself in the Spanish language and culture. Taylor showed us that learning also occurred outside of the classroom setting and outside of real-time and face-to-face interactions with Spanish speakers. Taylor immersed himself in Spanish by watching YouTube, scrolling through Instagram media that interested him, and connecting with Spanish speakers online using language apps, such as HiNative. Through technology, Taylor was able to learn Spanish and learn about other cultures.

Other Media Sources: Television and YouTube

In addition to the technology sources above, we cannot underestimate the impact that television and radio have on one's ability to acquire a language. Amelia explained that her primary source of language acquisition is through viewing television and listening to radio in Spanish. She stated that it is truly amazing how you can become used to a language and pick up words just through watching television.

Ina (2014) found television viewing to be an effective and purposeful independent learning of a foreign language, especially with subtitles, due to the ability to "entertain children-students and motivate better than anything else so students put more effort to understand the teaching material" (p. 3). Therefore, through consistent viewing of television/radio, students are able to be exposed to a plethora of vocabulary and grammar structures that they just would not in an hour's class time.

Similarly, Taylor demonstrated how he took advantage of scaffolding opportunities that YouTube had to offer:

> The good thing about YouTube is that you can see captions, or no captions. That's really good for learning a language because it's like training wheels. Once you take them away, you are only paying attention to the words, but if you have them, then your mind is trying to make connections with what you are hearing and what you are reading . . . . Some videos have very fast, very thick Spanish accents. This type of video is something where I would watch like one to five minutes of it and be like, "Oh my gosh! I can't understand!" But a good thing about YouTube is that you can slow it [the speech] down. Now, I can understand the words he is saying. I can take a notepad and write the words down and be like, "Wow! What fun words that he is using!" YouTube really allows you to individualize your study and really immerse yourself into culture and things that are not even cultural, but in Spanish. (Interview with Taylor, June 13, 2019)

Taylor revealed how he used tools, such as captions and slowed speech, to improve his learning experience. When videos were too fast or difficult, he was able to use these tools so that he could understand the language and make note of new vocabulary. Afterwards, he disabled the tools and was able to understand the language at a normal speed. These features offered Taylor helpful opportunities for scaffolding, which he described as training wheels. This is a great strategy for students who are not able to fully immerse themselves through traditional methods like study abroad.

Social Media Accounts

Furthermore, Taylor described how YouTube and Instagram accounts allowed him to become immersed in not only the Spanish language, but also the Spanish culture:

> This account posts cool photos from places in the south of Chile. I like to read the descriptions of each of the posts because that is where some of the Spanish is. So, it is in a form like this where you are being visually stimulated, but you are also absorbing the Spanish around it because it's like, "Oh I see the visual context and now I am reading about it!" I feel like I am able to read because of context. For example, there are words like "la orilla" (shoreline) that I am able to pick up on because it goes with the context and it's helpful to absorb the words just like with immersion in real life. (Interview with Taylor, June 1, 2019)

Taylor highlighted how technology, such as Instagram and YouTube, could be used to provide a digital immersion experience. He explained that through accounts like Instagram and YouTube, viewers are provided with a visual context just as if they were engaging with Spanish in a real-life situation. Taylor explained how visual contexts allowed him to figure out the meanings of words, such as *la orilla*, on his own. By having the full context, Taylor was not required to rely solely on his imagination and therefore was able to absorb new vocabulary more easily.

Taylor clicked onto another page on his social media account. He demonstrated how he learned Spanish language and cultures simultaneously through certain accounts on Instagram such as "El país":

> El país is a publication in Spain. Obviously, they post interesting things about pop culture and connecting with the news in Spain and also internationally. This *[page on Instagram]* is about the vote that happened recently in Spain. It is just very interesting to see that side of the world, and you can do that with social media because everything is just so shareable now. (Interview with Taylor, June 1, 2019)

Through viewing accounts, such as "El país" on Instagram, Taylor was able to engage with Spanish cultures. I observed how he learned about pop cultures through examining comments about music artists Rosalía and Bad Bunny, how he engaged in festivals in Galicia, and how he stayed up to date on news stories and political events happening in Spain. Taylor claimed that social media allowed him to be a part of Spain's cultures.

Technology Immersion

Taylor was completely enthralled with Spanish. He stated, "I've put myself in a place where a large portion of my life is in Spanish through technology" (Interview with Taylor, June 1, 2019). Taylor was able to become immersed through technology. He started by putting his phone settings and Google Home in Spanish, where he set it to Spanish and had to perfect his pronunciation in order to be understood:

> I have to say, *Ok Google, enciende las luces. Ok Google, apaga las luces. Ok Google, ¿Qué hora es?* I do that kind of thing all the time, so that keeps me in Spanish. My phone is in Spanish, so every time I have to download a new app or ... I'm setting something up on my phone, I have to maneuver through things that I've never looked at before in that language, and that's a learning experience for me that I have willingly put myself into. But that's not studying for me, that's like living my life. (Interview with Taylor, June 1, 2019)

By completing small daily tasks in Spanish, he was able to keep the Spanish language in his working memory. Taylor willingly expressed his dislike for homework, but instead chose to practice Spanish while "living his life."

Application to the Classroom: Encouraging Students to Make Use of Immersive Opportunities

One of our main goals as educators is to inspire our students, and teachers can take away meaning from Taylor's experience and apply them to the curriculum. Teachers foster a love for learning when students are given space to explore their own interests through social media, podcasts, television programming, and music. Here they can develop whatever interest they have in another language. To foster language acquisition, students should be encouraged to create vocabulary lists of emerging words pertinent to their theme. More importantly, they should make use of opportunities to speak with people around them even if the only opportunity is through the use of technology. This proved to be very beneficial in Taylor's situation.

One of the most impactful actions that we can take as educators is encouraging students to seek out opportunities to use their Spanish language in a variety of settings. This can be a huge endeavor as a member of a monolingual community, as many students are. In the classroom, educators can encourage students to brainstorm ways that they can become involved with Spanish outside of the classroom. In the classroom an easy and practical way to foster this is by having students create a graphic organizer with different sections: music, television, podcasts, social media, apps, texts (plays, poems, stories, magazines), and their own personal interests. From day one, the class can start creating a list of how they can begin to immerse themselves in the language in these realms. The educator may start off by providing a few examples for each category to pique student interest, such as showing students particular songs, discussing popular television programs, and referencing social media content creators. This encourages students to explore the arts on their own time through the lens of their own personal interests. Later, after students have identified their interests, the teacher may provide an opportunity to share their experiences in class, like a television show they watched and liked, by summarizing the program or showing a clip of it in class. In turn, other students' interests are piqued, and it creates a domino effect.

Conclusion

In the introduction, I examined a personal experience from two of my high school classes that displayed polar opposite attitudes of a struggling student and one who was more successful. Will, a Spanish II student, openly expressed his opposition to learning Spanish by saying, "Why do we even have to learn Spanish anyway?" On the other hand, Carl, an Advanced Placement Spanish student, held a different worldview: "I have learned a lot from my diverse friends. They have taught me the importance of being open-minded and not closed off to ideas that differ from ours." While Carl's experience illustrated how his personal attitudes affected his motivation to learn another language, Will's attitude, perhaps, was indicative of his lack of awareness as to how to expand his learning beyond the textbook mentality and the benefits it could provide.

Over the years, it became apparent that a teacher must give instruction not only on content, but also on ways to be an engaged learner while still reaching state standards and maintaining expectations of the workplace. Through examining the experiences of my most successful Spanish learners, we are able to understand what they did differently—establish real-life connections, utilize the arts in Spanish, and use technology as tools to immerse themselves in the language and culture. The teacher must give instruction on how to become a good Spanish learner in order for students to acquire the ability to speak Spanish proficiently and communicate with the fast-growing Spanish-speaking population. In the best sense, students should be shown the tools that enable them to become more open-minded and engaged citizens in an increasingly diversified world.

From listening to and analyzing my most successful students' stories, I am better equipped to provide Spanish instruction that engages students in learning Spanish and to cultivate their cultural and linguistic empathy to understand and learn from others who are different from themselves. I learned there are a few elements I should include in my Spanish curriculum to improve my pedagogy: explicit instruction on how to incorporate real-life connections, using creative expression and the arts as they relate to students' personal interests, and using technology as a tool for a proficiency-based paradigm in concordance with ACTFL standards. As more of these approaches are regularly employed, students will be more receptive to learning Spanish not only for the credit, but with an awareness that language proficiency and cultural awareness are life skills and personal assets beneficial to their future.

References

Alipour, M., Bahman, G., & Zafar, I. (2012). The effects of songs on EFL learners' vocabulary recall and retention: The case of gender. *Advances in Digital Multimedia (ADMM)*, *1*(3),

p. 140. Retrieved from http://worldsciencepublisher.org/journals/index.php/ADMM/article/view/499

Cutshall, S. (2012). More than a decade of standards: Integrating communication in your language instruction. *The Language Educator, 35.*

González, N., Moll, L. C., & Amanti, C. (2009). *Funds of knowledge: Theorizing practices in households, communities, and classrooms.* Routledge.

He, M. F. (2018, October 16). Personal communication [verbal].

He, M. F., & Phillion, J. (2004). Using life-based literary narratives in multicultural teacher education. *Multicultural Perspectives, 6*(3), 3–9.

Ina, L. (2014). Incidental foreign-language acquisition by children watching subtitled television programs. *TOJET: The Turkish Online Journal of Educational Technology, 13*(4).

Krashen, S. (1982). *Principles and practices in second language acquisition.* Pergamon.

Lightbown, P., & Spada, N. (2013). *How languages are learned.* Oxford University Press.

Morris, M. (2016). *Curriculum studies guidebooks: Concepts and theoretical frameworks* (Vol. 2). Peter Lang.

Nussbaum, M. C. (1997). *Cultivating humanity: A classical defense of reform in liberal education.* Harvard University Press.

Psydeum Amelia. (2019, June 11). Personal communication [verbal].

Psydeum Amelia. (2019, July 20). Personal communication [verbal].

Psydeum Chandler. (2019, June 26). Personal communication [verbal].

Psydeum Chandler. (2019, July 6). Personal communication [verbal].

Psydeum Kimberly. (2019, May 10). Personal communication [verbal].

Psydeum Taylor. (2019, May 3). Personal communication [verbal].

Psydeum Taylor. (2019, June 1). Personal communication [verbal].

Psydeum Taylor. (2019, June 12). Personal communication [verbal].

Psydeum Taylor. (2019, June 13). Personal communication [verbal].

Psydeum Taylor. (2019, July 6). Personal communication [verbal].

Psydeum Taylor. (2019, July 7). Personal communication [verbal].

Psydeum Taylor. (2019, July 21). Personal communication [verbal].

Stevenson, A. (2015). "Why in this bilingual classroom ... hablamos mas espanol?" Language choice by bilingual science students. *Journal of Latinos and Education, 14,* 25–29. doi: 10.1080/15348431.2014.944704

Weaver, J. (2018, October 16). Personal communication [verbal].

World-Readiness Standards for Learning Languages. (2012). *Standards for foreign language learning: Preparing for the 21st century.* Allen Press.

· 5 ·

THE SPACE BETWEEN THE WALL AND THE BED

Stacey T. Brown

Very early on in my childhood, I knew I wanted my life's work to be wrapped up in words and language and how they create such a broad spectrum of meaning, emotion, knowledge, and experience for all human beings. I was fascinated at an early age by how much joy, mystery, enlightenment, and satisfaction I could get from reading. My parents read books to me regularly, but my interest was insatiable. I learned to read at an early age out of necessity. My mother took me to the library regularly, and as soon as I was done with the books I had read multiple times I was ready to go back. We went to a public library in the downtown area of where I was raised. It was in an old antebellum house that was situated on a beautiful lawn. The hardwood floors and stairs creaked as I investigated the collection of books. There were drafts in the building that created an eerie yet exciting feeling. The librarians were older in age and were dressed modestly, with short, cropped hair or hair that was in a bun. They were not excited about patrons or about people who loved to read. They were only looking for a place to read and to be with books, just like I was. So, there was this unspoken understanding that the library was a shelter, a safe space, where one could commune with an author, with language, in a very solitary and special way. This was a mutual space of solitude.

Another library opened up closer to our home. It was new and modern. It didn't have the same feeling. It definitely catered more to "children" and although I was a child, I liked the more "adult" space of the downtown library. There was no unspoken understanding at this new library that we were all there for solitude in a world that we could enter into and create in our own individual way. There were posters on the wall. There were reading circles and colorful rugs with shapes, numbers, and letters on them. It was not quiet. These people did not seem like they were serious about books. This was not for me. The only aspect of this library that I liked was that one of the librarians looked like a cross between a cat and a witch because of her hair and clothing. She was not friendly. She was not helpful. She really didn't even seem like she wanted to be there. It was as if she was waiting for a spot at the downtown library where she would find solitude with books and a culture more well suited for her.

My parents supported my love for reading, but my mother thought I was too attached to my books. She thought I should spend more time outside playing with children in the neighborhood. Summer where I am from is incredibly hot, and I was not interested in physical activity. The kids who lived nearby liked to play baseball. My brother was all for it, but I was not. I would find my way back inside to my books. I would lie down on the floor in the small space in between my bed and the wall so that my mother wouldn't know I was not outside and that I was reading. Of course, she would catch me from time to time. She actually thought I was lazy. This was when I started to understand that solitude, the time and space for reading, and eventually writing, would be something I would have to fight for throughout my entire life. Not only did the people in my family not understand my love for reading, they also did not understand my love of scholarship that began when I started school.

Kindergarten was a lovely experience for me. That was when kindergarten was a half day. I loved to learn and sing and talk and play while I was at school. It was fun! School was in the afternoon, so mornings were leisurely. My mom made me a full breakfast every morning, such as bacon and eggs. I got to lie around in my pajamas and watch a cartoon or read a book or play with my brother. It was great! Then, after school, it was time for my dad to come home. My mom made a delicious meal every night and we ate together as a family. Then, I could read or draw or play or watch TV with my family. All green lights. This school thing was a pretty nice addition to my life.

Then came first grade. Things changed. It was a full day. I did not wake up naturally on my own. My mom had to wake me up. I had to eat breakfast, get dressed, brush my teeth, and get in the car quickly! It was not pleasant. Then, once I got to school, it was not nearly as fun as kindergarten. It was much more structured. We had a lot more quiet time where we had to complete "assignments" and we could not talk to or play with our classmates unless it was recess. I really struggled with this. Recess usually meant I was sitting on a bench next to the teacher because I was in trouble for not following rules. I didn't understand why things were so different or why what I was doing was so wrong. Letters were sent home pretty regularly. There were parent conferences. I even got suspended once. My mom had to come pick me up from school. She made me stay in my room the rest of the day and night and she made something horrible for dinner. I still believe that was an intended part of my punishment. I was devastated. But, while I was in my room, isolated from everyone else, I found solitude by playing school. I set up my stuffed animals. I got out my books and read to them. I let them play and eat snacks, more like kindergarten. I drew pictures and played records and sang songs. I wanted school to be like that. I wanted to be that kind of teacher.

At some point that school year, my teacher decided that something had to change. I was not happy at school and she wasn't happy about that. She decided to start using positive reinforcement to highlight things I was doing right. She would send home "smile-o-grams" to my parents and they would put them on the refrigerator. I was still talking too much and doing other things I wasn't supposed to do, but I started to like the attention I was getting for the things I was doing right. My behavior started to change. I began to understand the rules and why they were in place. I began to understand that as much as I loved learning, and as quickly as I finished my work, it was unfair to others who took longer to learn and finish their work and I was keeping them from having the learning experience that I loved so much. I truly loved my teacher for what she did for me. I could cry as I write this because of what she did for me. I will never forget her or how she made me feel. That was when I knew I wanted to be a teacher. First grade. Done.

In second grade, the teacher read to us every day from Beverly Clearly and Judy Blume books. Those characters were kindred spirits. They were like me. I read every book I could from both authors. They created these realistic stories that I could relate to, yet there was this magic about those books, in the words, in the way I could fully understand how the characters thought, how I could create in my mind what their houses looked like, what they looked like, what their parents looked like, their dog, their cat, just like a movie. It was absolutely the most exciting thing I had ever experienced, and all of that stemmed from words and language and creativity. There was an inherent connection between the storyteller and me. To be an author just seemed like the most amazing thing a person could possibly be. That was when I knew I wanted to be a writer. Second grade. Done.

I could go on from year to year, but clearly, very early on, a pattern was established that led me through school as an avid learner. I wanted to learn about everything. I wanted to read everything. I wanted to write about everything. I wanted to talk about everything. I never wanted it to end. I am still like that. I love learning.

Fast forward to senior year in high school. I had been a really good student all throughout school, taking advanced classes, making really good grades, having meaningful relationships with my teachers, and enjoying school all around in general. My senior literature teacher let us choose a book we wanted to read from a list that she had. I had no idea which book to pick, so she said "You are an intellectual rebel. I think this one is for you." It was *Crime and Punishment* by Dostoevsky (Dostoevsky, 2001). It changed my life. I could not believe that I wanted this main character to get away with what he had done. How did this author create this reaction in me? How did he do that? I was blown away. Then we got to pick another book. I chose *Song of Solomon* by Toni Morrison (Morrison, 2016). While Dostoevsky's book changed my life, Morrison made me want to change the world. Her story was so riveting and made me so angry and uncomfortable. I always tell my students that you should have at least one book that you want to hug because you love it and it makes you feel happy. You should also have at least one book that you want to throw across the room because it leaves you feeling so angry and unhinged. Eventually, you go back to that book because you have a responsibility to come to terms with it. Senior year was where that happened for me. My teacher was and still is one of my heroes. She was not only the kind of teacher I wanted to be, but she was also the kind of woman I wanted to be. She was strong and self-assured, yet vulnerable. She was intelligent and funny. She was challenging. She was beautiful. By then, I had read many books that I enjoyed, but also many books that made me think about life, books that caused shifts in how I viewed the world. I wanted more of that. Public school. Done.

I started college, but was really interested in making money more than I was in teaching. As much as I wanted to be a teacher, I thought studying medicine was the way to go. I truly was interested in medicine and in helping people, but I also knew that teachers didn't make much money. All that personal and intellectual growth had not fully manifested itself in my plans for the future. Yet.

In my first semester, I took the required classes that everyone has to take, but I was able to earn credit from my high school English class based on my Advanced Placement test score. So, I started off in English 1102 as a freshman. My professor was not a fan of this placement, and he made that clear on my first day in class, in front of all of my classmates. He assigned our first paper. I wrote it the night before in less than two hours. He gave me an F and wrote on the paper that I should make an appointment to come see him in his office. I was absolutely devastated. He told me that the paper was "fine," but he knew I had not pushed myself to do work that was better than what I had done in high school. He told me to rewrite it. So, I did. I did a more thorough analysis of the text and wrote a much better paper. He gave me an A. I began to read with more depth and analysis and pushed myself in classroom discussion. I continued to write papers for him that showed growth and improvement. He gave back one of my papers and didn't put a grade on it. He wrote on the paper that I should make an appointment to come see him in his office. Again, I was devastated. This time, he asked me what I wanted to do with my life. I told him I wanted to pursue a career in medicine. He asked me why, and I gave an honest answer. He told me that I was a talented writer and that I should become an English teacher. I laughed. He gave me one of the best pieces of advice I have ever received. He said, "You spend at least 40 hours of every week doing a job and getting paid for it. Make that job mean something. Make it something you love. Don't pick a career for money. That won't make you happy." I changed my major that day. I became an English major. I did not want to teach public school. I wanted to be a college professor. Freshman year of college. Done.

I continued my studies in English literature with a minor in History. I loved the non-fiction accounts of history as much as I loved English literature. My history professors were published authors and true historians that spun passionate yarns in class lectures about the lived experiences of real people who changed the world. I wanted more of that. I also explored other areas of literature, such as science fiction and fantasy. I developed a new passion for those genres. I fell in love with Renaissance writers and those of the Restoration. I pored over their plays, poems, and essays. I could not get enough! Then, I needed one last English elective to graduate. There was a women's studies class. I wasn't really crazy about the idea, but that was the choice I had to take. The professor, a woman, was "removed" from her position right before the class started, so I ended up with a male professor who had just moved to the U.S. from Malaysia. He was only a couple of years older than I was. He was so curious about American culture. In turn, he opened up so many experiences for us to learn about other cultures. My education thus far had been focused on European and American authors. He expanded that, through authors, women of other cultures. He was so passionate and knowledgeable about these women and cultures. It was just fascinating! That class changed the way I saw the world. It changed the way I saw women! It changed the way I saw myself. I am so thankful that I took that course.

I needed another elective in any area of my choosing, but by the time I registered the course options were few. There was a "deviant behavior" class. I spontaneously chose it. This was a pivotal decision that led me back to my curiosity about human behavior that originally sprung from fiction, as with Dostoevsky. The professor taught the class so objectively, and I liked that approach. While people can exercise deviant behaviors that are harmful to themselves and even to society, I became fascinated in more of an objective, "scientific" way about the psychology and sociology behind all of this, which I completely attribute to my current love of people and teaching. The objective and scientific approach that I still maintain in my love and "study" of people is one of solitude. I can detach myself from the emotions and implications of others' behaviors in order to study them and, honestly, to help them. To teach them!

Then I graduated. I was at a crossroads. I could apply to graduate school at that university or go somewhere else. I wasn't sure. Then my parents announced that they were getting a divorce after thirty years of marriage. My brother was in school at a university in another city. He asked me to come live there so we could be together and get away from the drama of my parent's unraveling marriage. So, I did.

I took a break from school, but lived in a thriving university community that was a combination of extreme political and social pockets of people. This allowed me to still embed myself as an observer and/or participant, at my choosing, in this complex, yet stimulating environment. I worked for a publishing company for a man who was once a university professor. Therefore, much of our publishing work was for people from the school campus who were academics. They would come in with their coffee and "shoot the breeze" with us and talk over their latest chapter. There were vibrant social and political discussions. Even as a very young and inexperienced person in this field, my opinions were invited and validated. My intelligence and creativity were appreciated, and even put to use.

As my brother and I sorted through our family strife and situated ourselves in the new structures that resulted in my parents' divorce, I made new realizations and affirmations about my life. I wanted relationships that were strong and meaningful, which led me to let go of people and situations and obligations that felt negative and toxic. The lifestyle of my twenties that had led to this point was largely based on a "seize the day" mentality, which naturally lent itself to relationships with people that weren't necessarily based on love and trust. That was a turning point for me, that led me in a much more positive direction towards a meaningful and intentional approach to life. That was when I met my husband. Here I was, in a very transitional place in this college town, not knowing where I was going or what I was doing, and then all of a sudden, I was leaving that place of confusing enlightenment to be with him. Although the college town was where I had planned to take root and start my master's program, love led me back home. His promise to me was that I would be able to continue my dreams.

In less than three years, we were married. I had a job in the meantime that allowed me to pay the bills and just figure out my next steps. This job did not require much of me intellectually or emotionally. Sometimes I miss that job! I didn't "take it home" with me. It was just a job. Yet, it was so incredibly boring and meaningless. I knew it was not forever. My mom suggested I teach at the high school level. I would start with a "provisional" certificate and go back to school for a few classes to get my teaching certificate. I get to go back to reading and writing? Sign me up! Although I did not believe that teenagers were my cup of tea, and neither was public high school, I did it. Getting back into college classes propelled me into where I am today, with a doctoral degree. I was unstoppable, getting a master's degree, then a specialist's degree. Shortly, I moved on to my doctorate. I truly enjoyed every single bit of it, although it was also completely harrowing and exhausting! I had my two children during those years. I worked very hard as a new teacher to establish myself. I moved to a new school after the first seven years at my first school. I fell in love with teaching and with the minds and personalities of high school students. I loved the collegial relationships that I developed, which have been long lasting, and I have grown tremendously as a teacher and as a human.

However, teaching is also where I found episodes of extreme isolation. I have never found it more difficult to read and write in my personal time. I always found space for that before I started teaching—my oasis, my escape. Teaching is so mentally and emotionally exhausting that I began to feel isolated from being an academic, from performing the activities that gave me the mental and emotional escape that I needed to rejuvenate and grow and thrive as a human. Pursuing my doctorate was the way that I *made* myself stay in an academic space. I forced myself into solitude. There was so much friction along the way, being a wife, mother, daughter, friend, teacher, but I found the time and space for scholarship. I read mind blowing texts and wrote papers that I was proud of. I was forced to realize that I could do things I didn't think I could do in my current "status" as a woman at this stage in life. This translated into my teaching, where I pushed students to realize their potential as well. There were moments of discomfort, where I took what I learned in my doctoral program and incorporated it quite awkwardly at first into my practice. My students didn't quite understand the changes or my vulnerability. I was taking risks, and it was hard! My colleagues didn't understand it either and that caused me quite a bit of distress in the work environment, where I definitely felt misunderstood and isolated. Luckily, I found comfort in those who were in the same doctoral program I was in, and my professors were a huge source of support as well. Those moments of discomfort and vulnerability led me to where I am now. I continue to face moments of isolation and insecurity, but because of experience, I know that they are temporary and fleeting and that they will lead to greater growth. So, here I am in my last decade of my teaching career. As I navigate isolation and solitude, I find it easier and easier to set healthy boundaries for myself and find the time and space I need in that metaphorical space of solitude, on the ground between the bedroom wall and my bed. This is the place where I can read and dream and be whoever and whatever I want to be, knowing there are no obligations whatsoever, while also navigating the space of the obligations that I do have, to my family, friends, and students, which are all the more important, meaningful, and worthwhile because of the balance I continue to develop.

References

Dostoevsky, F. (2001). *Crime and punishment*. Signet Classics.
Morrison, Toni. (2016). *Song of Solomon*. Vintage.

· 6 ·

TEACHER ON TRIAL: THE CASE OF THE PUBLIC INTELLECTUAL

Stacey T. Brown

Our whole lives are journeys, but sometimes we do not realize it until we embark upon personal conflicts that are inherently wrapped in wonderful adventures. The order of the universe establishes a continuum between trial and tribulation; not a duality, but a spectrum. We do not truly appreciate happiness without angst; achievement without disappointment; love without hate. I have always perceived my educational journey as happy one from the time I was a small child. My education, whether formal or personal, has always been tightly linked to my identity and self-worth. Like hooks,

> While I wanted teaching to be my career, I believed that personal success was intimately linked with self-actualization. My passion for this quest led me to interrogate constantly the mind/body split that was so often taken to be a given. (1994, p. 18)

I have always been a good student. It is one of my highest priorities. My life as a teacher has always been relatively seamless and joyful as well, aside from the expected aggravations that teachers endure due to meetings, paperwork, and time constraints. The discovery of my conflict as a student and as a teacher started when I began the Curriculum Studies program at Georgia Southern University. My education in Curriculum Studies has allowed me to take an archaeological dig of my so-called "scholarly" past to unearth the truth about myself as a student, an educator, and a human being. I now realize that the conflict wrapped in my adventure has served as the core of my existence and for that I am thankful. Whitehead says, "Education is discipline for the adventure of life" (1929, p. 98). I am using this opportunity as a cathartic opportunity to unearth my past, to define my present, and to predict my future.

When I began my studies at Georgia Southern, one idea became deeply rooted in the ground of my consciousness: solitude. As a married, white, southern mother, daughter, and teacher, how would I find time to be a student? I needed solitude. I consider solitude a rare natural resource in the field of education that is becoming endangered and unsustainable. Time is so economized in our society, particularly in public schools, that we do not value reading, writing, or thinking as critical for educators and we wonder why our students do not value them either. Giroux says, "I have argued that by viewing teachers as intellectuals we can begin to rethink and reform the traditions and conditions that have prevented teachers from assuming their full potential as active, reflective scholars and practitioners" (2012, p. 14). My initial conflict was grounded in finding the time to read and write and further my own scholarship in order to better myself as a person and as an educator. The more I sought solitude, the more isolated I became. I began to splinter the words "solitude" and "isolation," connoting important differences in meaning that are largely consumed as synonymous. Solitude is a positive state, where time and space allow for creativity and erudition. In the transition to solitude, ironically, time and space are suspended, as the individual feeds on the food of solitude to gain important understanding about the world we live in based on the purity of freedom provided by this state. Whitehead matches the idea of solitude with this assertion: "The combination of imagination and learning normally requires some leisure, freedom from restraint, freedom from harassing worry, some variety of experiences, and the stimulation of other minds diverse in opinion and diverse in equipment" (1929, p. 97). Solitude is where we go to reflect and regenerate.

As I inserted myself into the world of Curriculum Studies, this lack of time and space kept me from the solitude I so desperately sought and the feelings of isolation began to grow. I felt malnourished as I struggled to spend time with my books. My writing was fragmented. My thoughts were jumbled. My emotions were shipwrecked. In addition, I was struggling to reconcile what I was learning with what and how I was teaching, and even living. I have this notion that I call the power of "I don't know" that stems from this particular facet of my experience as a Curriculum Studies student. Collins offers the positive aspects of the power of "I don't know," saying,

> Not knowing required me to think more broadly about the core ideas of my argument, the ideas that are larger than any political party, any media figure, and the specific expression of broader issues concerning democracy as they are expressed at this historic moment. (2013, p. 143)

The power of "I don't know" can be so much more profound than certainty. I was previously fairly confident in my teaching practice, although I was always reflective and always made changes based on experience in my pedagogy. This new type of reflection was different. My understanding of the world was so shaken, so unsettling, that I was unsure about everything. I did not know what I believed or why I believed it or how to even figure it out, much less apply it to my teaching. This experience is how I arrived at the power of "I don't know." I began to realize it was best not to act—yet. It was better to be in a state of traction and tension. In response to a plea for help, Dr. John Weaver, who would become my chair professor, suggested I not treat solitude as a scarcity to be found, but to intentionally carve out time and space for solitude, a metaphorical vessel within a metaphysical state of being, suitable for helping me transgress back into the sea of knowledge before me to navigate the storms of understanding and identity. I had to get off the isolated island of aporia, of intellectual isolation, and into a floating vessel of solitude where I could explore the aporia with intellectual freedom. Dewey says,

> Genuine freedom, in short, is intellectual; it rests in the trained power of thought, in ability to 'turn things over,' to look at matters deliberately, to judge whether the amount and kind of evidence requisite for decision is at hand, and if not, to tell where and how to seek such evidence. (2012, p. 60)

This freedom can only happen in solitude.

In the construction of this vessel, I decided to explore the philosophical differences between isolation and solitude and how they impact scholarship by writing about them for both of my professors one semester. During that semester, I also decided it was time to transfer some of what I was learning theoretically into pedagogical practice. Whitehead says, "Imagination cannot be acquired once and for all, and then kept indefinitely in an ice box to be produced periodically in stated quantities" (1929, p. 97). Much of that semester pushed me further into isolation, due to the uncertainty and the state of "I don't know," but it translated into a space of therapeutic reading and reflective writing in solitude once I was able to establish that carved out time and space, that place of flow where time and space do not even exist. At that point, I decided to come forward and share my newborn knowledge and beliefs with others, particularly in my classroom. Because I shifted gears mid-school year, I had to explain my "new" beliefs and practices in the classroom and eventually defend them within my department. While students reacted positively, many of my colleagues did not. The reaction I received placed me back in a state of isolation and aporia. When others questioned or rejected what I put into practice, I was defensive, confused, angry, and scared! I realized that maybe I was not yet deeply established enough in my beliefs and practices, at least not enough to defend them. It was not time to put theory into practice. I was not ready to leave my solitude. I was still in traction, in an in-between space, oscillating between old and new knowledge and understanding. There was still more investigating to do. Whitehead supports this need by saying, "Do you want your teachers to be imaginative? Then encourage them to research" (1929, p. 97), but the current school setting does not provide for this time, nor do they support the idea. The only reason I was able to carve out the time and space of solitude was because I had the responsibility of being a doctoral student. I forced myself into this metaphysical state. I continued to read and write, semester after semester, reflecting, questioning, and developing. I continued to wrestle with ideas and perspectives and identity. These were the growing pains that came from struggle and challenge that eventually led to inspiration and enlightenment; indeed, intellectual freedom. There were also tears, like the waters that shape the rocks in a riverbed. These burning tears created the flow and direction of the waters I navigated as a human being. This was my experience in solitude. It allowed me to make sense and find Truth and prepared me to emerge from solitude as an active participant in the political discourse of education.

My growing pains and emotions continue to emerge as I become liberated. I say *become* because, "Liberty is a practice" (Foucault, 2007, p. 165). I am not, and will never be, truly liberated. Foucault says that

> The liberty of men is never assured by the institutions and laws that are intended to guarantee them. This is why almost all of these laws and institutions are quite capable of being turned around. Not because they are ambiguous, but simply because "liberty" is what must be exercised. (p. 165)

Initially, this liberty made me feel isolated. Whenever I shared what I was learning with others in the school community, there were those who were incredulous, even critical. I learned to guard my knowledge and keep it to myself. I only wanted to retreat further. I did not understand that "schools are not neutral sites and teachers cannot assume the posture of being neutral either" (Giroux 1988, p. 127). I was allowing what I know to leave me vulnerable and that made me retreat. I felt more and more misunderstood and wondered how much of a price I was willing to pay personally for my education and my beliefs. I also wondered if I had what it takes to become more than a scholar, to become a non-neutral public intellectual. As a teacher and a human being, Foucault reinforces the point:

> This is the situation that we are in and that we must combat. If intellectuals in general are to have a function, if critical thought itself has a function, and, even more specifically, if philosophy has a function within critical thought, it is precisely to accept this sort of spiral, this sort of revolving door of rationality that refers us to its necessity, to its indispensability, and at the same time, to its intrinsic dangers. (2007, p. 168)

After several readings of Foucault and his philosophy of power, I decided I was ready to put theory into practice again. I began to realize I could not simply remain a secluded scholar, cozy at my desk, drinking hot tea, listening to classical music, and musing over student papers. I began to feel motivated to fight against the disdain I received for my ideas and my teaching methods. I felt obligated to share what I had learned from Curriculum Studies in order to allow my students to find Truth for themselves. I also realized that my new beliefs and practices were not static, that it was okay for them to be questioned and that I should be receptive to dialogue about them. Solitude, as a construct of time and space, began to take on new shades of meaning. Foucault says, "Space is fundamental in any form of communal life; space is fundamental in any exercise of power" (p. 170). I now realize that I must not only find solitude in order to do the work of a scholar, but that I must establish time and space to share my work with the public. Miller combines solitude with activism: "My dichotomous self welcomes the floater, the watcher, and, merging, I become, for a moment anyway, an active agent in my world" (2005, p. 70).

I remember sharing my dissertation idea of isolation and solitude with Dr. Sabrina Ross, who became a member of my dissertation committee. We were talking about my form of inquiry, and I assumed that mine would be philosophical. Dr. Ross said that there were certainly shades of philosophy there, but my form of inquiry was undoubtedly political. I was shocked, even in denial. I have never considered myself a "political" person. I had never liked inserting myself in the arena of politics in the school setting and I did not like talking publicly about them. I now realize that "Politics is everywhere; there can be no escape into the realms of pure art and thought or, for that matter, into the realm of disinterested objectivity or transcendental theory" (Said, 1994, p. 21). She went on to explain that my topic applies to oppressed groups and that I, myself, was part of an oppressed group. I could not lobby for solitude or against isolation without public discourse. My topic could not stay in isolation or my life would become a self-fulfilling prophecy and I would remain in exile. I could not just write a dissertation to "get things off my chest"! I had an obligation to be public and political; to stand up for myself and for others who are oppressed. This was another moment that moved me to tears because I did not intend for this to happen, but at the same time I knew this was an inevitable, exciting part of my future. Miller asserts that we must learn to operate in "doubled spaces-spaces of both insulation and inclusion" (2005, p. 78). At the time, I thought that doubled spaces might be possible for Miller but not for me. I began to learn that it is a practice and that it is a mode of survival that allows us to "carve out such spaces" (p. 80) of solitude that allow us to operate as public intellectuals.

I have always had good relationships with my students, but when I began to incorporate what I was learning from Curriculum Studies into my classroom, it transformed my teaching. I would now consider myself more scholarly, which was my initial goal, but also more political and outspoken. I initially wanted scholarship for myself. Now, I want it for everyone. I do not teach students to believe my Truths, but to find their own. Greene addresses this challenge to teachers:

> Yet the serious teacher is in constant tension. On the one hand, he knows that he cannot tell his students how to invent and choose themselves... On the other hand, he knows he has to take deliberate action to enable diverse students to learn how to learn; and sometimes this deliberate action must take the form of engineering, or behavioral control. (1973, p. 92)

My interpretation of Greene's behavioral control implies engineering that encourages critical thinking and educational risk. I encourage my students to join me in taking risks. We challenge ourselves and we learn from our failures. This was a big shift for my high school students who were very uncomfortable with failure. It was a big shift for me, too. It has made me a more confident teacher, but I have learned to be more confident in the power of "I don't know," which means that based on what I read and write, based on intellectual discourse with others, based on new experiences in educational practices, my knowledge and beliefs may inevitably change. This is where real growth begins. As I tell my students every year, if we keep doing what we already know how to do, how are we learning anything new? How are we growing? We must branch out and climb up and take leaps. We must embrace the growing pains.

As I began to see myself more as a public intellectual, I began to bring controversial issues into the classroom in very creative ways, which, again, brought attention to my students and me, and it was usually negative attention. We were doing things differently. I began to feel even more isolated from my peers. Some of these colleagues brought their concerns to the attention of the administration. I was fairly new at this school, so everyone was already trying to figure me out. Students in my classes began to tell students in other classes who began to tell their teachers what we were doing in my classes and the oppression began. The isolation grew. I found less and less time to read for my doctoral classes because I felt so persecuted. I started to question everything that I was doing. I began to question my entire existence! I felt that my whole identity was being attacked. I was a teacher on trial. When I was called into the office by administration and presented with a list of accusations, my response was that they were all true. Members of the administration, upon further explanation of my practices, had no further questions and I was proclaimed innocent. My students were meeting the goals set before them and even surpassing them. Regardless, questions and complaints about my teaching persisted within my department because what I was doing was different than how others were doing it. I was not utilizing the prescribed, standardized practices that were a part of the culture in the department. A large part of my teaching philosophy is embodied in Whitehead's assertion that

> New directions of thought arise from flashes of intuition bringing new material within the scope of scholarly learning. They commence as the sheer ventures of rash speculation. They may fortunately obtain quick acceptance, or they may initiate a quarrel of scholars from which all tinge of speculation has faded. (1933, p. 108)

I was officially in exile.

I was once called an "intellectual rebel" by one of my favorite teachers in high school. I have always considered that to be a compliment, and it was intended to be so. I do not consider myself an actual rebel as an adult, as in someone who intentionally defies or breaks rules, but I am no conformist. I have learned to assert my intellectual freedom and have gained confidence in going against the grain (creative insubordination?). I find creative ways to meet the common goals and resist standardized practices. With the demands to conform, I did not respond to the suggestions of my colleagues at all. I simply stayed silent and continued to teach the way I had all year, instilling critical thinking in an effort to "connect the personal with the political, the practical with the theoretical, and the local with the global though passionate participation in and critical reflection upon teaching, learning, inquiry, and life" (He, 2010, p. 471). Whitehead demonstrates his support of this idea by stating, "It is our business-philosophers, students, and practical men to re-create and reenact a vision of the world, including those elements of reverence and order without which society lapses in to riot, and penetrated through and through with unflinching rationality" (1933, p. 99). Asserting my intellectual freedom and working among oppressors placed me in a position of exile.

It took me a really long time to heal from this indictment. I felt outside of the circle of that establishment; in exile. I had no sense of belonging, but I began to find courage. Freire says that "Courage, as a virtue, is not something I can find outside myself. Because it comprises the conquering of my fears, it implies fear" (2005, p. 75). Even armed with courage, I began to feel paranoid about how my colleagues perceived me. While my administration was very supportive of what I was doing, I felt they were also protective of my accusers. I didn't really know who they were. Their identities were protected. Therefore, I suspected all of them. I was not punished, but I certainly was not defended. I wanted to quit. I even expressed this to my administration. I knew I would not actually do it, but the feeling of exile was unbearable. I fought against this isolation, realizing that

> The pursuit of full humanity, however, cannot be carried out in isolation or individualism, but only in fellowship and solidarity; therefore, it cannot unfold in the antagonistic relations between the oppressors and the oppressed. No one can be authentically human while he prevents others from being so. (Freire, 1970 p. 85)

This brings to light the importance of relationships in any organization, but particularly among academics. More and more we see relationships that are forced because we teach common subjects or grade levels or ability levels. We are not always free to work alone or to work with those with whom we have common interests, ideas, and teaching styles. Of course, it is appropriate to have systems of accountability for what teachers are expected to do to ensure that students are being educated to their maximum potential. However, it is difficult to forge important academic relationships under forced constraints.

The initiative to bring teachers together to produce common curriculum can actually leave them feeling isolated, misunderstood, and unsupported. If there were more organic opportunities for teachers to come together in the spirit of intellectualism, then teachers would flourish. If I was given a seat at the table of my critics before the judgment began, how would things have been different? What could we all have gained? Where was the time to discuss our ideas and hone our craft when the required discussion, from which I was excluded, was how we would create standardized benchmarks and common assessments? Why must we all teach a unit exactly the same way? Where do our unique gifts, talents, and interests enter into the classroom? How will our students be inspired when we are not? Schools should be a place for teachers and students to engage in academic discourse. Schools are not businesses. Students are not human capital. Relationships are more important than partnerships. That is also true of the relationship between teachers and students:

> Loving our students requires us to help them nourish their own self-love and self-trust. If I hope to be a good teacher, I must defend my students, especially against myself. I will teach then, not credulousness but critical awareness, not easy belief but skepticism, not blind faith but curiosity. I want no reverence for what I say; I want no disciples. (Ayers, 2004, p. 93)

This is important. We cannot be homogenous in our beliefs, but we can be harmonious in our discussion and tolerance of them. We need to understand that

> philosophical thought does not bring its concepts together in friendship without again being traversed by a fissure that leads them back to hatred or disperses them in the coexisting chaos where it is necessary to take them up again, to seek them out, to make a leap. (Deleuze & Guattari, 1994, p. 203)

This does not happen in a standardized classroom. We must provide our students a safe space for this process as we build a space of our own and together, we flourish.

Teachers can create unique "uncommon" non-standardized ways of teaching that allow students to be successful on standardized tests. We must advocate for intellectual freedom, for ourselves and for our students. Freire helps us understand that

> The revolution is made neither by the leaders for the people, nor by the people for the leaders, but by both acting together in unshakable solidarity. This solidarity is born only when the leaders witness to it by their humble, loving, and courageous encounter with the people. (1970, p. 129).

This happens in classrooms that allow for critical thinking, individuality, vulnerability, and a safe place for mistakes and resistance. Illich describes this phenomenon:

> Healthy students often redouble their resistance to teaching as they find themselves more comprehensively manipulated. This resistance is due not to the authoritarian style of a public school or the seductive style of some free schools, but to the fundamental approach common to all schools—the idea that one person's judgment should determine what and when another person must learn. (1970, pp. 41–42)

Through careful study and examination of the world we live in, through different lenses in our classrooms, we redouble our resistance to "traditional" schooling. We must refuse to be "docile bodies" (Foucault, 1979, p. 138) and choose to be teacher and student activists. Ultimately, "Transformative intellectuals need to develop a discourse that unites the language of critique with the language of possibility, so that social educators recognize that they can make changes" (Giroux 1988, p. 128).

I spent the first part of my teaching career and the first part of my doctoral studies believing that I could be and wanted to be a cloistered, private intellectual, and that I would read and write all for myself. This drove me into isolation, first of all because I have never read less in my life than I did when I first started teaching. This is antithetical to the purpose of teaching! I forced myself to become a doctoral student so that I could immerse myself in intellectual acts because they were not happening within the school where I was teaching! We must advocate for the school as a center of academic discourse, for both teachers and students. We must demand time and space, the solitude we need, to hone our craft. At the same time, we must come forward and share our beliefs and ideas with others, as public intellectuals. As Giroux points out teachers

> must speak out against economic, political and social injustices both within and outside of schools. At the same time, they must work to create the conditions that give students the opportunity to become citizens who have the knowledge and courage to struggle in order to make despair unconvincing and hope practical. (1988, p. 128)

When we simply act as facilitators, presenting materials that do not align with our intellectual ideals, and interests, we are no longer teachers. We are merely clinicians. As a doctor of education, I intend to practice education, just as a medical doctor practices medicine. Teachers should be trusted to hone their craft and create their own materials. While it is appropriate that teachers should be evaluated and measured in quantitative ways, much of what teachers do is qualitative. Education can be clinical and standardized and students can score well on exams that way, but don't we also want them to immerse themselves in the knowledge that is necessary for those exams in meaningful ways that help them also find out who they are and why they matter and what they want to be in the world? Shouldn't teaching include the heart and the soul, not just the mind? When teachers practice education and hone their craft in profound and meaningful ways, magical things happen in the classroom. Rose accurately describes this through an experience of his own:

> I saw the effect of high expectations: teachers taking students seriously as intellectual and social beings. I saw what happens when the teachers distribute responsibility through a classroom, create opportunities for students to venture opinion, follow a hunch, make something new. I saw the power of bringing students together around common problems and projects–the intellectual and social energy that results, generating vital public space. (2009, p. 151)

Through my doctoral studies, and through educational practice, I have learned to be authentic and to lose the shell of that traumatized person I was when my teaching was in question. Ayers reminds us that,

> Teachers in an open, democratic society must learn to think freely and without fear, to have and to use minds of our own, to discover and to make sense for ourselves ... This is required of us if we hope to teach students who will continue to develop minds of their own. (2004, p. 10)

I am naturally a happy, peaceful person and like to be friendly with everyone. For a while, I didn't feel like I could do that. So now I hold my head up and I smile in the halls and say hello, like I always did before any of this happened. I have made peace with my oppressors, even if all of them have not made peace with me. I treat them with kindness, despite how they treat me. I realize they are also oppressed, maybe even more than I was. Following Freire, I believe that

> As the oppressors dehumanize others and violate their rights, they themselves also become dehumanized. As the oppressed, fighting to be human takes away the oppressors' power to dominate and suppress, they restore to the oppressors the humanity they had lost in the exercise of oppression. (1970, p. 56)

I realized that the source of my oppressors' frustration stemmed from the fact that teachers "who are not concerned with inner well-being are the most threatened by the demand on the part of students for liberatory education, for pedagogical processes that will aid them in their own struggle for self-actualization" (hooks, 1994, p. 17). I also realize I will always be either in exile or "in-between in exile" (He, 2010, p. 478) and will operate in "doubled spaces" (Miller, 2005, p. 78). Said says "Exile means that you are always going to be marginal, and that what you do as an intellectual has to be made up because you cannot follow a prescribed path" (1994, p. 62). The intellectual rebel still residing in me finds this incredibly exciting, and Said agrees:

> If you can experience that fate not as a deprivation and as something to be bewailed, but as a sort of freedom, a process of discovery in which you do things according to your own patter, as various interests seize your attention, and as the particular goal you set yourself dictates: that is a unique pleasure. (1994, p. 62)

This is not to say that I do not adhere to my ethical responsibilities as a citizen and educator. Said warns us that "The intellectual is supposed to be heard from, and in practice ought to be stirring up debate and if possible, controversy. But the alternatives are not total quiescence or total rebelliousness" (1994, p. 69). I believe this is important in order to be taken seriously as an intellectual.

During this difficult period of my life, when I felt so isolated and disrespected, two key figures emerged. One was a fellow teacher who reached out to me. We had intriguing, collegial discussions about what we were teaching and planned curriculum together. We were both comfortable with having creative control in our respective classrooms, while also doing many things exactly the same way. She also became one of my defenders. The other figure is the colleague who encouraged me to pursue my doctorate in curriculum studies. As I grew in my writing and became more confident in my teaching, he and I also became close colleagues and he continued to encourage me as I progressed through the Curriculum Studies program. That led me to realize that it is important to reach out to others who are exiled and oppressed. Mentoring and supporting others is another important role in being a public intellectual. I want my struggle to mean something, so I use my experience to reach out to others who might be experiencing what I went through, those who feel exiled, misunderstood, judged for their beliefs and practices. This is another way I practice education, outside of the classroom, outside of students, outside of school. It was hard for me to find people I could trust when I was going through my time of persecution. I don't want others to experience that. These academic relationships are so important in order to build a world where education is a place for intellectual discourse, where difference is respected, where we learn from one another, even when we do not agree with each other, where we respect each other's right to practice education differently.

After reading about and working with other amazing writers, professors, and educators who have experienced isolation, oppression, and exile, I realize I would rather experience isolation, oppression, and exile than be in the state I was in before entering Curriculum Studies. I feel more alive and aware. Like hooks,

> I am grateful to the many women and men who dare to create theory from the location of pain and struggle, who courageously expose wounds to give us their experience to teach and guide, as a means to chart new theoretical journeys. Their work is liberatory. (1994, p. 74)

As a result, I have grown as a person. Said states that

> it is a spirit in opposition, rather than in accommodation, that grips me because the romance, the interest, the challenge of intellectual life is to be found in dissent against the status quo at a time when the struggle on behalf of underrepresented and disadvantaged groups seems so unfairly weighted against them. (1994, p. xvii)

Public intellectuals like Said have helped me discover the importance of my activism as a teacher. My teaching is so much more meaningful and rewarding to me and to my students. Collins says that, "The search for justice is an ongoing, principled struggle that resists disciplinary power relations and gives meaning to every day life" (2013, p. 26). I see my state of tension and flux in isolation, solitude, and in-between spaces as necessary and positive.

Now that I have more of a grasp on how to carve out the time and space of solitude, I navigate more smoothly. I am bolder and more resilient. I realize the storms are going to come and that they are necessary. I am equipped for the weathering. Curriculum Studies has led me into inlets and coves of new literature and ideas that have helped me to transcend the murky and dangerous waters of exile onto a land where I find others who share my plight. But I will never remain a landlubber. My journey will always take me back to the sea of solitude where I read and write and make meaning and go forth to share it with others. I realize that I can be the most isolating force in my own life. In seeking solitude in order to be a private intellectual, I had created a prison from which I was not able to emerge. Said says:

> For in its essence the intellectual life—and I speak here mainly about the social sciences and the humanities—is about the freedom to be critical: criticism is intellectual life and while the academic precinct contains a great deal in it, its spirit is intellectual and critical, and neither reverential nor patriotic. (2000, p. 397)

Becoming a public intellectual rather than a secluded scholar allows me to exist as an intellectual in both private and public settings, as a more well-rounded, self-actualized person.

Promoting the idea of public scholarship and academia within the school, for both teachers and students, could transform education in mind blowing ways, and that can only happen through intellectual discourse and academic freedom, where we do not standardize and pre-package curriculum. When teachers can create lessons and units that come from a place of continued research and scholarship, those lessons and units can still meet standards and can prepare students for standardized assessment. Standardization may have its place, but there should be limits that protect teachers and allow them to hone their craft. Teachers should practice education, not facilitate it. We are practitioners, not clinicians. There should be time and space for solitude in the educational system for both teachers and students. Not every moment should be economized. Productivity happens in inert states as well as active states. Professional development should further teacher scholarship and should promote intellectual evolution. Meetings should allow for intellectual conversations about teachers' own research interests, readings, and writings. To avoid pushing teachers into exile and isolation, rather than judging one another and demanding that everyone do everything the same way, we should support each other and learn from one another, realizing that even when we cannot be homogenous in our beliefs, we can be harmonious in our discussion and tolerance of them.

While I continue to teach, one of the newer roles I fill now as an educator allows me to support and defend teachers in a very unique way. I am not an administrator, but do hold a supervisory role. Because I am still in the classroom, in the trenches, with them, I still share the experience of teaching with them. I can relate to the challenges and difficulties in their current political and educational climate. I can be a mediator, an intermediary force, for teacher and students, teachers and parents, and even teachers and administrators, and that gives me great satisfaction! I do not think I could ever leave the classroom completely or not work closely with high school students. That is what ignites the greatest fire within me. However, working within an educational world that is united as a community is just more than I could have ever imagined when I wanted to be a secluded teacher-scholar. The confidence I have gained through my doctoral studies and through the application of what I have learned has truly allowed me to transcend so much of the fear and isolation that held me back as an educator and a human! I am also working with a former student who is now a college student and am serving on his committee as he writes his thesis! This is not at all what I thought I wanted when I became a teacher, but it is definitely what I want now as an educator. With a little less than a decade to go in my career, I am hopeful that I will continue to evolve as a public intellectual who co-creates passionate educational communities that promote intellectual freedom and academic discourse!

References

Ayers, W. (2004). *Teaching toward freedom: Moral commitment and ethical action in the classroom.* Beacon Press.
Collins, P. H. (2013). *On intellectual activism.* Temple University Press.
Deleuze, G., & Guattari, F. (1994). *What is philosophy?* Columbia University Press.
Dewey, J. (2012). *How we think.* Renaissance Classics.
Foucault, M. (1979). *Discipline and punish: The birth of the prison.* Vintage Books.
Foucault, M. (2007). "Space, power and knowledge." In S. During (Ed.), *The cultural studies reader.* Routledge.
Freire, P. (1970). *Pedagogy of the oppressed.* Continuum.
Freire, P. (2005). *Teachers as cultural workers: Letters to those who dare to teach.* Westview Press.
Giroux, H. (1988). *Teachers as intellectuals: Toward a critical pedagogy of learning.* Bergin & Garvey.
Giroux, H. (2012). The war against teachers as public intellectuals in dark times. *Truthout.org.* 17 Dec. 2012, 8:22.
Greene, M. (1973). *Teacher as stranger: Educational philosophy for the modern age.* Wadsworth Publishing Company, Inc.
He, M. F. (2010). Exile pedagogy: Teaching in-between. *Handbook of public pedagogy: Education and learning beyond schooling* (pp. 469–480). Routledge.
hooks, b. (1994). *Teaching to transgress: Education as the practice of freedom.* Routledge.
Illich, I. (1970). *Deschooling society.* Marion Boyers.
Miller, J. (2005). *Sounds of silence breaking.* Peter Lang Publishing, Inc.
Rose, M. (2009). *Why school? Reclaiming education for all of us.* The New Press.
Said, E. W. (2000). *Reflections on exile and other essays.* Harvard University Press.
Said, E. W. (1994). *Representations of the intellectual.* Vintage Books.
Whitehead, A. N. (1933). *Adventures of ideas.* The Free Press.
Whitehead, A. N. (1929). *The aims of education and other essays.* The Free Press.

· 7 ·

SEEKING THE FUNDAMENTAL, ELEGANT, AND SIMPLE

John H. Cato

Every journey starts at a place and at a time, and my teaching journey started in college the spring of 1993. My college had a required core, and although I was a declared computer science (CS) major, during my sophomore year, I was required to take physics. In fact, that was the first physics course of my life. Although I had some vague ideas about what I would learn in the class, what I could not have foreseen was that physics class was going to change the trajectory of my entire life.

On the first day of class, I sat in my assigned seat, in class order. We sat in order of the "best" student in the class to the "worst" student in the class. By luck, on day one, I was assigned to be the section marcher, or the student responsible for essentially taking roll, passing out papers, and other odds and ends. I was also responsible for calling the class to attention when the professor walked in.

When class started, I immediately knew something was very different. My professor began by stating the course would be our first "real" course in logic. He also asked us some questions which I thought I knew the answers to but quickly found out that I had all kinds of misconceptions. He explained how many more things I thought I understood were in fact wrong, and said we would be systematically chipping away our misconceptions until we understood Nature as it really is. He also explained that when we had questions, we should email him the questions so that the entire class could benefit. And if we had difficulty with homework problems, again, email. Then, he gave the first lecture, and I remember thinking, I wish I could be so logical. The ways he connected ideas and explained concepts were something I had never experienced before. He had such an ability to take something complicated and make it so incredibly simple. I knew on that very first day I wanted to learn to think like he did. I knew on that very first day I might want to study physics. I knew on that very first day I might want to be a teacher.

After a few weeks, one night, I had a question about one of my homework problems—I can still remember the problem. I crafted my email, I sent it, and I waited for his response. To this day, I can still remember the opening to his reply: "You really have a great mind for physics!" To be honest, that was the first time I can recall anyone ever telling me I might be good at something. I knew I was doing well. But for him to say I had a great mind for physics is what really opened me up to believing I might be good at it. I knew after that email that I not only wanted to study physics, but I also wanted to teach it! I met with my professor about changing my major, and he was nothing but supportive. Consequently, I switched my major to physics, and set out to become a physics teacher.

After college, I was headed to grad school to get my Ph.D. in physics. But due to my father-in-law's illness, my wife and I decided to defer. But I had to have a job. So, I found myself teaching math and physical science at a private school for a few years. When it came time for me to resume grad school, we had laid down roots. My plans had changed, but not my goal. I still wanted to be a physics teacher. So, I got certified to teach high school physics, and I was hired to teach physics at a local high school.

Although I had wonderful college physics professors, I still had a great deal of hard work to do in order to actually become a good teacher. However, during my first few years, becoming a good teacher was probably the furthest thing from my mind. I was, truthfully, just trying to survive. I found myself having too many students, too many preps, too many emails, too many meetings, too many duties, and too little time. I found myself simply overwhelmed by the volume of work—much of which had nothing to do with teaching physics.

After a few years of teaching, I knew if I was going survive and continue teaching, I was going to have to find a way to address my workload and make it manageable. Reflecting, I recalled Dr. Joe Pizzo's speech to West Point's Physics Honor Society, Sigma Pi Sigma. In that speech, Dr. Pizzo submits that physics is what a physicist does, and that what physicists do can be summed up in three operational adjectives: fundamental, elegant, and simple. And as Dr. Pizzo stated, to the best of my recollection, physics is a way of organizing our complicated universe into a few fundamental and elegant models with the goal to make it as simple as possible. I knew what I was going to have to do was find a way to bring that way of thinking into my classroom. I was going to have to find a way of reducing the complexity of the classroom to its fundamental components and make an elegant model with my goal being to make teaching, both the action of teaching as well as the professional obligations of being a teacher, as simple as possible. Consequently, I began considering how best to accomplish that goal.

The first thing I did was to figure out what I really wanted to "teach" my students. To that end, I developed three overall goals which have served me for much of my career. They are:

Goal 1: Introduce students to how Nature really works.
Goal 2: Develop logical, critical, and analytical thinking skills.
Goal 3: Introduce the students to the high-tech world they are about to go into and operate.

Introducing students to how Nature really works is my foundational goal because it's the reason I first fell in love with physics. Consequently, I want to share that with my students. And helping my students develop their thinking skills is important because regardless of whether my students go into physics or not, they will need logical, critical, and analytical thinking skills in every part of their lives. Finally, introducing students to the high-tech world is important because every day, every aspect of their lives is so dependent on technology.

Having developed those goals allowed me to focus my lessons like never before because I knew the overall points and purposes of my course. Teaching no longer was about getting through the content or writing tests or grading papers. Instead, each day I thought about what I could do to make my students progress towards accomplishing my goals.

Next, I needed to find a way of making my life simpler as a teacher. Out of that pursuit came what I call, for the lack of better words, my overall teaching philosophy. While this chapter is autobiographical, I do hope my example can benefit other teachers as well. I can summarize my philosophy in a brief outline below:

(1) Establish high standards, otherwise (generally) the response will not be effort-filled. It is key to physics (at least) that successful students put forth the effort, since the subject is not always innately clear.
(2) Once the standards are established, expect the students to be honestly trying to understand, treating them as responsible individuals. Homework is a teaching tool. Those who want to learn will use the homework as the tool it is. This will provide the springboard for questions and other explorations.
(3) Because of (1) and (2) above, ensure that the instruction is as direct and to the point of understanding as possible. Don't waste the students' time.
(4) Hence, listen to what the student questions are really saying, as opposed to what the words are indicating. Because the "language" is new, the students may not have the vocabulary yet to truly express their interest and/or confusion. Generally, behind each question there is a conceptual level of understanding that needs to be tweaked. Listen for that!
(5) Develop the conceptual awareness. Once the concepts are established, the problems become significantly easier to handle. Once we've reduced the physics to equations, it becomes a math problem. The beauty of the science is the conceptual understanding!
(6) Finally, "Socratically" involve the students. Lecturing is boring and non-involved. Causing the students to respond and be active in the classroom presentation aids in the conceptual appreciation, and therefore their longer-term understanding.

After developing my course goals and my teaching philosophy, I believed I had greatly progressed towards my desire to reduce teaching to being fundamental, elegant, and simple. And for the next ten years, I continued to refine my techniques and improve my teaching strategies. But I also saw changes occurring in education from such things as federal policies like No Child Left Behind and Race to the Top, things which I fundamentally disagreed with—like focusing on achieving 100% graduation rates and tying teacher pay to student performance.

In Georgia, teacher pay is an interesting thing because it is based on both the teacher's highest degree attained and their number of years of service. When I started teaching, I already had a master's degree in computer science. And I did not want to get a doctorate in education. Not only did I disagree with many of the current policies in education, I also thought if I went to graduate school in education, I would have to take courses on pedagogy and testing and learning—ideas I really did not believe in. As evidenced by my goals and philosophy, it was clear to me I believed good teaching was far more than good assessments, scripted classrooms, word walls, and gimmicky clown-show educational tricks. I simply was not interested in anything they had to offer.

One day, a colleague and friend told me about the program he went through. He attained his doctorate in curriculum studies from Georgia Southern University, and he highly recommended I attend an informational dinner about the program—and I accepted. I had no idea what curriculum studies was, but I certainly knew what curriculum I was not interested in studying.

At dinner, I heard about the program. I was extremely surprised to hear that not only did they support many of the ideas about education I had developed, but I would be allowed to pursue my particular interest inside of curriculum studies because the field was very broad. Therefore, I decided to enroll in the program and see if it was for me. And after the first class, I knew it was. I had finally found a home in education. I had found an educational program that espoused many of the same beliefs about education I believed. I went on to attain my doctorate, and I bring a great deal of that experience into my classroom.

And in my classroom, I try and engage with my students on a personal level. Consequently, it's not uncommon for someone to feel comfortable enough to ask me personal questions. Usually, a question I get at least once a year in every class is, "Why are you a teacher?" After I explain why I am a teacher, what they often follow up with is, "No, why don't you do something more lucrative?" At this point, I take the time to explain to whomever asked the question that I consider the question somewhat insulting, because they are insinuating that teaching is a job that is not worth me doing. Implied in the question is that teaching is a stupid profession for me because I should be doing a job with much more status or that is much more lucrative. Why do people perceive teaching to be such an undesirable profession? Why am I thought less of because I am a teacher? Also, the question implies that what motivates me should be money. It's implied that I am stupid for not going into a career where I can earn the most money possible. Granted, many professions pay much more than teaching, but does that make those jobs more important?

Perhaps those questions underscore a more important issue that exists just below the surface. Maybe students ask why I am a teacher because they don't see teaching as a profession? They are certainly capable of observing for themselves how much of what I have to do and how I have to do it is dictated to me by school administrators and politicians. Students are certainly aware of how their parents feel about schools and the comments that are made by parents at school board meetings. And they are aware of statements made by politicians about education to drum up support for new laws and policies. Moreover, students are certainly aware of how presidents have signed into law legislation which mandates ridiculous requirements that can only be achieved by lowering the standards essentially to the floor for everyone. In short, behind their question really lurks the question, why would I choose a profession in which so much of my job is dictated to me by people who are not motivated at all by educating students?

Truthfully, I see their point. And it very much sums up my belief that people—students, parents, politicians, etc.—don't really view teaching as a profession. I take my career very seriously, and I take my role in the classroom very seriously, and I approach what I do from a perspective that while many parts of my job are mandated, I do have some say in how those things get implemented in my classroom. Therefore, I try and always shape my classroom in such a way that I both satisfy the requirements and I also can personally live with doing them. I focus on what I think really matters most in the classroom—my relationship with my students. I firmly believe few people learn in any environment in which they have an antagonistic relationship with the teacher. If my students are going to buy into physics, they first have to buy into me.

In my two decades of teaching, I have seen a lot of changes—changes in me and my beliefs about education. Changes in the policies that have dramatically altered the learning environment. Changes in how people feel about teaching as a profession. In spite of all those changes, many of which are negative, one thing hasn't changed after all these years: why I still teach. In spite of it all, the fundamental, elegant, and simple reason I still teach is because I love physics, and I want to share my love of physics with my students.

· 8 ·

THE HIGH A: OPERA'S HIGHEST NOTE SHOULD BE EDUCATION'S, TOO

John H. Cato

I graduated in 1997 with a degree in physics, and I began teaching high school physics in 2004. What attracts me to physics, and ultimately what *drove* me to major in it, was physics provides the explanations and laws for understanding how the universe works at its most fundamental level. Once understood, those laws also could allow me to predict the outcomes of experiments based simply on those laws. Physics, therefore, allows us not only to be able to solve problems, but it allows us the ability to predict outcomes of experiments. And the kinds of problems we can solve are not just the problems at the end of a chapter, such as finding the speed of a car driving down the road or of a ball rolling down a ramp. Rather, physics allows us to solve problems and make predictions that result in paradigm changes for how we see the world and the connections between ideas.

In studying physics, one of the main ways we are taught to think about trying to make these connections is with models. A model is a simplified representation of phenomena that helps us think about complex phenomena in a more understandable way. For example, atoms are very complex particles, and trying to understand how atomic interactions work is very difficult. But we can think about that complicated particle by simplifying it to a model in which we think about atoms being like little, tiny solar systems with the nucleus being like the sun and the electrons going around it like planets orbiting the sun. In fact, we even use similar names, like "orbits," when describing the atom. As another example, although pendulums and vibrating violin strings are not the same thing, we can model them as oscillating systems which have amplitudes, frequencies, and wavelengths. If we are careful about how we model them and restrict our models to how they both oscillate around an equilibrium position with a periodic motion having specific frequencies of oscillation, we can see that one model can handle both systems. Indeed, developing and using models are very important tools in physics (Knight, 2016).

Furthermore, Knight (2016) goes on to detail that there are two primary types of models, descriptive models and explanatory models. In descriptive models, we are trying to describe behavior, like how a pendulum can be modeled as an oscillating system. And in explanatory models, we are trying to explain our observations, like why did something happen? After coming up with an explanatory model, we use it to form theories from which we can base predictions. If the predictions match our expectation, we say we have a pretty good theory and that the model is a reasonable way of thinking about the system. But if the predictions are not very good, then there is a problem with either the theory, the model, or both.

One very important model used extensively in physics is oscillating systems. Oscillating systems are all around us, from grandfather clocks to violin strings. Oscillating systems have two core features that must be addressed: (1) oscillations have to take place around the equilibrium position, and (2) the motion has to be periodic. For example, think of a child on a playground swing. When she is just sitting on the swing, it hangs vertically down and no motion is occurring. We call this the equilibrium position. It is a position of stability, and something has to act on the swing in order to get it to move away from this position. Once she starts to pump her legs or if someone pushes on her, the swing will start oscillating back and forth, and she is always being pulled back to that equilibrium position by what is called the restoring force, which in this case is gravity.

When we want to describe the motion of the swing, we might want to describe things like how high the swing is going or how long it takes the swing to make a round trip oscillation. We call those concepts the amplitude of the system and the period of the system, respectively. The amplitude of the system is how far from the equilibrium position the object moves. For example, when referring to the girl on the swing, we could say her height is related to her amplitude: the higher she goes, the farther away she is from where she started. That would mean if she has big swings and is reaching big heights, she has large amplitudes, but if she has small swings and is only reaching small heights, she would have small amplitudes. While the amplitude describes how big the oscillations are, the period describes how long they take. The period of oscillation is how long it takes the oscillator to complete one full cycle. For example, the period of the swing would be how long it would take the girl to go from one side of her motion all the way to the other side and back again.

Finally, another property of oscillating systems is they have energy. Essentially, there are two kinds of energy at play: potential energy and kinetic energy. For a swing, the potential energy is related to the amplitude of the swing, and its kinetic energy is related to how fast the swing is going. While the swing is oscillating, it is always changing heights and speeds, as the potential energy and kinetic energy of the swing are always changing. But what's really important to understand is that the total energy of the swing is constant unless something is removing energy from the swing. For example, the swing would go back and forth forever if its energy were constant. But we know swings lose energy—their heights get smaller with every swing and their speeds get smaller with every oscillation due to factors such as air resistance and friction. Therefore, it is important to understand that real systems lose energy over time, ultimately resulting in the system returning to its equilibrium position.

Now that we have the ability to describe the motion of oscillating systems, we need to consider that oscillating systems vary in their complexity, and that has to be accounted for in our model. In general, when developing models, it's helpful to start with the simplest kind first. Having a basic understanding of the simplest system allows us to see what factors affect the system and in what ways they affect the system, and the simplest model of oscillating systems is called simple harmonic motion. In simple harmonic motion, the amplitude of oscillations is sinusoidal, meaning that if we made a graph of the system's position over time, the graph would look like a sine wave. The system would always have the same amplitudes and an oscillation would always occur with the same period. Moreover, in simple harmonic motion, no additional energy is needed to keep the system oscillating because it never loses energy. Once set in motion, it oscillates with the same amplitude and period forever.

One interesting finding with objects that are in simple harmonic motion is that the period of motion is not affected by the amplitude. They are independent of each other. That result seems counterintuitive, but experimentally has been verified. It seems then that an object undergoing simple harmonic motion has some kind of "natural" period of oscillation with which it oscillates. In fact, it does! We call it the oscillator's "natural frequency," where frequency is related to period in that if the period is how long it takes to complete one oscillation, the frequency is how many oscillations it would complete in a specific amount of time. The natural frequency, then, is the frequency with which an oscillator on its own wants to oscillate.

Most real systems, however, cannot be modeled as simple harmonic motion. As we know, if we push a child on a swing only one time, with each successive oscillation, the swing's oscillation gets smaller, and after a minute or two, unless we push again, the swing stops because it is losing energy. We know that we have to continue pushing on the swing to keep it going. These kinds of systems in which we continue adding back energy to keep them going are called driven oscillating systems. Thus, pushing a child in a swing and keeping her going is an example of a driven oscillation.

Since most oscillating systems lose energy over time, we have to have an external force to drive them. It turns out that what matters is how closely the oscillator's natural frequency is to the frequency of the driving force. If the driving frequencies are very different from the system's natural frequency, the system will oscillate, but the amplitudes, or the distance from the equilibrium position, will be small. As the driving frequencies get closer to the natural frequencies, the oscillator's amplitudes get bigger and bigger. And when the driving frequency matches the natural frequency, the amplitude is its maximum. In fact, when the two frequencies match, the amplitudes can become quite large. Moreover, when the driving frequencies match the oscillator's natural frequency, we say the system has reached a phenomenon called resonance. Probably the most frequently cited example of resonance is the opera singer who breaks the wine glass with her voice. When she sings and her voice's frequency (the driving frequency) matches the wine glass's natural frequency, the wine glass oscillates with such a large amplitude it shatters.

Education as an Oscillating System

As a physics teacher, one of the desired learning outcomes I want for my students is to be able to apply physics models to applicable systems. As examples, when students encounter systems where things have discrete values that fill up in specific ways, I want them to understand they can model that system like the shell model of the atom. When they see systems that can be modeled by things like locality, momentum, and position, that system can be modeled like a particle. Or when a system can be described by concepts like amplitudes, frequencies, and drivers, that system can be modeled by a driven oscillating system. In fact, we have incorporated physics models into many other fields of study, from simple concepts like the "work force" in business, to more comical examples like how we will say someone has "animal magnetism," to even explaining the observation we make about couples when we say "opposites attract." We even see physics models and concepts being used to describe such abstract concepts as government spending and tax cuts. For example, one can see former Treasury Secretary Robert Rubin (1995–1999) evoking inertia when discussing politics and government spending. During his interview for the documentary I.O.U.S.A (Creadon, 2009), Rubin states, "the natural inertia in the political system [. . .] is toward federal programs [. . .]. And, therefore, the inertia is toward spending on the one hand and tax cuts on the other hand." Moreover, physics models can be found inside of such areas as financial analysis, where there are "momentum indicators" which attempt to model how much umph is behind a price move and "stochastic oscillators" which attempt to model the periodic nature of prices over time based on specific drivers.

Indeed, education can also be modeled as a driven oscillating system. In order to model it, then, we need to consider which parts of education are part of the model and how they influence the system. Since student learning can oscillate with various levels of achievement, we can model the degree of student learning as our amplitude. High levels of student achievement would be large amplitudes and low levels of student achievement would be small amplitudes. If no achievement is made, then the system is just sitting there in equilibrium.

And in order to get our system oscillating, it needs to have agents, or drivers, acting on it. Those drivers are typically the stakeholders in the educational process. While there are many possible drivers in education which can impact student achievement, I am going to specifically discuss these five: students, teachers, administrators, parents, and state and federal policy makers.

Students as Drivers

One ubiquitous belief throughout education is all students can learn. And we know students play a major role in their own educations because there are many strategies and techniques that students can use to increase their learning. Moreover, different strategies will work better for each student, so each student needs to find effective methods for them and to use those strategies to increase their achievement. Furthermore, if students use ineffective study strategies or do not put in an appropriate amount of time to learn the material, then they are not maximizing the ways which can increase their learning. In addition, we can think about the level of student learning achieved by the student from their input as the student's natural frequency, or what amplitudes they achieve on their own from their own inputs.

What students tend to want, however, is not maximizing their learning. Rather, it is maximizing their grade. Indeed, it is not uncommon for teachers to hear questions or comments relaying this sentiment. For example, many times after a teacher assigns some work and asks if there are any questions, the very first question is, "Is this going to be graded?" And when it comes to students trying to decide what classes to take, they are not typically motivated by the rigor of the course or the competency of the teacher or the relevance of the material. In fact, many students will warn others about certain classes with comments like, "Don't take that class because it will ruin your GPA" (Knesek, 2022). Those kinds of comments clearly indicate the belief among students that what really matters about a course is its effect on one's GPA. In fact, Knesek (2022) writes that in general, "When students ask questions about assignments, quizzes, exams, or absences, it's almost always in reference to points and grades." Indeed, students constantly want to know what's being graded. If students ignore ungraded work and avoid rigorous courses or teachers, then it's reasonable to conclude students are avoiding them because they can negatively affect their GPA.

In addition to that, students tend to constantly want to be fed assignments that will pull up their grades. Studying harder to do better on upcoming assignments is not a tool in the current student tool bag. Instead, students are constantly asking for extra credit assignments to pull up their grade. As Knesek (2022) writes, "A favorite question is, 'Can I get any extra credit to raise my grade?'" Therefore, when students are not doing as well as they want, they tend to simply want things to boost their grades rather than working harder or learning the material deeper. Their motivation is simply how to achieve higher grades with less work, and hence, one main driver students tend to bring to education is their desire for high grades without necessarily learning the material and preferably with as little effort as possible.

If grades are such an important driver for students' motivation in their educational experiences, it is only reasonable to examine why. After all, in order to understand the system and in order for it to achieve maximum amplitude, we need to account for this student driver. So, why are grades so important to students? Perhaps psychologist Carl Rogers has an answer. When summarizing Roger's explanation, Knesek (2022) writes, "A person focuses on that which is important to the maintenance of the 'Self.' Students focus on grades and degrees because they think that will help them get a good job and advance their careers—maintaining the Self." Considering that so many students are competing for entrance into colleges, scholarships, and career fields where there are far more applicants than positions, students are really only acting in a way that's very natural: they are focusing on what matters most to them.

Teachers as Drivers

In addition to students, classroom teachers are major drivers in student achievement. In thinking about this idea, I asked myself, as a teacher, what can I do to maximize student achievement? Well, in general, I start by asking myself two questions: (1) "what do I want my students to learn by the end of my class?" and (2) "what do I want my students to be able to do at the end of my class?" In education, those two questions are often called "desired student outcomes" or "desired learning outcomes." And those two questions are what inform my classroom instruction to try and achieve high student learning. Indeed, what I want them to learn and what I want them to be able to do drive student learning in my classroom.

And what teachers want their students to learn could encompass an entire book—an entire encyclopedia of books. But I would say the main thing I want my students to learn and achieve is I want them to be critical thinkers. And what I mean by critical thinkers is my students can read and analyze arguments and interpret data in logical and analytical ways, and they can reach objective conclusions based on evidence. I want them to understand the basic principles of science and experimentation and be able to reach sound conclusions based on evidence. Therefore, what I do in the classroom attempts to drive my students to achieve their maximum amplitude by becoming better critical thinkers.

Now, many other teachers probably feel the same way. In addition to expressing the desire to encourage students to become critical thinkers, though, I also often hear grand statements such as, "What I want is what's best for the kids" or "All students can learn and achieve." True statements, but what is "best" for "all" students? What does it mean for "all students" to have "learned"? Or what does it mean for teachers to say they are more focused on "learning" as opposed to what students say they are focused on, getting higher "grades"? Well, one teacher might believe that learning is a process over time, but since grades are only a snapshot of learning at a particular moment in time, grades can't really indicate a measure of learning. Therefore, in order for "grades" to reflect the learning and growth that occurred, that teacher may allow students to retake assessments. Yet, another teacher may believe that is not what's best, and they believe students have to learn study skills and time management skills and preemptively be active in their education so that when the assessment date arrives, the student is ready. Consequently, that teacher may believe retests merely reinforce and encourage bad habits and lead to grade inflation without students having achieved deep learning. Yet, both teachers fundamentally believe they are doing "what is best." Additionally, one teacher may feel that allowing students to do additional work which can supplement student grades is perfectly acceptable and is good practice, yet another teacher may feel "extra credit" activities are merely things which pad grades without requiring students to demonstrate actual knowledge in a formal way.

In fact, making matters worse, at the end of the day, regardless of how teachers feel about such things as retests or extra credit, each teacher has to give each student a grade. And some teachers feel that the traditional grading system works against their personal belief about other factors being as important as grades, while other teachers feel that the traditional grading system is one of the things that we need to cling to as a way of leveling the playing field. As for teachers who feel that the standard grading system doesn't work for them, according to Walker (2021), they tend to state that "there are three major, long-standing objections to conventional grading practices. They don't accurately measure student learning. They are not intrinsically motivating. Perhaps most importantly, by leaning too heavily on non-academic factors such as compliance or punctuality, they are also endemically biased." Let's consider them in order. First, grades don't accurately measure student learning. Of course, by definition, grades can't be accurate since they are a made-up label that's generated from averaging a bunch of numbers. And teachers decide what the assignments are, and teachers decide what grade to assign students based on what was submitted. Since one teacher may assign completely different assignments and score them completely differently than another teacher teaching the very same concepts, two students who both earn a B may have been required to have widely different levels of performance to earn that score. One only needs to look at a 2007 lawsuit to see how that can play out in a real situation. According to Bailey (2007), the parents of a West Virginia student sued not only the teacher but also the entire school board because their daughter received an F on a biology project for being late. However, had that student been in a class with a teacher who did not have a late work policy, the student's project would have been accepted late, and it would have likely received a passing score. Or consider the 2002 lawsuit brought against Elizabeth Joice when one of her students failed her English final and consequently was unable to walk at graduation. According to Hymowitz (2002), Joice states, "[I] was told that the student was going to walk [in the graduation ceremony]" and she was forced by the school board to allow the student to retake the same exact exam so she could pass it and graduate. But another teacher may have a policy that allows students to retake exams or finals if those scores keep them from passing. In that teacher's class, the student would have sat for another exam and likely would have passed without the need for a lawsuit. The message is clear: it is often in a teacher's best interest to inflate grades and accommodate less than adequate work in order to appease parents and school officials, and that's really what "is best"—grade inflation.

Additional external factors have contributed to grade inflation becoming "what's best." For example, just consider the impact the pandemic has had on teacher grade inflation. According to Blad (2023):

> Washington state middle and high school students' grades in math, English, and science increased gradually in the decade before the pandemic, correlating with increases in state test scores.
> But in the spring of 2020, when COVID-19 sparked school closures nationwide, the percentage of Washington students with A grades in those courses spiked. Average grades in math, for example, increased from 2.36 on a 4.0 scale in 2018–19 to 2.70 in 2020–21.

It is clear that teachers do not agree on "what is best," and that disagreement certainly has a negative effect as a driver of student achievement, and external events like the pandemic have sent these effects into overdrive.

Administrators as Drivers

In addition to students and teachers, administrators are also agents who drive student learning. While I'm painting with a broad brush, very often, administrators are concerned with producing measurable student learning outcomes. So desired outcomes like producing better critical thinkers are not often desired learning outcomes for administrators. They tend to focus on such things as high benchmark test scores and high standardized test results—outcomes which can be measured. In an effort to find those measurable outcomes, administrators often turn to research.

Over the years, it seems educational fads come and go, and many of these fads originated with authors publishing a work and then selling their idea to school districts in the form of workshops. For example, when I first started teaching, there was "backwards design." There were workshops, year after year, on how that was the thing to improve education. Over time, it was replaced by things like "standards-based learning." And that was eventually replaced, too. Well, not replaced. Nothing in education really seems to be "replaced." It is more like the focus has shifted, and it now is focused on only doing those things in the classroom research says are "most effective."

Currently, a favorite source of research on what's effective is John Hattie's 2023 update to his 2009 book *Visible Learning*. In his book, Hattie details his meta study of research on what factors affect student learning and by how much, which he calls its "effect size." In short, his effect size is his way of describing the amplitudes of student learning which are achieved by various kinds of drivers. For example, administrators might want to observe teachers using strategies which have high effect sizes, perhaps ones with effect sizes greater than 0.4. Likewise, administrators would not want to see teachers using strategies which have low effect sizes, like ones below 0.4. Then, once students take standardized tests, administrators could compare the results and argue that teachers who do strategies A, B, and C get better results than those who do D, E, and F. And in order to increase learning for next year, teachers would be guided into using better strategies which have a higher impact on student learning and thus result in better test scores.

A great place to start with Hattie is his CLE, or his "common language effect size." A little effort to explain how he generates that is worthwhile. Hattie's method is to take research results from multiple studies, lump them together, average the results, and extrapolate the probability of success of how a "random student" who was exposed to effect X would do compared to another "random student" who was not. Here is a really simple example of his experiment that arrives at just one of his results which I think highlights some things to consider about his research:

> Study 1: X produces no effect on Y in elementary schools. CLE: 0.0
> Study 2: X produces a low effect on Y on students in middle schools. CLE: 0.06
> Study 3: X produces a medium effect on Y if X is well-designed. CLE: 0.4

Study 4: X produces a high effect on Y if X is well-designed and students are highly motivated. CLE: 0.7

Hattie averages those effect sizes to generate his average CLE: 0.29, which he defines as meaning "the probability that a score sampled at random from one distribution will be greater than a score sampled from some other distribution."

Now, let's apply some numbers to my sample experiments above. Hattie cites homework (I picked one that best exemplifies the issues) as having an effect size of 0.29, the same result as my sample data. Now, how does he determine that? Same as me. He lumps research on elementary school homework, middle school homework, and high school homework together. Next, he averages them together, ignoring specific experimental parameters. Then, he states that average CLE can tell us something about the relationship between X and achievement. Using my sample data or his CLE for homework, he is claiming an average student not exposed to homework would probably do as well as a student who was. Yet, even inside his own data are studies showing that's not at all true.

To answer the question, "Is that what he is really saying?" we have to first ask to whom Hattie was comparing the students in his final CLE effect size. As noted in his book, sometimes it's to a "control group," but at other times it's to the same students before the study. Recall, all of those research experiments used different comparative groups. Yet, he just sloshes them all together, which dramatically skews the meaning of his own generated CLE numbers. How can one compare CLE effect sizes between two tactics when the research on them didn't even compare them to like groups? For example, if one study shows homework has a CLE of 0.1 compared to a control group, yet another study shows homework has a CLE of 0.5 when compared to the same students before the study, one can't just say homework has an effect size of 0.3.

In short, there are a lot of things about his CLE numbers that are problematic, and his ranking of things that produce high achievement is not representative at all of the actual individual studies he used. It does not mean that there are not possible merits to the ideas, but certainly consideration can be made as to how they are used. For example, instead of administrators simply saying things like, "Look at CLE numbers and try and pick things 0.4 or higher," it could be, "What does low X look like? What does high X look like? Let's do things that have high X and not low X" and get away from his CLE scores and rankings. Using homework and feedback as examples, instead of saying "homework" has a CLE of 0.29 and is "not effective," perhaps consider "What does low quality homework look like? What does high quality homework look like? Let's do high quality homework." Or instead of saying "feedback" has an effect size of 0.7, we should say, "What does low quality feedback look like? What does high quality feedback look like? Let's give high quality feedback." In the end, however, administrators often drive student learning through the use of research and tend to focus on components that have measurable outcomes.

Parents as Drivers

Additionally, parents are another important driver of student learning. Unlike teachers and administrators, however, the parents' role is more complicated to generalize for several reasons. For one, we have already seen the effects parents have had on pressuring teachers to inflate grades or ensure student success through two lawsuits. But that's not the only way parents use lawsuits to drive education. Indeed, many parents have strong feelings about what should or shouldn't be part of a discussion in schools, and consequently, have used lawsuits in order to get schools to bend to their personal beliefs. As examples, many parents want voucher systems so their children can attend religious or parochial schools. Or parents want to remove from the curriculum specific scientific issues like climate change or evolution because they personally disagree with them. Or parents want to control what conversations a teacher can or cannot have with students. For example, Hadriana Lowenkron writes about a lawsuit against a school system for teaching "woke" ideology instead of academics. According to Lowenkron (2023), Jerome Eisenberg's daughter was enrolled at the Brentwood School, a prestigious school in Los Angeles. But Eisenberg was unhappy with his daughter's education after the George Floyd murder. As he put it, "The curriculum change shifted away from teaching students critical thinking skills—how to think—and started indoctrinating them into what to think." One might think that those kinds of legal battles are only happening in private schools. As cited in Lowenkron (2023), Jim Lee, director of strategic initiatives at the NAACP's Legal Defense Fund, states, "The majority of parents want their children to attend a school that is diverse and inclusive." But that doesn't seem to be the case if one looks across the entire country. Thus, parents tend to drive student achievement by focusing on cultural or personal beliefs which they want to either be a part of or removed from the school setting.

Because of such parent attitudes about those policies, some politicians in a few states have seized the opportunity to take on "wokeness" for political reasons. Take, for example, in 2021, the way Florida's current Republican governor Ron DeSantis mobilized Florida's legislature to take on Critical Race Theory (CRT). But perhaps the best example is when he declared a war on "woke" when he pushed through and signed into law legislation which, according to Izaguirre (2022), "forbids instruction on sexual orientation and gender identity in kindergarten through third grade." Again, these actions are being driven by the voters. According to DeSantis, as cited in Izaguirre (2022), "We will make sure that parents can send their kids to school to get an education, not an indoctrination." And although that law only targeted students from kindergarten until third grade, in May 2023, DeSantis signed a new law further expanding the restrictions in schools. According to Yurcaba (2023):

> The new measure prohibits sexual orientation or gender identity instruction in prekindergarten through eighth grade, restricts reproductive health education in sixth through 12th grade, and requires that reproductive health instruction "be age-appropriate or developmentally appropriate for students in accordance with state standards."

In addition to restricting school staff from those conversations, the law advanced the anti-woke agenda on a new front: pronouns. And Florida is not the only state to take on pronouns. For example, in Michigan, Dan and Jennifer Mead's daughter began referring to herself at school as "he," and he declared to school personnel his desire to be referred to with masculine pronouns. According to McEntyre (2023), the Meads sued the school and its board of education because "the district's policies violated their First and Fourteenth Amendment rights when it didn't notify and concealed that it was treating their daughter like a male." McEntyre writes the "district has adopted a non-mandatory guidance document from the Michigan Department of Education as the RPS policy for treating students as the opposite sex" and were not legally obligated to inform the parents. Consequently, the parents not only sued, but they also withdrew their daughter in order to homeschool her. In Florida, the state did not leave it up to the districts. According to Yurcaba (2023), the expanded "Don't say gay" law also "bars schools from requiring students or employees to refer to each other with pronouns that do not align with their assigned sex at birth. It will also prohibit trans school employees from sharing their pronouns with students." Therefore, regardless of a student's desired pronouns, the biological sex at birth determines the only legally allowed pronouns that may be used to refer to a student. As these examples show, through lawsuits and using the power to elect politicians willing to take on "their causes" in public school, parents are certainly a strong driver of public education.

Politicians as Drivers

Finally, politicians are system drivers, and they are tightly connected to parents. Since elected officials have constituents, and many of those constituents are parents, it's logical to connect much of the legislation passed by politicians to the desires of their constituents. And as previously detailed, there seems to be a strong connection between the actions of the politicians and parental constituents. But those policies are not the only ones which politicians use to drive education. These bureaucrats also tend to focus on students having marketable job skills and college/career readiness. For example, back in 2008, many states, Georgia included, applied for and received President Obama's Race to the Top grant. Essentially, Race to the Top granted monies to states which created specific educational reforms. While some components focused on turning around failing schools or increasing student test scores, many of the components were designed to be accountability measures of schools, and one accountability measure was ensuring students left high school either prepared for college or prepared for a career.

There is a good reason to suspect students are not prepared for college or a career. Take, for example, the yearly Post Graduation Readiness Report (PGRR). According to Hornbuckle (2023), the 2018–2019 PGRR indicated 75% of graduating high school students felt at least somewhat unprepared for college or a career. Additionally, the report indicates more than half of college students changed their major at least twice. Lucariello (2022) goes further and indicates that according to the PGRR, "which polled over 500 students from the 2019 through 2022 graduating classes, [. . .] 75% of high school graduates are not ready to make college and career decisions."

To satisfy Race to the Top's college and career accountability component, Georgia created its College and Career Ready Performance Index, or CCRPI. According to the Georgia Department of Education (2024), "CCRPI is a comprehensive school improvement, accountability, and communication platform for all educational stakeholders that will promote college and career readiness for all Georgia public school students." Indeed, Georgia's CCRPI attempts to measure how well each school is preparing students to either go to college or go into a career.

Remarkably, this single score is supposed to measure completely whether or not a school is preparing students for college or a career. Even if we entertain that as possible, what "effect" has the CCRPI really had on student learning? Well, I would argue, the effects are pretty predictable. For one, since a school's CCRPI score is largely based on student performance on End of Course (EOC) standardized assessments, school administrators emphasize improving EOC scores. Subjects that do not have an EOC are off the hook, and ones that do are constantly under the watchful eye of administration. Additionally, since poor behavior greatly affects student learning, politicians have pushed state-wide programs which have artificially reduced the number of behavior incidents. For example, in Georgia, a program called Positive Behavioral Interventions and Support (PBIS) is currently being implemented. The thinking is, if students have positive interventions, their behavior will improve, the number of referrals will decrease, problematic students will become good students, passing rates will rise, and graduation rates will rise. While it is true the effects of implementing PBIS might have led to an overall decrease in the number of referrals, which makes the school appear "better," it would be hard to connect any real academic success to PBIS.

And having a higher graduation rate is a good thing because states need to be able to offer an educated workforce to potential companies looking to come to the state. As Indiana Governor Eric Holcomb stated in his 2022 State of the State Address, "While education is the starting point, we must do more to align our state's K–12, higher ed, workforce, and economic development efforts. There is power in their synergy." And let's be honest, it's really about money. As Conney (2023) writes:

> The reason educational attainment and per-capita income are so inextricably linked is simple: more highly educated people means more people are employed in the high-wage knowledge economy, and more high-wage knowledge-economy jobs migrate to or are created because of existing talent concentrations.

In short, if a state can attract companies that need educated workers, those workers will make more money and therefore pay more tax and spend more money in the state.

Are We Achieving Resonance?

If education, then, is being modeled like a driven oscillating system, with the many drivers influencing student achievement, are we achieving resonance?

There is little doubt that in a world filled with pervasive technology in virtually every field, and specialized skill sets required for many jobs, our graduates need to possess the skills needed to both acquire and use rapidly advancing technologies and the specialized languages that exist in today's workplace. In short, our students need to be proficient in both mathematical thinking and reasoning and in reading comprehension. Yet, according to Kirsch (1999), "Numerous reports published in the last decade have indicated that a large portion of the United States population lacks adequate literacy skills, and many employers say they cannot find enough workers with the reading, writing, mathematical, and other competencies required in the workplace" (p. xi). For example, consider a report generated by the nonpartisan board the National Assessment Governing Board (NAGB), which was created by Congress in 1988. The NAGB releases a periodic report—formally called the National Assessment of Educational Progress (NAPE) but commonly called The Nation's Report Card—which assesses the state of the nation's educational system. Looking at several different reports sheds some light on the overall state of the system. According to the NAGB (2022a) report on reading, only 37% of 12th-grade students performed at or above the proficient level. To put that in perspective, two out of three high school graduates read below the proficient level. And in mathematics, our students are even worse. And in a different NAGB (2022b) report on mathematics, it is reported that only 24% of 12th graders are at or above the proficient level on mathematics. Together those two NAGB reports are quite telling: America's graduating high school students are not proficient in either reading or mathematics.

It seems clear from those results that students overall are reaching a very low amplitude in student achievement. Additionally, after decades of pontification and concerted effort to reform the American education system, many American students are still graduating from high schools and colleges without meaningful critical post-education skills like critical thinking skills. They often have to seek out low skill jobs that rely on repetition or undergo significant job training before employment. Or they are graduating with skills that are not in high demand, leaving many high demand jobs unfilled. It seems clear our system is not achieving resonance.

But is achieving resonance even possible? I argue yes. One only needs to look around the world and see that not only do other countries achieve it, they do so quite regularly. According to DeSilver (2017), we see countries like Singapore, Hong Kong, and Japan routinely leading the world in math and science scores. And we also see countries like Singapore, Hong

Kong, and Canada routinely leading the world in reading. But it is clear our focus on giving students standardized tests or basing educational policies on parental attitudes about diversity or focusing on meaningless stats like graduation rates when many of those graduating do not have the skills to be either immediately employable or ready for college are not moving the needle towards success.

Consequently, if we want to achieve resonance, we have to get all the drivers working together. We need students, teachers, administrators, parents, and politicians all working towards the same goal: achieving maximum student learning. Instead of students who are grade-oriented and focused on solely attaining high GPAs, we need our students to embrace learning critical thinking skills and doing all the work assigned from the mindset of building skills. We need them to put all their efforts into learning to be self-learners and not relying on retests and extra credit to pass courses. We need our students to seek out hard classes and not just fill their course load with classes in which they can get easy A's. We need teachers who will hold the line. We need teachers who will demand the best from their students and not give in to the temptations of allowing students to skate through a class. We need teachers who set the bar high and do not lower the standard simply to appease parents or administration. And we need administrators who will accept not every student will pass a class or even graduate. We need administrators who will hold students accountable for their behavior and not allow the students to indefinitely repeat behaviors ad nauseum. We need administrators who focus less on effect sizes and what teachers can do to make up for students having poor student skills and study skills, and focus more on making sure the teachers have the resources and backing to be rigorous and have high standards. We need parents who want to send their children to school in order to receive a high caliber education. We need parents who hold schools accountable for letting students graduate who do not have the skills necessary to go to college or enter the workforce. We need parents who question teachers about what skills their children need to become better students and better thinkers and not question them about whether their lesson plans are political or what pronouns the teachers are using. Finally, we need politicians to stay out of the classroom. We need for them to stop passing legislation which undermines the very thing they claim they want: students who can leave high school prepared to either enter college or the workforce. What we need is all drivers working together pushing students to become better thinkers with meaningful critical thinking skills. In other words, if students, teachers, administrators, parents, and politicians are all driving student learning with matching frequencies, are all seeking to achieve the same desired outcome, like Finland, Hong Kong, Singapore, and other high achieving countries, we, too, can achieve resonance.

Education is a very challenging field to be in because there are many different stakeholders who have vastly different goals for their desired student outcomes. From the students to the teachers to the parents to the school administration to the politicians, we all drive student achievement. And if we can learn a lesson from physics, when we all push and pull on the students in different ways and with different goals, we achieve very little. But if we can all get on the same page and emphasize the same goals, then perhaps our students can finally achieve what we all want, what results in opera's high A—resonance.

References

Bailey, C. (2007, March 14). Parents sue after daughter is given an F at school. *West Virginia Record*. https://wvrecord.com/stories/510591815-parents-sue-after-daughter-is-given-an-f-at-school

Blad, E. (2023, November 13). Students' grades may not signal actual achievement, study cautions. *Education Week*. https://www.edweek.org/leadership/students-grades-may-not-signal-actual-achievement-study-cautions/2023/11

Cooney, P. (2023, May 23). The connection between educational attainment and economic development. Michigan Future Inc. https://michiganfuture.org/2023/05/the-connection-between-educational-attainment-and-economic-development/

Creadon, P., O'Malley, C., Gibson, S., Wiggin, A., Golub, P., Bonner, W., & Incontrera, K. (2009). *I.O.U.S.A.* Distributed by PBS Home Video.

DeSilver, D. (2017, February 15). U.S. students' academic achievement still lags that of their peers in many other countries. Pew Research Center. https://www.pewresearch.org/short-reads/2017/02/15/u-s-students-internationally-math-science/

Georgia Department of Education. (2024). *College and career ready performance index*. Georgia Department of Education. https://www.gadoe.org/CCRPI/Pages/default.aspx

Hattie, J. (2023). *Visible learning: The sequel*. Routledge.

Holcomb, E. (2022, July 11). 2022 state of the state address. https://www.indystar.com/story/news/politics/2022/01/11/gov-eric-holcomb-state-state-read-his-speech/9135192002/

Hornbuckle, M. (2023, June 29). *Post-graduation readiness report*. YouScience. https://www.youscience.com/post-graduation-readiness-report/

Hymowitz, K. (2002). Fail me, I sue. *City Journal*. https://www.city-journal.org/article/fail-me-i-sue

Izaguirre, A. (2022, March 28). "Don't say gay" bill signed by Florida gov. Ron DeSantis. AP News. https://apnews.com/article/florida-dont-say-gay-law-signed-56aee61f075a12663f25990c7b31624d

Kirsch, I. (1999). Preface. In A. Sum (Ed.), *Literacy in the labor force* (pp. xi–xii). U.S. Department of Education. https://nces.ed.gov/pubs99/1999470.pdf

Knesek, G. (2022). *Why focusing on grades is a barrier to learning*. Harvard Business Publishing. https://hbsp.harvard.edu/inspiring-minds/why-focusing-on-grades-is-a-barrier-to-learning

Knight, R. (2016). *Physics for scientists and engineers* (4th ed.). Pearson.

Lucariello, K. (2022). National survey finds high school graduates not prepared for college or career decisions. *THE Journal*, 12/05/22. https://thejournal.com/articles/2022/12/05/national-survey-finds-high-school-graduates-not-prepared-for-college-or-career-decisions.aspx

Lowenkron, H. (2023, May 22). Parents launch a legal war on woke at elite schools for "indoctrinating" their kids with their "preferred political fad of the moment". *Fortune*. https://fortune.com/2023/05/22/school-war-on-woke-parents-lawsuit/

McEntyre, N. (2023, December 21). Michigan parents sue school district for using male pronouns, different name for daughter: Suit. *New York Post*. https://nypost.com/2023/12/21/news/michigan-parents-sue-school-district-for-using-male-pronouns-different-name-for-daughter/

NAGB. (2022a). *NAEP report card: Reading*. The Nation's Report Card. (n.d.) https://www.nationsreportcard.gov/reading/nation/achievement/?grade=12

NAGB. (2022b). *NAEP report card: Mathematics*. The Nation's Report Card (n.d.) https://www.nationsreportcard.gov/mathematics/nation/achievement/?grade=12

Walker, T. (2021). "Amazing and very challenging": More educators rethink grading. NEA. https://www.nea.org/nea-today/all-news-articles/amazing-and-very-challenging-more-educators-rethink-grading

Yurcaba, J. (2023, May 17). DeSantis signs "don't say gay" expansion and gender-affirming care ban. NBCNews.com. https://www.nbcnews.com/nbc-out/out-politics-and-policy/desantis-signs-dont-say-gay-expansion-gender-affirming-care-ban-rcna84698

· 9 ·

NEVER SAY NEVER

Mary K. Davis

Before I share further how my journey into teaching began, I think it is important to share with you that there were three things I never wanted to experience in my life. We all have said "I will never." My three "nevers," in order, were: (1) I would never live further south than North Carolina, (2) I would never work for the state of Alabama (I have no explanation for this one), and (3) I would absolutely never be a teacher. Even more specifically, I would never be a high school teacher. These three items are important to me as they all came to pass and each played an important role in my journey into education.

My story begins in college. I attended a small college nestled in the mountains of western North Carolina. I was incredibly fortunate to have the opportunity to continue to play softball, a sport I truly loved. As the time drew nearer to depart for North Carolina, I had begun to grow very nervous. I am originally from Ohio. I had never been further south than Kentucky. When I got to school and was moving into the dorm, I panicked. I did not know a soul and was moving eight hours from home. I was so homesick and lonely. I cried for weeks wanting to go home, back to my safe, familiar state of Ohio. This is where my first never came from; North Carolina was as far from my family as I ever wanted to be.

As time continued, I began to settle into college. I made new friends, poured myself into academics, and spent a great deal of time on the softball field. Not only did softball give me an outlet, but it came with a built-in set of friends. As my collegiate career closed, I graduated with a double major. I earned a Bachelor of Science in Accounting and a Bachelor of Science in Management Information Systems with a minor in Computer Science. I was very excited to charge into the business world with all my newfound knowledge, much like most young graduates. I was very fortunate to find a job at a great small hardware and software engineering house where I not only honed my business skills, but was also provided the opportunity to gain experience in computer hardware and software design. I was completely enthralled with how all these little pieces came together to create games or point of purchase devices. I thought that was the greatest job in the world. I worked with great people, in a great place, learning a dynamic job.

Remember when I said I never wanted to live further south than North Carolina? Well, I met this wonderful man from Georgia. This man wanted to be an elementary school teacher. I did not think much about this other than that he would always be employed. I thought it was cute and fun. At that time, my very limited understanding of elementary school teachers consisted of coloring and hugs. I now know how difficult it is to be in elementary school. Well, that teacher from Georgia asked me to marry him and we now live in Augusta, Georgia. While I hated leaving my fabulous job, we decided it was easier for me to find another job in business than him, especially with teaching contracts coming out once a year and the limited window of employment opportunity. This is the first ironic twist of fate that led me to teaching.

Once we moved, the jobs I selected were tied to education, but in a different scope. I worked as a bookkeeper in a local high school for a year. I hated it. I was bored and lonely. I missed the challenge and learning that went with my previous job. I missed the people that I worked with. The people in my new job were not as welcoming. They had done things a certain way for a long time and here I came with different ideas and experiences. My husband suggested I look for a new job. I began applying different places to see what adventures awaited me. I applied for a position at a satellite campus for a university. While the satellite campus was located in Augusta, it is important that you know the home campus was located in Alabama. I was really hoping this job worked out. I was excited at the thought of learning something new. Well, I did not get the job—yet. Upon learning I was not the candidate, I quit my job as a bookkeeper knowing I would eventually find something, anything.

Within days of putting my resignation letter in, I received a call telling me that the position with the university was open again and asking if I was still interested. As a result, I now worked for the state of Alabama. My second "never" had become a reality.

I was excited at starting something new, learning new things, and working with new people. I was learning budgeting, financial aid, purchasing, human resources, and class scheduling. I loved the dynamic environment of education, learning what it took for students to walk in the door and receive their education. I enjoyed helping adult students meet their goals and achieve their diploma, but it was far enough away from the teaching that I did not really equate it to education. Yes, it was an educational institution, but I was not doing education things. The closest I got to the education side was becoming a student again. I took advantage of the tuition assistance program and earned a Master of Science in Management with a concentration in Organizational Behavior and Effectiveness. I loved this program. I have always enjoyed learning about the dynamics of business, the culture within organizations, and the different styles of leadership. While I was in school learning about leadership, management, and communication, I was able to put those theories into practice and learn a great deal while at that job. I learned a lifetime of human resources in a very short amount of time, including how to handle disgruntled employees, being spit and screamed at, lawsuits from the Equal Employment Opportunity Commission, and how to handle your secretary having an affair with your boss. All of that learning could be a book within itself. I was at that job for seven years before we parted ways. While I still liked the job, I did not love it anymore. There were three humans I loved more.

While working at this institution, my husband and I had three beautiful babies. Once we had our first child, a boy, I cried every day going to work. I hated dropping him off at daycare. It was like my heart broke every time I walked out his door. I would go over to the daycare on my lunch hour as often as I could just so I could hold him or peek at him. I feel like once we finally settled into a routine, our daughter came along. I was able to take a very long maternity leave with her. The pregnancy was very difficult, and I was on bed rest for most of it. It was not long after that we learned we were expecting another baby boy. It was this last child that really changed my path.

Our first two kids were relatively healthy. Of course, they brought home all the viruses and ailments kids bring home from daycare, but all in all, they were pretty healthy. Our third was born in October of 2009 and had RSV within the first six weeks. He was hospitalized for a few days as his oxygen levels went up and down. Once he came home and settled in, I thought he would be like the other two—a cold here, an earache there—but that was not the case. His poor little immune system was weak and he caught everything. I was home more than I was at work. I felt guilty when I was at work, and guilty when I was home.

One cold and wet rainy day in February of 2010, I took him to the doctor again. This time he had another ear infection and needed tubes. I was worn out, emotionally and physically. We had just left Target with his prescription when I received a call from the daycare. The first words I heard were "everybody is safe, Sissy is fine." At this time, our daughter was only 14 months old. My heart stopped. Fortunately, I was around the corner from the daycare and rushed over to see Sissy. The class had gone outside for a bit of fresh air. They were not outside long before they had to line up to come back inside. The story was she had lined up, but got out of line to follow her teacher to another child and when the class filed into the classroom, our daughter was left outside. No one noticed our child was missing until another teacher from another class looked out the window and saw her. I started crying. The daycare was located in front of an apartment complex. My mind was racing—what if someone took her? What if she got out of the fence? At that moment in time, all I felt was fear. Before leaving the daycare with my daughter, I put in notice we would not be returning. Daycares, at that time, required two weeks' notice, which was perfect because my job did too.

As a result of this day, I put in notice with the daycare that we were pulling our kids out and put in my resignation with the university. I do want to mention that my husband and I spoke about me quitting my job to stay home many times. We knew the change would be financially tight as I was making a good income; however, I had faith we could make it work. I found ways to financially contribute to our household, like odd jobs and a small part-time job that fit our schedule. I learned to make all kinds of things to keep our food expenses down. He was always supportive of me staying home; however, it took a little while to understand the stress he felt with being the only paycheck. I was so lucky to be able to stay home for three years. Three years was a short period of time, but they were the best years. I enjoyed every minute of taking care of my kids and our home.

As the kids grew and started school, I knew I would need to enter the workforce again. I absolutely did not want to go back into the business world full time. I had cherished being home with my kids. I was adamant I wanted to be home when they got home from school and when they were off. I wanted to go to their sporting events, school plays, and whatever else they were involved in. How was I going to find a job that allowed that? I pondered this, I prayed about it, I worried about it. One of the biggest reasons I hated daycare was that I did not want other people raising my kids. Where was I going to find something conducive to my wish list?

It just so happened that a teaching position came open at our county's alternative school. In what subject, you may wonder, as I did not have a teaching certificate? Business. Oh, the irony. I did not want to be a teacher. I did not want to be a high school teacher. At an "alternative school"? What did that even mean? We did not have those in Ohio—we had career academies. After all the back and forth, and my husband's strong encouragement, I applied for the job. Just to be clear, I did not want the job. I was applying for the experience of the process as I had been out of the workforce for a while.

I went into the interview with nothing to lose. What was there to lose when I really did not want anything? I did approach the interview with an open mind and wanted to get reacquainted with interviewing and meeting new people. I used to be the one hiring, so I was excited to be on the other side and improve my skills as an interviewer by being the interviewee. It did not occur to me that I might get the job and what that would mean. I was offered the job. Again, oh, the irony. Here I was being offered a job I did not want, doing something I did not know how to do, with teenagers. Here was my third "never" coming back to haunt me.

When the phone call came offering me the job, it was explained to me what steps I would need to take in order to obtain a teaching certificate. I would need to go back to school. The program I would need to complete was through the University of Georgia, called PACTE. It was a program designed for new teachers going into Career, Technical, and Agriculture Education. Before making the decision, my husband and I discussed the pros and cons this new experience would bring. I was concerned about my youngest kid, as he was only three years old. I was adamant I did not want him back in daycare. Fortunately, we had a support system that would be able to provide for my son. The other two were in school, so it was not as big of an adjustment for them. We were able to have someone come into the house to get the two older kids on the bus and take our youngest to his Mother's Day Out program and then spend the day with him until I was able to get home. Finally, the last concern I had: I really did not want to be a teacher.

Well, needless to say, I am now a teacher. I accepted the position that set me on a journey full of adventures that continues to this day. I was thrilled to enter the workforce again as it would alleviate some of the financial stress, put me on the same schedule as my kids and husband, and provide more opportunities to grow and learn more than I could ever imagine possible. I was also excited to start in the small learning environment the Alternative School would provide—even though I did not know what type of environment it would be. I just knew it was small.

To say the alternative school was an adjustment was an understatement. I am not sure which aspect was a larger adjustment, teaching or working in a punitive alternative school. I had left the world of Elmo and Paw Patrol for teenagers going through a metal detector and turning out their pockets. I understood kids dabbled in drugs, but did not realize THC was added to melted ChapStick and eye drops by middle and high school kids. I am not saying I am naive, but I also had never been confronted with some of challenges kids face like abuse, living in drug infested houses, gangs, and a parent, or parents, jailed. I can honestly say I learned a lot from this environment, and at times, enjoyed it. However, I am thrilled, and thankful, to be in a calmer and more stable environment.

As the years progressed, I became more acclimated to education. I started to get bored at the alternative school. Most of the classes I taught had been transitioned to online format or students were so far behind, they took additional required classes to catch up to grade level. It was at this time I began to think about going back to school. Earning a Doctorate was a goal, but one I did not think I was capable of achieving. My husband had entered a program a few years earlier and I did not want to put additional strain on our family by going back as well. However, there were some good reasons to go back at that point. All our kids were in school, so childcare coordination was not as big of a deterrent. My husband had started the program, and I could follow in his footsteps. He was paving the way for what I could expect, and we could be done within a year or two of each other. We would be done with school by the time our oldest entered high school. The workload was not as big of a concern, at least for me, because I enjoy reading and writing.

I have to make a conscious effort not to romanticize the past when we were in school and say it was all a great experience. It was hard, emotionally and mentally draining, and came with so much guilt. There was lots of crying and exhaustion. When I started the program, the professors told us we would experience loneliness because there were only a few people that understood what we would be going through. Current coworkers would not truly understand because they were not experiencing the same thing. They were correct;

it was lonely, but I did have something others did not. I was so grateful to share this experience with my husband. He would watch the kids while I had to work, and I would watch them while he worked. We tried, as much as we could, not to work at the same time and to get the kids out of the house when one of us was working. We are very fortunate to have great parks in our community!

Once the dissertations were finished, and we graduated, it seemed as though something was missing. I missed the cohort I had visited and learned with once a month. I missed being on a campus and soaking up the atmosphere. I missed the reading and writing. As this chapter was closing, another was opening. I transitioned from the alternative school to another school within our county. This transition included a content change. I was excited about this change because it is a dynamic field that requires constant learning.

While I believe teaching is a very difficult profession to enter at this time in our society, I believe it to be one of the most exciting, challenging, and dynamic professions. There is so much noise, it can be hard to remember the objective; however, every day provides glimmers of joy, hope, and excitement. Even though my time with my students is relatively short, the impact they have on me is probably far greater than the one I have on them. I absolutely do not want to downplay the impact teachers have on students; I am only trying to point out that I learn as much from them as they do from me. They are just beginning their journey, and their canvas is relatively blank. It is truly exciting and humbling to watch students grow, listen to them mature, and see their faces light up with understanding when something finally clicks. The responsibility of teaching is tremendous, and the stress is overwhelming, but the reward is unmatched.

· 1 0 ·

THE POWER STRUGGLE IN EDUCATION

Mary K. Davis

It was a rainy Wednesday morning and I sat looking at a new book in front of me wondering what knowledge Michel Foucault's *Discipline and Punish* would present to me. I wondered if it was a narrative, a series of narratives, or a historical account of certain laws. As I pondered the contents of the book, my mind began to wander to the title of a course I had taken in school, Power and Schooling. What does this mean? There are so many hands in the proverbial pot when it comes to educating a child. There are parents, teachers, administrators, county-level assistants and superintendents, and state-level bureaucrats; this does not include entities that are lobbying for their interests at each level. Then there is the child—what power do they hold? As I regained focus, the question that lingered in my mind was what exactly is this power and who holds it?

As I contemplate this question now, I cannot help but wonder why education takes the top-down approach. This is not Google or Amazon, fulfilling a product for a profit; this is education. Education is above profit; it is a service, a community project of sorts, the village raising the child. Education is supposed to assist in turning tiny humans into contributing members of society. Schools, in conjunction with the parents, are to educate these young minds and mold them into great thinkers. While we, as educators, choose to be in the classroom to impart knowledge and nurture young minds, we must remember that education is often thought of as a business. Thinking about education as a business, monetizing it, evokes all kinds of emotions. These emotions can include anger, frustration, and resignation, to name a few. Children cannot be educated without funding. However, where there is money, there is profit, competition, and accusations. Generally, educators follow what is in the best interest of the children, but with the top-down model, it is curious to ponder that the higher you go, the best interest of the child wains. Pasi Sahlberg (2011) reminds us in *Finnish Lessons*:

> [...] educational systems are facing a win challenge: how to change schools so that students may learn new types of knowledge and skills required in an unpredictably changing knowledge world, and how to make the new learning possible for all young people regardless of their socioeconomic conditions. (p. 1)

What a model it would be if our leaders were concerned with both moral and economic outcomes (Sahlberg, 2011, p. 1). This would be a bottom-up model allowing parents, children, and teachers to hold more academic freedom that is so desperately needed.

Power is a tricky idea. Power has several definitions in the Oxford Dictionary to include "the ability to control people or things," the "ability or opportunity to do something," "strength or influence in a particular area of activity," and "the influence of a particular thing or group within society" ("Power," 2017). As there are many dimensions to the definition, there are just as many when you put it into practice. We talk about power as if it is absolute, ready to corrupt and take all that is good with it. When I think of power, I think of Thor holding a lightning bolt ready to strike at any time; anyone that gets in the way is removed. However, when you think of power in the context of education, the roots from that word grow into different areas, like a vine; power used for good flourishes, and if used for bad, withers. Many throughout the education process hold power as it is highly concentrated at the top, but wains the further down the mountain it tumbles. Imagine a ragged, craggy mountain top; there are those that sit high atop shouting down edicts, changing rules as the year progresses, holding school systems accountable to lofty goals. There are those sitting a little lower on a mountain side, again, shouting orders down, all the while looking up for approval and waiting for the next edict to come racing down. Then there are those closer to the bottom, juggling edicts, ensuring students are making progress and meeting the standards set forth from high atop the mountain, all while trying to teach children how to interact with each other, listen to instruction, practice standardized test taking, and engage in learning. Look at ground level and you will find the parents and the students, looking up towards the teachers, hoping their child will receive a quality education from kind, compassionate, competent teachers. Looking to the right of the parent, sitting on a tree branch not too far away, you will find the media blasting off the latest statistics for failing schools and expounding on what lousy job educators do. If you look to the left of the parent, standing on a craggy rock ledge, you will find charter schools and voucher programs all clamoring for the money that is falling from high atop the mountain as well as capitalizing on the calamity the media is portraying. All of these entities are looking for the power to educate the child, or "commodity" in some cases.

Some believe the child holds the power to their learning. One would like to think they have the ability to determine how they learn best and at what pace. Sadly, this is not the case. In the best circumstances children have teachers that guide them using their best learning method into material that is challenging and engaging using current resources and materials. Not all children are exposed to a solid education, taking place in solid buildings using current and plentiful materials. This is the difference between empowerment and oppression; both can be disguised as power.

It can be argued that education is oppression. Oppression is holding someone back by exercising power or authority over them. This can be done mentally, physically, emotionally, or through horrible conditions. Through discipline, those in authority are exercising their power over the students. Michel Foucault (1977) quotes La Salle in *Discipline and Punish* stating:

> By the word punishment, one must understand everything that is capable of making children feel the offense they have committed, everything that is capable of humiliating them, of confusing them: . . . a certain coldness, a certain indifference, a question, a humiliation, a removal from office. (p. 178)

When a child is disciplined, is it with fairness and compassion or is it with humiliation and embarrassment? Was the discipline doled out in a private setting or a public one? It matters to the child. Was it the action that was disciplined or the child? Because that matters also. When a child is embarrassed in front of peers, this can lead to tempers flaring, tremendous classroom disruption, and a loss of trust and respect from the student. If the offense was worthy of discipline, that is not oppression; however, if the offense was not worthy of discipline, or that degree of discipline, that is oppression. This is a fine balance for teachers to maintain, as the result can be a shift in power within the classroom dynamic that can take a positive learning environment into a negative one quickly.

One reason teachers may use oppressive discipline is because they feel oppressed as well. The pressure is tremendous for students to succeed. Students are on a set schedule, following predetermined rules, learning standards that have been set forth by the people high atop the mountain. There is very little wiggle room for creativity, learning at their own pace, and deep critical thinking and expansion on a topic. The education of a child is like an onion. They begin learning a topic in kindergarten, and by the time they reach high school, one hopes they have peeled the onion back enough to gain some mastery on the topic; however, with increasing testing and subject requirements, mastery is not likely to happen. Not all teachers and students are given the same opportunities for success. Jonathan Kozol (1991), in *Savage Inequalities*, shares his experiences of visiting the worst public schools in America to shed light on the oppression of our students and expose the inequality taking place in our current system. Teachers and students talked to him and he listened, something our current education system ignores. He gave a voice to their frustration, pain, and despair. Kozol (1991) writes of the importance of listening: "It occurred to me that we had not been listening much to children in these recent years" (p. 6), and he goes on to state "The voices of children, frankly, had been missing from the whole discussion" (p. 6). To gain true authentic voices in education, we must let them be heard, for as Kozol (1991) recognizes, "children often are more interesting and perceptive than grownups are about the day-to-day realities of life in school" (p. 6). We must allow their voices to be heard; by not hearing them we are oppressing their thoughts and voices along a journey that is truly theirs.

The inequality that takes place in education is a different beast; to some it is empowerment, while to others, it is oppression. Individuals with the power to control funding find it emboldening to oppress others, not admitting they are overpowering and oppressing those that need it most. Because of this greed and power, they are contributing to the withering of communities and future generations. To those experiencing the effects of those decisions through dilapidated buildings with holes in the walls or floors, lack of heat and air conditioning, and even a school that is flooded with waste from time to time, this is oppression. Kozol (1991) informs us of the learning environments causing more stress and harm to the child—how can learning be the priority? While the schools Kozol (1991) writes about are in predominantly black urban areas in places like Chicago, St. Louis, and New York, pockets of underfunded and impoverished schools are everywhere. This educational atmosphere is not to be tolerated in any stable middle to upper socioeconomic area. This obvious inequality is adding insult to already injured youth. The inequality and bitterness of these oppressed students can be highlighted when Kozol (1991) writes "The most important difference in the urban systems, I believe, is that they are often adjacent to the nation's richest districts, and this ever-present contrast adds to the heightened bitterness to the experiences of children" (p. 90). We have generations growing up with bitterness, anger, and frustrations as the inequality of educations grows wider and wider. This racial and socioeconomic inequality stems from the power of funding. Money, greed, and power drive the educational train that sparks fear in the hearts of many when educational inequality is challenged. Freeing the oppressed children and community becomes unimportant and without urgency when those in power feel threatened.

Parents, guardians and advocates for their children have tremendous power and influence. Children want to please their parents and crave reassurance they are doing things the right way. Parents send their children to school for many reasons, including education, socialization, maturation, and, yes, how to conform and fit in. Adults know their children need to learn to identify with a group, make some friends, and eventually conform to the rules society sets forth. Children look to their parent(s), their first teachers, to confirm and accept what the teacher says and to acknowledge him/her as the authority in the classroom. If the parent(s) do not support the teacher, the academic year could be a long one for all involved. It takes a partnership to educate a child. This is a shared endeavor among the shareholders to provide the best opportunity for the child to grow and matriculate.

This shared responsibility is also a transfer of power that takes place between parents and teachers. This transition is not acknowledged publicly; it may not even be consciously recognized. However, parents feel a loss of control when their child begins kindergarten. This may subconsciously be a recognition of a loss of influence or power, although this feeling wanes as the child grows older. This loss of control is the beginning of the transfer of power. The kids may have attended a prekindergarten or a Mother's Day Out program, but there is not the accountability for these programs as there is for public schools. Gone are the days of staying home "just because" or taking the student out early for ice cream. There is now a rigorous schedule and standards that must be met. With the transfer of power, there is a sacred trust that accompanies it. This trust is a risk on the part of the parent. This trust is grounded in professionalism and humanism. This professionalism comes in many forms. I, as a parent, believe I know what is best for my children. However, as Gert Biesta (2006) points out in *Beyond Learning*, "Parents generally send their children to school because they want them to be educated, but it is up to the professional judgment and expertise of the teacher to make decisions about what this particular child actually needs" (p. 21). As parents, we want what is best for our children; as teachers, we want the best for your children. At times, parents need to trust in the teachers, step back, and allow their children room to grow. Teachers are held to high standards and strive to maintain a positive learning environment and educate every student to the best of their ability. Parents must trust the educators to do just that.

Some would say the teachers hold the power over the children. Maybe they do to some extent. I suppose that depends on what type of power we are talking about. The goal of the teacher is to educate the child. Part of that education is allowing the teacher enough room and freedom to teach the children how to think critically. Immanuel Kant believed "It is not enough that children be trained; the most important thing is they learn how to think" (Buchner, 2015, p. 123). During a time when teachers are constantly criticized for shoving information at students, it is even more urgent and important that students are provided tools that will serve them throughout their life. This is a gift and a different form of power; this is empowerment. Empowerment is providing the tools to succeed, teaching to critically think, to nurture self-determination and eventually allow the students to make their own decisions.

For teachers to be able to empower students they must be empowered themselves. Part of the journey for empowerment among teachers is a personal, intrinsic journey. For good instruction to take place, bringing a classroom to life, teachers need to transform themselves into who they want to be. Parker Palmer (1998) states in *The Courage to Teach* that "we teach who we are" (p. 2). This is a profoundly simple statement. If a teacher is unhappy with themselves, their teaching may be angry, short tempered, and impatient. If a teacher is content, their teaching may be fun, creative, and good natured. Teachers must constantly evaluate who they are and how they handle situations. Palmer (1998) stresses, "If I am willing to look in that mirror and not run from what I see, I have a chance to gain self-knowledge—and knowing myself is as crucial to good teaching and knowing my students and my subject" (p. 3). Good teaching needs self-awareness to thrive, reach each student, and bring forth the potential locked inside. Knowing yourself is empowering, and that empowerment will be felt by the students as they begin their journey to knowing themselves.

Once a teacher feels empowered, they must dig deep within themselves to use that empowerment through courage and grace. Palmer (1998) muses, "The courage to teach is the courage to keep one's heart open in those very moments when the heart is asked to hold more than it is able" (pp. 11–12). There are moments teachers can feel the heart harden towards a child, when the offenses committed daily in the classroom take away valuable time and patience. How can we serve this child when making eye contact has become a challenge? We must constantly remember they are still children, someone's child. How can we, as teachers, boast of our positive learning environment, safe classroom space, or even our positive experiences if we are unwilling to soften our hearts towards our most troubled students? Our job is not to judge; it is to educate and serve. It is to listen when a student does not know where he is going to sleep that night and the only reason he came is because he has nowhere to go. Palmer talks about integrity, remaining true to ourselves while treating every child with fairness, kindness, and compassion, evaluating pieces of us for our heart to remain open.

Paulo Freire (1970/1993), in *Pedagogy of the Oppressed*, discusses another characteristic of a good teacher, and a necessary element of education. Freire (1970/1993) often mentions treating people with love, humility, and true kindness. He repeatedly mentions that having ulterior motives is not treating people with a pure heart and therefore is an act of oppression; this is the same, if not worse, with our students. Our students depend on us, and expect us, to treat them with fairness and kindness; this is a basic human expectation. Freire states that "True solidarity is found only in the plentitude of this act of love, in its existentiality, in its praxis" (p. 32). I interpret this to mean that in order to free both the oppressor and oppressed, there needs to be a codependent relationship between the two, each willing to become even more vulnerable to each other, each recognizing the human heart and willingness to work together. bell hooks also discusses vulnerability throughout *Teaching to Transgress*. hooks (1994) writes, "That empowerment cannot happen if we refuse to be vulnerable while encouraging students to take risks" (p. 21). Students should hear our vulnerabilities through the stories we share regarding our experiences. Part of learning and engaging is listening to stories of those that walked before us. Sharing our own sorrows, triumphs, struggles, and failures teaches children it is all right to open and share pieces of themselves. The classroom should be a safe place, both physically and emotionally;

in some ways this is more important than the content we are trying to master. They need to learn it is good to be themselves, to feel what they feel, and express themselves in an environment that is free from judgement. When the intention in the classroom is to help and work together, the relationship will succeed as the oppressor will see the oppressed as human, not an object. However, when the relationship fails it is because the oppressor will always choose what is in his/her best interest—a greedy, exclusive relationship. This is true self-awareness and empowerment that enables the teacher/student relationship the opportunity to thrive and succeed.

The classroom is a form of empowerment for the parents and the teachers. Even though the classroom is the teacher's domain, it is also the foundation for a community. The classroom is the common ground for shared power and empowerment for the parents and the teachers. The sense of community in the classroom is extremely important as it truly takes many to educate our children. Teachers are quick to welcome parents into their classroom to volunteer, observe, or read a good story. Even though volunteers are more prevalent in elementary school, there is a place for them in middle and high school, and they are just as important to both the school and the child. Parents must embrace this opportunity whenever they can. Staying connected to the classroom empowers students; they are proud their parent came in, proud they are concerned and interested in their education. Not all parents are able to come in and help; maybe they cannot miss work, maybe they are in school themselves, maybe it is a health issue. There are ways to stay connected to the classroom whether it is through cutting out future art projects at home, sending in glue sticks, or accompanying the class on a field trip. It does take a village to educate a child.

Staying connected to the classroom is important. There are two sides to this proverbial coin. Children of parents who are able to participate more may receive preferential treatment from the teacher. A bond develops between the parent and teacher as that teacher is watching over and keeping safe the most precious gift, the child. However, on the other side of that, a stranger is influencing and changing that child. This can result in another power struggle. Many parents do not take kindly to a teacher stepping in to help raise their "precious." Some teachers complain about lack of parental support. However, teachers must not give up on these parents, for it is the distant, resistant parent that may need additional support and encouragement to become involved. It may not be the teacher at all; maybe the parent does not speak English, maybe they were not successful in their education, or maybe, as Jonathan

Kozol (2007) writes in *Letters to a Young Teachers*, they "remembered misery and failure and prolonged years of humiliation" (p. 23). Even parents need kindness and compassion from teachers. Teachers are in a unique position to build community support and wellbeing through their classroom. They can bring families together through children with positive reinforcement, encouragement, and mentoring. Most teachers take an interest in their youngsters, their likes and dislikes, hobbies, and talents. They listen, encourage imagination, and nurture and cultivate dreams. It should be understood that not all teachers want connections with their children, not all are teaching to serve the student. Some wield their power over children, not through empowerment, but through fear.

Fear is detected when teachers hold power over students based on their authority alone. However, this is not power; this is another form of oppression. Whether it is discipline or performance, the expectations from the teachers may be more than a student can handle. An example is a first grader sitting quietly for long periods or berating a high school student for a bad test grade in front of peers. This is two-fold. Are the expectations from the teacher in line with what the students are capable of adhering to, or are they so stringent a student is destined to fail? If the expectations are too high, students will never obtain approval from the teacher, thus turning into a discipline or classroom management concern. When a classroom turns from critical learning into a placeholder or, in some cases, a destination to avoid jail time, the teacher is responsible for that shift in empowerment to oppression. Ta-Nehisi Coates (2015) talks about this oppression in his book *Between the World and Me*. Coates (2015) discusses the fearfulness and despair he felt as a young black child growing up in Manhattan. There is a note of despair to his tone as he laments, "When our elders presented school to us, they did not present it as a place of high learning but as a means of escape from death and penal warehousing" (p. 26). What a different experience he would have had if racial and academic equality were truly strived for. He further states, "I sensed the schools were hiding something, drugging us with false morality so that we would not see, so that we did not ask: Why—for us and only us—is the other side of free will and free spirits an assault upon our bodies" (p. 26). Would there have been a necessary, constant fear of keeping his body safe? By not challenging and teaching his young mind early, he felt unfit (p. 27). Had his education been of equal quality as those in surrounding areas, how would his life have been changed? I cannot begin to pass judgment on his teachers, but it is curious that if they had practiced the self-reflection Parker Palmer says is necessary, would they have increased the vigor and rigor of their classrooms to reflect the urgency and importance of education? It is a thought to ponder upon as the oppression of Coates's classrooms had a large impact on his life.

One of the reasons teachers may subconsciously oppress students is they feel oppressed. They are looking towards their boards of education, the state, and the federal machine trying to ensure they are meeting the standards so kids are not left behind, and have every opportunity to succeed. They are teaching a predetermined curriculum about which they had little, if any, input. Their success, in many ways, will be determined by the outcome on standardized tests taken by nervous boys and girls who want to move on to their next year. Teachers determine success by the mastery of skills, like multiplication, the correct sequence of World War II, or correctly identifying all fifty states on a map. In addition to juggling requirements, they are constantly bombarded with negative feedback that they are not doing enough. The rigor is not high enough, their test scores are low, and the system is failing. In many cases, the teachers are evaluated on the results of the standardized tests, determining if they have a contract for the next year. All the while, kids are fearful of those same tests. What power can be gained by these tests? While many teachers have an administration allowing them the academic freedom to be creative and take initiative to ensure skills, like critical thinking and reasoning, are learned as well, many teachers do not. Because of this constant fear felt by teachers, they are pushing information onto students and punishing those that cannot keep up or perform accordingly. Jack Gerson (2004), in "The Neoliberal Agenda and the Response to Teacher Unions," in *The Assault on Public Education*, writes "Students are encouraged to focus on "getting the right answer" as the goal, rather than encouraging curiosity, inquiry, critical thinking, conceptualization, and the problem-solving process" (p. 104). Has our education system become about the ability to regurgitate information for the purpose of test taking? Gerson (2004) believes this to be true as he reiterates, "The effect is to sort schools by poverty level; low-income students are taught to give the right answer or get shoved out—to the military, to the street, or to prison" (p. 104). So, if our impoverished students are unable to perform well, due to outside issues, why are we compounding them by punishing students for not performing well on tests? Power. It is powerful to hold money and funds from those who need it most. This perpetuates the cycle of the "haves" versus the "have nots," opening the door for reform and competition. Reformers believe they can do it better; their way is just what education needs to succeed. However, how is their way different from what we are doing now? The teachers are usually less qualified; they do not have the pedagogy or experience, classroom management skills, or mentoring to succeed. Another factor reformers refuse to acknowledge is poverty.

Reformers want to address education, but fail to address poverty. As Jack Gerson points out, "no campaign to 'close the achievement gap' can succeed if it does not make priority to close the poverty gap by providing jobs, restoring and expanding essential public programs, and raising income levels for low-income families" (p. 104). Derrick Bell (1992) writes, in *Faces at the Bottom of the Well*, "abstract condemnation of racism and poverty and the devastation of our communities is inadequate and ineffective" (p. 125). How can students be expected to learn when they are hungry, uncertain of their next meal, sick, worried, scared? Adults do not function well like that either, yet all that is ignored and dismissed as inadequate education, and bad teachers are blamed. Gerson discusses adding wrap-around services to low-performing schools, teacher training and support, and supporting the community. What advantages this would give to youngsters. Yes, it is a change and yes, it takes time, but our future's children deserve better.

Diane Ravitch (2013) discusses in *Reign of Error* the theory held tightly by reformers, saying "Reformers often say that poverty is an excuse for 'bad teachers'" (p. 91). Her theory is that if all students were educated equally then all would eventually head to college and someday poverty would be wiped out. However, this is not the case. We know that not everyone is bound for higher education, nor should everyone be. What is true is that the theory of the Obama administration that "poverty can be overcome with good teachers" (p. 91) is false. Good teachers cannot overcome the effects of poverty and it is ignorant to believe so. Ravitch (2013) makes a compelling argument that reformers believe competition for a quality education will eventually fix both education and poverty. Ravitch (2013) points out, "Our society has grown to accept poverty is an inevitable fact of life, and there seems to be little or no political will to do anything about it" (p. 93). Our political system fails to understand, or maybe ignores, that to provide an equal opportunity for all children, we must share in the responsibility to change the system. Politicians are fearful of changing this system and reallocating resources as it allows individuals to be on equal footing. Poverty is a horrendous beast; its consequences and effects reach far beyond the classroom. Poverty affects many aspects of a child's life; it affects motivation, well-being, emotions, attention span, academic performance, and it forces focus on survival tactics (Ravitch, 2013, pp. 93–94). This oppression takes the power away from the community and places it in the hands of the government, big corporations, and other entities that want to exploit impoverished individuals. The community is a place of security and familiarity. It is a place you should be able to walk down the street and greet neighbors with a smile; the school should be a safe, energetic place of learning and achieving. However, when a community is in an area where poverty is high, and that community ceases to be safe, it becomes survival of the fittest and that will take precedence over any education a child will receive. The community does not have the power, the children will not thrive, the cycle will never be broken.

Standardized testing became a means to prove public education is in crisis. It became the measure by which politicians and elitists could declare public education is failing and more options are needed. Instead of decreasing achievement gaps, it expanded them; instead of providing equal education for all, it increased inequality. In addition, failing test scores were used to enact changes both in the function and the governance of education (Garrison, 2009, p. 2). Garrison (2009) reiterates this in *A Measure of Failure* by stating, "Standardized exams were developed as markers of failure, and stood as justifications for and symbols of the change reformers sought" (p. 3). This is an abstract thought or claim based on individual goals. If the public education system works, it cannot be reformed, it cannot be privatized, and a profit cannot be made. For politicians and elitists to maintain power, there must be something to declare crisis over, and that something is substandard education provided by our public schools. The battle cry of reformers is that if students are underperforming, we must enact change. If our students are doing well on testing, the tests are not rigorous enough and the test requires revision. These same individuals fail to look at equality of resources: are the buildings in good condition, are the textbooks up to date and plentiful, is technology up to date, are there enough supplemental curriculum supplies for teachers? These questions remain unanswered. To fully provide education would be to decrease the power that comes with that one word: fail.

Standardized tests do much more than allow politicians to play Chicken Little. The results of the tests allow schools to rank the students based on achievement. This achievement ranking perpetuates the belief that worth as a student, even as a human being, is tied to the ability to perform on an assessment. It discounts intelligence, learning styles, and assessments completed by the teacher, thus reducing students to a number received on a test. It perpetuates a hierarchy that is difficult to break, even when a student closer to the bottom earns a much higher test score. It discounts the effort students put into the course and the dedication of the teacher to provide the best instruction and remediation possible. As tensions increase on all sides—parents, teachers, society, government officials—it has become evident that testing has failed. Garrison (2009) sums up this failure this way:

> Far from being able to "close the achievement gap" and promote opportunities for minorities, "standards-based" reforms have so far resulted in opposite of the rhetoric that supports the practice: more and more children are "left behind" as dropouts appear to be increasing and curriculums have barrowed as (mostly) working-class and minority youth are condemned to a regime of test-prep and little more. (pp. 103–104)

This quote shows us the depth at which we are failing students. Our system is leaving them behind without a thought to the consequences and continued repression of young minds. As we fight against making our children a commodity, it is important that we acknowledge the power of play and interaction with others. This is a direct contradiction of teaching to the test where repetition and rote memorization are encouraged and the only ways a student can be successful. Martha Nussbaum (2010), in *Not for Profit: Why Democracy Needs the Humanities*, describes Winnicott's theory regarding the importance of play for small children. Nussbaum (2010) points out several times the importance of children developing empathy, sympathy, and interaction with and towards other people. She states this starts at home and is nurtured in the school. Winnicott believes that "Play is a type of activity that takes place in the space between people" (Nussbaum, 2010, p. 99). Children learn to get along with others first from playing at home with parents, then siblings, until the comfort circle expands to include other children. Eventually, play turns from the playground to the athletic field or band practice, both a form of art. The play they learned at a young age has evolved: "it connects the experiences of vulnerability and surprise to curiosity and wonder rather than crippling anxiety" (Nussbaum, 2010, p. 101). As adults, we look to the arts as well. We look to music, literature, watching the dance of an athletic competition, paintings, theater, or the wonderment of nature.

We would not have acquired this appreciation for the arts had we not been introduced through our home life and had it reinforced through teachers. Play and appreciation for the arts empowers children, and eventually young adults, to try new things, seek new talents and sometimes even fail. Even though failure is not an option in today's academic setting, failure is quite good for children. It teaches kids to try harder, to work deeper and more critically, to accept their shortcomings, and with enough practice and courage, to try again.

Eventually, they will succeed. Failure also teaches children to appreciate the talent of others and accept each other for the talents possessed. Learning to play nice in the sandbox empowers students to treat others with kindness and compassion as well as to work hard to achieve their goals. This is not something that can be taught in the classroom specifically; this is learned through interaction with peers, parents, and teachers. Reformers want to bombard us with how our schools are failing, but the fight is about more than test scores and money; it is about the whole student and both teaching and learning respect for all.

For all the talk of reforming education, there has not been a successful program put forth with the best interest of all students in mind. In 2001, President George Bush called his reform "No Child Left Behind" and the Obama Administration called his "Race to the Top" in 2012. There has been a nationwide call to increase charter schools and voucher programs under the guise of creating more equality. However, no program or reform did more damage than No Child Left Behind (NCLB). The writers and policy makers aimed for the moon when drafting and debating NCLB. They had great hopes and expectations for what they could achieve. Policy makers, and George Bush, ultimately decided on four strategies to draft this legislation upon. The first piece was to strengthen Title I accountability among local and state school officials. This strategy aims to test each child on the progress made during the academic year. In order to test each student and be able to compare them, clear standards must be in place for teachers to use as a guidebook. By being able to compare students, data was also gathered and compared on key descriptors including gender, socioeconomic status, race and ethnicity, and spoken language. Those schools that did not make "adequate progress" were deemed inadequate schools and publicly shamed and embarrassed. Teachers were fired, administrators scolded and moved, and children left in uncertain, stressful, and tenuous environments. Not only is this a less-than-optimal learning environment, it is probably a less-than-optimal choice for the community as a whole. At no point did the writers of NCLB ever take into account poverty and the climate in which the child is growing up. When a child is worried about going home to an abusive family, they probably will not concentrate on *Huckleberry Finn*. When the student knows he or she must walk home through a street corner of drug dealers or gang members, the periodic table is not quite so important. Instead of addressing issues like the ones above, this policy served to further oppress an already oppressed group. Presidential administrations are out of touch with what communities deal with and what it takes to educate children. It should not be administrations making these decisions; it should be the communities themselves.

The second portion of legislation created within NCLB was increasing academic choices for parents and students. This piece of legislation is tied into school accountability. If a school was unable to maintain "adequate yearly progress" (AYP), then parents and guardians were provided a different option. As Ravitch (2013) points out, "Students must be given choices other than traditional public schools, such as charter schools, vouchers, and online schools" (p. 3). This is not a new concept to parents and students; parents have always had the opportunity to send their children to private schools. What is relatively new are the ideas of charter and voucher schools. Charter schools, voucher programs, and private schools are meant to be a better option to their failing public school. Charter school enrollment exploded as a result of NCLB. One of the concerns with charter schools is the for-profit business model and the lack of academic oversight. Because of the financial backing from the private company, the company's priorities and, in some cases, politics dominate the landscape at those institutions.

One of the first charter schools was the Lancasterian School. According to *Schooled to Order: A Social History of Public Schooling in the United States*, by David Nascaw (1979), "schoolrooms were arranged in strictly hierarchical fashion, more appropriate to a feudal kingdom than a New World republic" (p. 20). As Nascaw (1979) points out, this was true "No matter that the system as such appeared to violate every norm of democratic and republican social life" (p. 21). All that mattered was the discipline was strong and the respect for authority was ingrained in the young lads. After all, the main purpose of this authoritarian style of education was to keep indigent boys from roaming the streets, keeping crime low and brawls at a minimum. These schools were supported by successful businessmen and charities, who sent their children to elite private schools to ensure a proper education. As a result, there was very little academic oversight, learning a craft was more important than mathematical skills, and recognizing authority was priority. As more research is established, and the numbers are crunched, charter schools do not appear to be more successful in educating our youth, but they are successful in luring funding away from public schools that need it the most.

One of the other options mentioned in NCLB was voucher programs, designed for the educational dollars allocated to a student to follow him/her wherever he or she goes. The first voucher program was tried in Washington, D.C. This was touted as a scholarship program allowing students from poor performing schools to transfer to higher performing schools. One of the concerns with this program, and charter schools for that matter, is the transfer of funds away from the public school, when funding is at an all-time-high concern. This removal of those dollars also removes resources, thus perpetuating the lack of resources in low-income areas.

Education is a struggle, a constant tug of war. Whether it is a rope held by students and teachers, teachers and administrators, students and administrators, administrators and county officials—the list goes on and on—there is a power struggle. Everyone involved wants to believe they are doing what is in the best interest of the child, but we know that is not always the case. The power holding education is a reflection of the struggle currently happening in America. America is at odds with itself; there is a great deal of anger in our country. We can deny it, but as polarizing as our last election was, it is evident. This anger is fear in disguise. We, as citizens, are fearful of what we do not see, what we may not understand. This is the same in education. We are fearful of the unknown. Ronald Takaki (1993) in *A Different Mirror* reminds us of our diversity and how we can appreciate it when he writes, "America's dilemma has been our resistance to ourselves—our denial of our immensely varied selves. But we have nothing to fear but our fear of our own diversity" (p. 427). He continues with "To get along with each other, however, requires self-recognition as well as a self-acceptance" (p. 427). If we listen, truly listen, to each other, to the narratives told by those that came before us, to the struggles, concern, fears, and triumphs, we could learn a lot from each other. We could accept our differences and empower all of us to move forward as one group. This is true in education as well. If we could focus on the needs of the child, the well-being of our educational foundation, I feel confident we could heal our system.

Sir Walter Scott (1808) had a saying: "It is a tangled web we weave when we first practice to deceive" (p. 93). That is what education is now: one large, messy, tangled web. Our educational system is full of deception and manipulation. Those in power want us to believe every child has the same opportunity as the next, but we all know that is not true. Those in power are not only manipulating the narrative, but the money as well. There must be change. We as educators must work to change this unjust system. Edward Said (1994) writes, in *Representations of the Intellectual,* "The central fact for me is, I think, that the intellectual is an individual endowed with a faculty for representing, embodying, and articulating a message, a view, an attitude, philosophy or opinion to, as well as, for the public" (p. 11). It is our job, as educators and the educated, to untangle this web. William Schubert (2009) eloquently states in *Love, Justice, and Education*, "We relish continuing this conversation . . . experiencing the action it inspires . . . assuming that it will lead to new realms of love, justice, and education" (p. 227). We must empower those that can speak up to do so, we must correct those that need correction, and we must free the oppressed from oppression. This will take time; this is true reform.

References

Bell, D. (1992). *Faces at the bottom of the well: The permanence of racism*. Basic Books.
Biesta, G. J. J. (2006). *Beyond learning: Democratic education for a human future*. Paradigm Publishers.
Buchner, E. F. (2015). *The educational theory of Immanuel Kant*. Forgotten Books.
Coates, T. (2015). *Between the world and me*. Spiegel & Grau.
Foucault, M. (1977). *Discipline and punish: The birth of the prison*. Pantheon.
Freire, P. (1970/1993). *Pedagogy of the oppressed*. Penguin Books.
Garrison, M. J. (2009). *A measure of failure*. State University of New York Press.
Gerson, J. (2004). *The assault on public education*. Teachers College Press.
hooks, b. (1994). *Teaching to transgress*. Routledge.
Kozol, J. (1991). *Savage inequalities: Children in America's schools*. Crown.
Kozol, J. (2007). *Letters to a young teacher*. Three Rivers Press.
Nascaw, D. (1979). *Schooled to order: A social history of public schooling in the United States*. Oxford University Press.
No Child Left Behind Act Public Law PL 107–110. (2001). https://www.congress.gov/bill/107th-congress/house-bill/1
Nussbaum, M. C. (2010). *Not for profit: Why democracy needs the humanities*. Princeton University Press.
Palmer, P. (1998). *The courage to teach: Exploring the inner landscape of a teacher's life*. Jossey-Bass.
Power. Def 1, 3, 6, 8. (2017). In *Oxford English dictionary online* (2 ed.), Retrieved from http://www.oxfordlearnersdictionaries.com/us/definition/english/power_1?q=power
Ravitch, D. (2013). *Reign of error*. Vintage Books.
Sahlberg, P. (2011). *Finnish lessons: What can the world learn from educational change in Finland*. Teachers College Press.
Said, E.W. (1994). *Representations of the intellectual*. Vintage Books.
Scott, W. (1808). *Marmion: A tale of flodden fields*. Archibald Constable.
Schubert, W. H. (2009) *Love, justice, and education: John Dewey and the utopians*. Information Age Publishing, INC.
Takaki, R. (1993). *A different mirror: A history of multicultural America*. Little, Brown, & Company.

· 1 1 ·

DR. COACH DAVIS

Thomas J. Davis

In order to provide my story, I must start with what I believe makes me unique. I was, let us just say, a blessed and lucky little person at the age of zero, and I did not want to take the opportunity at a second chance at life for granted. When I was born, I was blue and had a very small chance at survival. I was diagnosed with Transposition of the Greater Vessels. In layman's terms, my heart pumps backwards. I have never known anything different, so it is the everyday normal for me. There are also mental and emotional components that go along with the physical. I believe that because I have had to face the world differently, the wear and tear come from the mental and emotional stresses of my condition more than the physical. The most prevalent example I have is when it is time for my yearly check-up. I get very concerned and overly anxious about what my cardiologist might find or see. I know physically everything is going well, but there is a worry that grows exponentially the week leading up to the appointment. So far, all my worry and anxiousness has been for nothing, but it is the process I go through every year. My concern is that something will need to be addressed, and it will affect how much I can do or the time I have left with my family. I would be able to tell if something were to not be right, but I allow myself to overly worry and believe in the minute percent of a chance that something might be wrong. Because of this, I cause more stress for my family and myself as I look forward to that day to be over. Of course my health is important, but it does not help to fret and worry continuously. Most people that know of my condition take it in stride, probably better than myself in some instances. But some people, which are very few because I do not tell many, give me a gasp and ask a handful of concerned questions. I answer them as in-depth as they can understand, turn around, and continue with whatever task I was doing before the conversation started. This is how that conversation usually goes when someone has questions:

> "What is something about you we don't know?"
> "I've had a couple of heart surgeries."
> "Really? Why? What happened?"
> "I was born with a closed circular system and I couldn't get oxygen to my blood. They did the Blalock-Hanlon when I was born."
> "What does that mean? What is that?"
> "They cut me open from here to here (under right pectoral, cutting to the right, to under the right shoulder blade), and inserted a balloon to create a three-chambered heart for a while."
> "What was the other surgery you had?"
> "It's called the Mustard procedure. That's the name of the doctor who developed it. They took the atrium portion of my septum and made a baffle out of it to create a fourth chamber. They then had to replumb everything, so my aorta goes to my lungs and my pulmonary veins go to my body. Basically, the right side of my heart pumps blood to my body and my left side pumps it to my lungs."
> "Do you have any issues?"
> "No. I go for a check-up at the pediatric cardiology unit once a year. I know, an old guy walking into a pediatric office, but I'm comfortable with them and they have been great."
> "Hmm, so that's what's wrong with you?" (some laughter)
> "Yeah, I guess so." (much less laughter)

And that is about it. The most entertaining conversations I had as a student were when the service academies would call during my senior year in high school. They would introduce themselves and talk about all the opportunities I would have if I joined. I would then tell them my story, and then I would get, "Well, sir, you have a wonderful day and good luck." I started trying to cut them off before they got into their telemarketing spiel to try and save them some time.

Okay—I tell you all of that to tell you this: I was extremely lucky to be a student-athlete that got to compete at a high level. My cardiologist presented my case to a convention of cardiologists and they did not agree with his philosophy. His philosophy was if the benefits outweigh the risks, he would allow me do whatever I felt that I could do, to an extent. Once the risks outweighed the benefits, we would have to take another approach. Well, it never reversed, and at this point, he was talking about a 17-year-old athlete who was offered a college scholarship, and that idea did not coincide with the medicinal thinking at the time. People who have what I have are not supposed to be able to do the things I have done. That part of my life was full of some of my most rewarding successes, detrimental defeats, and the best life lessons I've gotten. I was also extremely blessed to have the coaches I did that brought out the best of who I was at the time. I got into education because I wanted to give back to the next generation of student-athletes the way my coaches gave back to me. Everything has to start somewhere, and this is the start of my beginning.

As a student-athlete at my high school, I played for a legendary coach. He won five state championships there and three more when he left to open a new high school in our county. He was the one teacher in the school everyone was afraid of. He was tough, demanding, serious, and wanted each student and player he encountered to be their very best. He knew how to motivate young people and pushed them well beyond their self-perceived limits. As a freshman with a heart condition, he was not real sure how to handle me. Tuesdays and Thursdays in his first period weight training class were running days. Pitchers were afforded the luxury of swinging a sledgehammer into a load of sand. Privately to me he would say, "They've got seventy-five reps, you can do fifty." When we ran the mile for time, he would say, "Try to make it in ten minutes, but don't die on me trying if you can't." He said it in a way that he was looking out for me, but I took it as a challenge to match what his other players could do. I could do more, and wanted to do more, than he thought I could, because I did not want to seem as though I could not handle the demands a *normal* student-athlete should be able to handle. He was a great motivator and taught his students and players the importance of a good work ethic and to never think they have reached their limit. There is always another step that can be taken or another challenge that can be met. After my sophomore year, he left to open a new school and our next coach came in that summer. He had the same expectations as my first coach, but he had a different style. He was a good motivator, understood baseball, and wanted the best for his students and players, but he was more open as a communicator and could talk to his players about anything. It was a little looser atmosphere with him, and players were more open with him and each other. These are the two men that really inspired me to become a teacher and a coach. I was able to see them influence countless students' lives and make them better people by pushing them to be their very best, including myself. When I went off to Montreat College and played baseball there, the coach there was a mixture of both of my high school coaches. Although I was three hours from home, I felt a little better knowing that he bore some similarities to my hometown coaches: tough, demanding, a good communicator, wanting his players to be their best on and off the field. He gave me a sense of comfort, of home.

Whitlock (2007) discusses the idea of homeplace and that there is a sense of comfort and accessibility to it. She writes, "I write to shape homeplace into an idea that I can embrace, one that will embrace me right back" (p. 82). The idea is that homeplace can be anywhere that one feels comfortable. For me, my homeplace has long been the field, and more specifically the mound. I feel at home and share it with people I love and enjoy. By understanding Whitlock's (2007) message, I have become more aware of how to see the world and where I fit in. My story is not only about acknowledging my homeplace, but also finding ways to remove my sense of comfort so I may grow and develop into a more well-rounded person. As an educator and a coach, I believe this is important so I can better reach my students and players. As a parent, I believe this is important so I can better prepare my children for the challenges they will face when they venture into the world on their own. The similarities among my coaches are the things that really matter when it comes to athletics. Coaches must be able to reach their players and help them understand that they can be better than they were when they got there. Throughout that process, becoming a better player is almost inevitable. These three men understood that and made a lasting impression on a great number of young people. Once I became a teacher and a coach, I wanted to instill the same qualities these three men instilled in me, to push my students and players to be the best they can be. As a middle school teacher and coach, I worked to prepare those students and players for their high school experiences. As a high school teacher and coach, I work to prepare them for life beyond high school, regardless of the possibility of athletics being involved in their future. I have many conversations, especially with my juniors and seniors, about the lessons they have learned from their respective sports and how they can apply what they learn to their individual school experience or life situation outside of school.

Athletics has been a big part of my life. I was never very social or brave enough to take a chance at many things, but athletics helped me to shed the lack of courage and try something new. I had just enough skill to be good, and while I was on my journey, I learned a thing or two about life along the way.

There are lessons throughout athletics that elude the smartest and most short-sighted people; but those lessons are embraced by the ones who see the big picture clearly enough to understand why the lessons are important and how they can be applied to their own lives.

As a college athlete, athletics gave me an opportunity to work for an education while still competitively playing baseball. As a teacher and coach, athletics has given me an opportunity to impact student-athletes and make a positive difference. I am passionate about this topic because I can see how student-athletes can grow and change through the lessons they learn from their individual sports. These lessons are all transferable in some way among the different sports, but when the student-athletes put the dedication and commitment into both their athletic ability and the life lessons that are being taught, they mature and become better people, which in turn provides the fuel for them to become better athletes. Athletics also gives some student-athletes a purpose to complete school and a reason to strive for academic success. In my case, I would not have been successful in the academic portion of my high school career if not for athletics. Baseball is what forced me to keep my grades up and work towards the goal of graduation. I am not a good example of a great student, but I am a great example of a struggling student who figured out how to use my athletic ambitions to be the motivator in my academic struggles. I see some of my players going through the same things I did as a high schooler, struggling with school the same ways I did. I take it upon myself to help them recognize the issues keeping them from being successful and to teach them how to overcome them. Because of the athletic opportunities I have had, I am where I am today with the opportunity to continue the education and molding of young student-athletes. I also understand that the lessons they can learn during their time in athletics will help them to grow, mature, and see the world in a variety of ways. Hopefully, I will impact them in a positive manner and influence them to do well once they leave our program.

While I will concentrate on the athletics portion of high school, I do not want to minimize the importance of a solid education and the various learning dynamics that take place in the classroom. Without the academic foundation in the classroom, the connection to the lessons on the field is lost. When the connection between academics and athletics is made, the connection to the reality of the world is much greater. What is learned throughout students' academic careers is important to each one of them in a unique way. All students are geared toward certain disciplines and topics, but it depends on how they apply the knowledge they acquire and the extent to which they allow it to influence their lives. The level of influence can turn into passion, which brings those students to life; it invigorates their passion for learning. Those types of influences and passions are evident in athletics as well. Athletics becomes a part of a student's identity whenever they choose to take that role on. While I do teach literature to juniors and seniors, I am also the head coach of the high school baseball team. Because of my experiences in athletics and the classroom, I feel I am in a unique position to share my story and the lessons I have learned through athletics.

I became a literature teacher because I see the power of words and stories. I enjoy reading and I believe stories can give us new perspective on a subject, teach us a new lesson, or show us a different path to achieving a goal we have in mind. Very rarely do I have a student who plans on becoming an English major in college, so I teach the stories in a way that my students understand the important messages the author is writing to convey. It is not always about the characters and the plot; it is more about the makeup and development of the characters, the actions that create the plot, and the lessons they can take from the stories. Since I teach the upperclassmen, I believe it is important for them to see how other people, fictional or not, work through problems and make decisions that affect them for the rest of the time we get to know them. The reality of going out into the world is more imminent for those students, and I work to find readings they can learn from and adapt to their own lives. I do not perpetuate the "concept of banking" in my education practices. Banking is the premise that the teacher knows everything and the student knows nothing. I can guarantee that I do not know everything about anything that I teach to my students. I do not want to be the one that rules the conversation. I want my students to use their critical thinking skills, develop their own perspectives, and contribute to the learning process. Although I am the one responsible for delivering educational and helpful information to my students, I must not forget they have a contribution to the conversations as well. Their intellectual property can enhance our endeavors that we take together through education in the classroom and on the field. We must communicate constantly so they can feel as though they have an investment as we take on the formidable learning process we all go through.

I enjoy being an academic teacher and a coach. I get to see how our athletes are in the classroom. When I talk to a coach about players or write a letter of recommendation for them, I can give a better description of what those student-athletes are like academically, as I often get questions about what our student-athletes are like off the field. I feel as though I can give a more accurate answer because I teach a core subject. My students and I will get into conversations about colleges and the varying levels of degrees. The question always comes up: "What degrees do you have?" I go through the ones I have and discuss my experiences in them. Then I get the response, "But you're a coach, and you have a doctorate? How does that work?" For some reason, that one is hard for them to believe. I have brought some of the books I have read to class to discuss with my students certain points that may be beneficial to them. I believe them seeing their teacher still in school has a positive impact on them, especially with me being a coach, as coaches are not usually seen as academics by trade. Hopefully, they see the dedication I have for them in the classroom, on the field, and to myself and family as I continue my educational journey. My players know of my schooling and I believe it is good for them to see a person in a leadership role have the desire to continue learning. I want them to understand education can continue throughout their different life stages.

Reference

Whitlock, R. U. (2007). *This corner of Canaan: Curriculum studies of place & the reconstruction of the South*. Peter Lang.

· 12 ·

ATHLETICS AND EDUCATION: ALL MEN WERE CREATED EQUAL, THEN SOME BECAME ATHLETES

Thomas J. Davis

> Two roads diverged in a wood, and I took the one less traveled by, and that has made all the difference. –Robert Frost

The word *student-athlete* is a unique term designated for a small population of students from each school. These students are generally seen as the ones who can handle the academic and athletic balance that must happen for them to be successful while trying to find their own path and identity. There are many factors that figure into this intense identity and they must find ways to be successful in both paths of life. At times, student-athletes can be perceived in a negative light. They can be considered mean, aggressive, unintelligent, narrow-minded, selfish, coddled, and lackadaisical. Many people believe athletics to be just activities, something to do when nothing else will suffice. Athletics were once classified as easy to understand, simple hobbies meant for the students who were not scholarly enough or had little talent in the arts. Craig Lambert (1998) discusses the idea of the "dumb jock" and how that person is viewed. He says:

> The left-handed compliment he's a brain reflects our opposition of mind and body, thought and action, intellect and sports. Our culture enshrines many tiresome stereotypes; among them is the "dumb jock," who excels on the playing field but is a dolt

> in the classroom or anywhere else that requires mental power. The jock's musculature supposedly continues above the neck. (p. 25)

It takes special student-athletes to be able to excel at both sides of their scholastic careers. The ideas of before have been replaced with the understanding that the student-athlete is a dedicated, respectful, and hard-working person who is driven to make the most out of their opportunities. There are lessons from both aspects they can learn that are interchangeable and that can be beneficial to them. For this to be a reality, the student-athletes must realize what they are attempting to accomplish, and then discover qualities about themselves and learn to utilize them to complete this daunting task successfully. To be more than a novice in any athletic activity, the athlete must understand it takes determination, tenacity, and a dedication to work ethic to hone the craft he aims to perfect. It is a craft, not a social experiment or experience, not a continuous activity or career for the weak-hearted or over-emotional, but a craft that must be developed, built-upon, expanded, and made as consistent as possible.

Alongside the pressures of maintaining high levels of performance, tough standards and expectations, mountains of unwarranted attention, and the everyday grind of being a student, there are also many societal pressures that come with the identity of a student-athlete. As young members of society, there are many struggles that come along with even being just a student trying to find an identity. As a high school student, there is a struggle with finding an identity among the different social groups within the school. There is a wide variety of possibilities to lay the foundations of being an artist, musician, military member, scientist, actor, singer, a lover of foreign or the English language, and an athlete. Once one of these is chosen as the student's desirable identification group, the question then becomes "What am I willing to give up to be a part of this group?" Between the ages of 14–19, it is hard enough to grow up and deal with all the normal changes that adolescents go through, much less attempt to decide and understand a future that may possibly be a grand opportunity. Identifying with one of these groups means that the other possibilities are now less of an option because of the severe time constraint that goes along with balancing both the extra activity and the required academics.

As high school student-athletes continue in their sports, they have an opportunity to extend their identification with their specific group. Although they are older and accustomed to the demands of their identification, they are not always wiser. The distractions multiply along with the pressures of on-the-field performances and the newfound academic stress that can make their time there difficult, especially if they decide to continue this identity at a top-tier university. Attention (positive and negative), fame, opportunities to speak to the press, social media outlets, and contemplating going professional are just a few of the issues that they try to juggle as students only 18 or 22 years old. Yet, at this level, the identification of their academic ambitions will also change the way they behave and interact with others. They must be able to set themselves up for a life after athletics and all the difficulties that come along with it, including adapting back to life without a group to identify with.

***

> There are so many different things they can learn through competing in high level sports: how to deal with disappointment, how to persevere, how to bounce back from challenges, how to work together. –Matt Tanney

There is much more to learning than what is in the textbooks and grade-level standards. Lessons that last well beyond the ones taught in class can be learned outside the confinements of the latest curriculum guide. Immanuel Kant believed that play is necessary for the development of children. In *The Educational Theory of Immanuel Kant*, Kant (1908/2015) lays out many of his theories on education and how they apply at different stages of youth. One of Kant's (1908/2015) theories is, "Running is a healthy movement and strengthens the body. Leaping, lifting, carrying, hurling, throwing at a mark, wrestling, racing, and all such exercises are excellent" (p. 160). Kant (1908/2015) believed in the use of physical activity and that it could advance the mind as well as the body. These types of activities were considered important enough to become part of the school curriculum. Schubert (2009) argues for the significance of play based on the theories of Dewey. Schubert (2009) writes:

> Too often, even play is distorted by imposition of purposes in most Earthling schools. Without such imposition, play is likely the source of the greatest Earthlings learning, though too often Earthlings designate it as mere leisure pursuits, and thus do not value the role of play in learning. (p. 79)

For many students, play is a way for them to learn not just academic lessons, but also lessons that carry beyond the classroom. When students are involved in play, the different activities incorporate multiple skills at one time. These activities also force the students to make decisions that advance them further along in the activity. Play is not only for leisure, but it can, and also should be, used for enhancing learning opportunities so students can get the most out of their education. Although athletics are taken more seriously at the higher levels of school, the students are still learning simple lessons as they amplify their skillset. They also continue to expand their skillset not directly related to their sport. Schubert (2009) continues, "Children know that play is the most worthwhile kind of work" (p. 79). Not only do students enjoy their learning experience during play, but they also have a sense of satisfaction and accomplishment once they complete the task, activity, or game. Lessons other than the academic ones being addressed are developed such as working with others, communication, learning new perspectives, problem solving, and sharing, which can all be beneficial in the students' development. This is the skillset students must cultivate as the requirements for them are ever evolving in our fast-paced world.

Athletics can teach lessons and drive the athletes to be better people. Herbert Marsh and Sabina Kleitman (2003) discuss this very idea in their article "School Athletic Participation: Mostly Gain with Little Pain," where they state, "Marsh argued that AP—athletic participation—could enhance school identification, involvement, and commitment in a way that enhances more narrowly defined academic outcomes as well as the nonacademic outcomes" (p. 206). To expand on this statement, Marsh (2003) continues, "AP fosters identification with the school and school-related values" (p. 206). Athletes have a unique advantage of being able to take the lessons they have learned and shape and adapt them to their own unique lives and situations. Just as with artists and musicians, the finely specialized abilities must come from the development of the early forms of those raw skills.

Athletics can influence the lives of the participants and help them to shape their own idea of the world and how it works. There is a culture within athletics, each sport having its own set of written and unwritten rules, concepts, theories, ways of doing things, and a language it speaks. Chris Barker and Emma Jane (2016) discuss what makes up a culture and how it is built. They propose, "Indeed, all cultural practices depend on meanings generated by signs. Consequently, culture is said to work 'like a language.' This makes all cultural practices open to semiotic analysis" (p. 89). I have always been under the impression that the people make the culture, and the culture makes the people. Athletics has that relationship in a variety of ways. In high school sports, some areas are deeply tied to and defined by the athletic successes and failures of their local high school. Certain locales are identified by their football, baseball, soccer, or softball prowess. In college athletics, the cultures are spread much broader across the states. College prospects from all athletic programs have chosen their collegiate teams partially on the culture that has been developed there and in the surrounding community. There is a relationship between the two that influences both parties for a great deal of time afterward. Richard Anderson (2004) asserts an assumption of meaning that is created through our environment and social surroundings: "Human existence is intrinsically linked to meaning—to comprehend meaning, to communicate meaning, and, in our most distinctively human capacity, to create meaning" (p. 279). There is a great deal of meaning that comes from the sports athletes play. When championships are being played, the stadiums or arenas of the visiting teams are full of their home fans cheering them on. The connection between those fans and their teams is a deep-rooted relationship. At times, fans will allow the success or failure of their team to define their mood, livelihood, and value. This is not healthy, but it is a by-product of the athletic-minded and athletic-centered society we live in.

Athletics influences the athletes' lives in the areas of academics, social life, identity, and access to athletic and life opportunities. The change to a life that happens by being a student-athlete does not disappear once that part of life is over. The relating of what the student-athletes learned over the course of their participation in athletics to their personal and professional lives often occurs. As Christine Green (2008) writes,

> Sport participation is commonly believed to develop positive character traits, to assist young people to become better citizens and more successful adults, to reduce delinquency rates and risky behaviours, to assist with moral development including a sense of fair play, and to instill a strong achievement orientation. (p. 130)

The students who participate in athletics come to understand what they can take from those activities and apply to their own lives.

***

He who can, does. He who cannot, teaches. –George Bernard Shaw

Now, this quote is a semi-cordial way to say the ones who are less skilled are the ones who teach others how to do something. I do not believe this applies to the profession of teaching.

I think it is different when it comes to athletics. When quality players stop playing and begin coaching, it is usually not because they are poorly skilled. They may not have had the skills to reach the next level, which is usually the professional ranks, or there is not a professional team for them depending on the sport. Some are tired of waking up sore and going through the consistent regimen of the required fitness or physical demand of the job. Rarely do I find them not smart enough or skilled enough to coach another generation of players. Coaching is really teaching; it is just a different classroom. Being able to coach is a way for former student-athletes to stay connected to the game they love. Some coach multiple sports, either out of love for it because they were multi-sport athletes, or out of necessity at their respective school; but relating to athletes is transferable no matter what sport they coach. Athletics provides them with an opportunity for teaching. Robert Bullough (2001) discusses the characteristics of good teaching and outlines this with his twelve points that he uses as a guide. He writes, "Whenever students are being helped to see major concepts, big ideas, and general principles and are not merely engaged in the pursuit of isolated facts, good teaching is going on" (p. 106). Athletics are not about winning and losing. They are about what the students learn while participating in them. As they progress as players, the athletes' views on these concepts grow, mature, and become part of them.

The many lessons, differences, opportunities, difficulties, challenges, and realizations that we can learn from sports are limitless. Sport brings people together for an opportunity for healthy competition, but often there are many other causes and opportunities that are present themselves outside of and within that competition that make a much more profound impact on the world. The levels the majority of these lessons are learned from are the amateur ranks, high school and college; and the ones bringing these lessons to life are the student-athletes who are sacrificing their time and body to bring these to us amongst a great competition.

Finding an identity is hard enough for people who live a "normal" life. At times, it can seem easier for athletes because they belong to a certain group, but there is no easy way to be an athlete. They identify with their sport easily enough; but like the cliques in a high school, each sport has its own types of personalities, mannerisms, and behaviors. This, at times, makes identifying with their teammates much harder than identifying with the game they love to play. In other words, each sport has its own identity.

There is also the dilemma of the multi-sport athletes. How do they work equally at all sports and fit in with both groups? Those multi-sport athletes are then in season much longer than one-sport athletes, so there is a tighter restraint on time and efficiency that they can contribute towards their academic life. The in-season life is often filled with longer days that are needed to prepare for the next competition. In some ways, athletics can act as a prison and the student-athletes are the inmates. Yet, unlike prisons, these inmates have chosen to be a part of the institution. Michel Foucault (1995) mentions that Louis-Pierre Baltard called prisons "complete and austere institutions" (p. 235). As Foucault describes the functions of the prison, it fits the institution of athletics as well. He writes:

> In several respects, the prison must be an exhaustive disciplinary apparatus: it must assume responsibility for all aspects of the individual, his physical training, his aptitude work, his everyday conduct, his moral attitude, his state of mind; the prison, much more than the school, the workshop or the army, which always involved a certain specialization, is "omni-disciplinary." (pp. 235–236)

Everything described as responsibilities of the prison are also responsibilities, or assumed responsibilities, of athletics, and by extension, the athletes themselves. Rarely can someone manage all these aspects of life at one time successfully; in some cases, a few are ignored entirely. Yet student-athletes are expected to handle these with ease and perform their best every time they compete. So, once a student decides to add "athlete" to the end of the title and identify with that select group, there is an automatic agreement and expectation that all these facets will be looked after in a complete and austere manner. This is not always fair to the student-athletes, but it is a group they have elected to be a part of and identify with until another path is laid before them, and a decision often has to be made.

Students that choose to belong to a group begin to take on a different persona. They are trying to identify with their new group, and they are part of an ever-changing youth. At times they may feel like displaced persons. Derrida (2000) talks about this in his book *Of Hospitality*. He writes, "'Displaced persons,' exiles, those who are deported, expelled, rootless, nomads, all share two sources of sighs, two nostalgias: their dead ones and their language" (p. 89). He is discussing the feelings of these displaced persons and how they still relate, or want to relate, to their past or physical place from whence they came. This can also apply to the students that choose to identify with a specific group. Once this happens, in a way, they are now displaced persons. They no longer belong to the old group or old ways of living and must now quickly adapt to their new life. The dead ones Derrida (2000) refers to are the friends or ways of life that were once a part of the newly identified student's life. The language is the way they used to communicate or terms that were once applicable and a way to associate with people outside of their new group. The change, and the pace of that change, that student-athletes must accustom themselves to are massive and rapid to a high school student.

John Wooden was a legendary basketball coach at UCLA. His teams won 10 national championships in a 12-year span, 7 of them in a row. He is one of only four people, Tommy Heinsohn, Bill Sharman, Lenny Wilkins being the others, to be inducted into the Hall of Fame as both a player and a coach. What many people do not know is that he was a high school English teacher after graduating from Purdue as an honor student. He understood the message his players needed to hear, and he impacted them well beyond the basketball court. He focused on the character of the player along with the skills needed to play the game. One of the lessons he hammered home with his players was this: "Be more concerned with your character than with your reputation, because your character is what you really are while your reputation is merely what others think you are" (2004, p. 68). Players often identify with their sport so much they forget there are many more important aspects of life than just their athletic life. Life as a student-athlete can be more difficult than a professional athlete for a few reasons: (1) there is an academic standard that has to be met every semester with no real room for mistakes; (2) these student-athletes are part of the culture of great importance society puts on sports, and they tend to forget who they really are and not allow their character to develop and shine through their public persona; and (3) these student-athletes have other talents and skills in addition to their athletic ones and they tend to forget and neglect those as the use of their athletic skills dominate the majority of their day.

Becoming a member of a team can be nerve-wracking. Then there are the multiple sport student-athletes who can belong to two very different groups whose dynamics are vastly diverse and must adjust at the turn of the season. There are also the student-athletes who have talents for the arts. These two groups have the potential to be polar opposites when it comes to personalities, dynamics, politics, and friendships.

* * *

Education is not the filling of a pail, but the lighting of a fire. –William Butler Yeats

Athletes who want to succeed must continuously learn all they can about their sport/position as long as they are playing. Life and education are the same way. To succeed in life, we must continuously learn all we can to have a better understanding of the world we live in. Education, like anything else, is what we make of it. If we fully buy-in, it will be a great life-altering experience. Academics should not weigh us down; they should not be a burden for us to bear. Being academically successful takes just as much work, if not more, than being athletically successful. Many student-athletes have talents in their respective sports that are already established, or they would not be playing for their high school or collegiate teams. Some of them do not have as much talent academically as they do athletically, so they must work harder and differently than others. As a high school English literature teacher, I understand that all material that is covered is not life-or-death important for life after schooling. Very rarely do my students who have gone on to be bankers, lawyers, HVAC technicians, or automotive mechanics use any of the Shakespeare I taught them, at least not on the surface. I would hope they learned through Shakespeare, and everything else we covered, more about the process of learning and what it takes to come to a successful conclusion. I want my students and players to be inquisitive, to always want to learn more. Academics should light a fire, whether it is a desire to learn more as we travel through life, or as a light for a path to find success at the end of the journey. Each side, the athletic and the academic, takes work. How each student-athlete defines work will determine how successful they will be and will plot the course they will take to get there. Donald Hall's (1993/2003) book *Life Work* discusses the concept of work and how it takes on different meanings for every individual. He discusses an artist named Henry Moore and how he would spend countless hours working on models and drawings. He quotes Moore on his idea of the secret to life. Moore says,

> The secret of life is to have a task, something you devote your entire life to, something you bring everything to, every minute of the day for your whole life. And the most important thing is—it must be something you cannot possibly do! (p. 54)

When people find an avenue to use their skills, they get the sense of enjoyment and fulfillment from it, and it does not take on the social definition of "work." Hall (1993/2003) writes, "I've never worked a day in my life" (p. 3). Although athletes enjoy their respective sports, that does not mean they do not have to work at developing their skills for them. The one thing athletes cannot be in their sports is perfect. There will always be an aspect of their skills they can improve on and develop. They take these aspects and look at them like small, individual projects they can work on as they aim to have the best possible finished piece at the end of their career. Hall (1993/2003) recalls a story about Roger Clemens, a pitcher for the Boston Red Sox at the time, and a career seven-time Cy Young Award winner. He was a hard-throwing right-hander who worked to get better. In reference to a quote from Clemens, Hall (1993/2003) writes, "Asked why he worked so hard he answered, 'People write articles about how you're blessed with the right arm. . . . That might be true, for some people, but I had to work to get where I'm at" (p. 39). Clemens would work continuously through a variety of exercises and drills that he thought would help improve his skills. There is nothing wrong with obsessing about work, but work cannot become the obsession. A satisfaction is essential for work to continue to be productive. There will always be certain things about work people do not like to do, but the process of doing the work is what is appreciated. The same goes for the classroom. I have taught student-athletes who seem to work all the time, either on their athletic skills or their academic classes. Those students have found success because of the work they have done, but also enjoy the process of making themselves better and becoming a more equipped person. Unfortunately, it feels like the sense of work in the classroom is becoming lost as the generations change.

We are in the age of instant gratification, and the concepts and skills of studying, dedication, critical thinking, and relentlessness are not as understood by the generation in school now. As a teacher, I see them struggle to apply themselves for a full class period (50 minutes). Checking phones, changing music, taking a break—these are all distractions that keep them from achieving success because they do not, or cannot, stay focused for a considerable amount of time. There is also the use of artificial intelligence (AI) that hinders their work. The students look at AI as a tool to make schooling easier. As they use it to supply answers, solve math problems, and write essays and papers, the work the student has to put in has been significantly diminished, yet they still see it as a success if they are correct, or not caught. I believe the greater success that has the most meaning is when the students accomplish an assignment on their own. They learn two things about themselves: (1) they have the cognitive ability to complete the task, and (2) they can push through the setbacks and self-doubt and find success at the completion.

Although the athletic side of "work" is much different than the academic side, there is still an emphasis on the academic side that is missing. Once these student-athletes reach the collegiate level, their athletic attributes seem to out-value their academic ones. Many times, the student-athlete loses sight of what can be learned or gained from the opportunities that they are talented enough to experience. The passing of classes, the promise of money, fame, notoriety, setting records, awards, and reputation are all discussed, but rarely are the academic, altruistic, or life-after-sports perspectives ever included in these discussions. While students identify with being an athlete, they lose sight of everything outside of athletics at times because of the pressure put on them to succeed on the field or court. The other side of that is the academic side can be just as demanding and harsh, but the student must find a field that he/she is passionate about and have the discipline to make that commitment. Once that is accomplished, the "work" is taken out of the equation and it then begins to feel like play, which for a student-athlete, is the key to success.

Something I consistently tell my players is that there are two sides to the student-athlete; they can be as athletic as they want to be, but if they are ineligible, they are doing nobody any good. Academic and athletic achievements have a correlation, and when one does not go the student-athlete's way, the other usually suffers the same fate. What many student-athletes forget is the student side of the equation. Athletics can only get them so far. There must be a willingness and drive to excel and compete in the classroom as well. In fact, research shows that positive athletic programs can enhance the education experience of the students. Daniel Bowen and Colin Hitt (2013) support this idea by saying, "Successes on the playing field can carry over to the classroom and vice versa. More importantly, finding ways to increase school communities' social capital is imperative to the success of the school, not just the athletes" (para. 18). There is a direct correlation to the number of positive experiences that a student encounters in athletics and academics. Any and all positive attributes for the school can help build the community around them and garner support for the students and their activities. Both can affect each other in a way that can also improve the character of the student-athlete. Plato (375–380/1991) said it best in *The Republic*:

> He who is only an athlete is too crude, too vulgar, too much a savage. He who is a scholar only is too soft, too effeminate. The ideal citizen is the scholar athlete, the man of thought and the man of action (Book 3, 410 a–d).

According to Plato, student-athletes are the individuals who can succeed in all aspects of life. They have a good balance between the worlds of academics and athletics. Academics are equally important to the overall development of the student-athletes we teach and coach. This type of identification is much tougher for a student-athlete to make and maintain. An idea from Serres (1995) comes into play here as he talks about fitting in. In *Genesis*, he writes,

> The unique relationship between two singular units reveals specificity in space. An elaborately cut key has the same relationship to the original lock. It has no relationship to other locks. [...] Made smooth, the key becomes a pass key. The one multiple relationship gets easier and easier the more indeterminate the one is. If it is determined, it excludes much, it denies, the symbol fits no one, the key is almost of no use. (p. 29)

I think the point he is making that can be applied here is each person has a uniqueness about himself/herself. These student-athletes must make the academic identification in the field they have a passion for. The next step is to identify with the types of academic demands and opportunities they will want to experience. While this used to only apply to college students, this now applies to high school students with the introduction of pathways. These allow students to earn a certificate in a certain field such as certified nursing, engineering, and cyber security. These can help set up a student to be ahead of the game, academically speaking, as far as what their course load will be at their prospective college or university. With the completion of pathways, students do start post-secondary school with more of an interest in the academic side of being a student-athlete. On the other hand, making the academic identification now comes earlier in their careers, and for some of them, that aspect is tougher to see clearly and accomplish at the younger ages. This is a time in their lives when the concept of Self-Determination Theory (SDT) would apply (Ryan & Deci, 2000). The students who complete a pathway in high school who are looking at it as a possible career choice will experience a mixture of motivations. They could see it is a chance to set themselves up for a college program, a chance to sharpen their skills for a career choice, an opportunity to explore the option within a particular field, or any other intrinsic motivation that fuels them. They could also see it as a chance to remove themselves from a certain situation, make a good salary, have opportunities for travel, or any other extrinsic motivation they deem beneficial.

Coaching is teaching, it is just a different classroom. A lot of it has to do with having a comfort zone. As a teacher I am comfortable in the classroom. I know how it should flow and how the connections can be made. As a coach I am comfortable on the field—sometimes more comfortable than in the classroom. To me, the field is just a larger, more open classroom that offers more opportunities to teach the young men I coach. For student-athletes to be successful, whether in the classroom or on the field/court, they must step out of their comfort zone. Michael Coffino (2018) talks about this in his book *The Other Classroom: The Essential Importance of High School Athletics*. He states:

> Taking leave of personal comfort zones is a worthy end in and of itself. The benefits of stepping outside the stubborn edges of comfort are many: (1) challenging ourselves to perform at peak; (2) becoming comfortable with risks that help us grow and equally so, being willing to fail; (3) inspiring us to be more creative; (4) aging better and staying sharp; (5) facing and overcoming fear, especially of the unknown; (6) giving us more life choices and identifying paths that allow us to evolve continually. (p. 40)

As an educator, all of what he says is what we try to do through our curriculum. Whether it is interpreting Shakespeare, figuring atomic numbers, deciphering polynomial equations, or understanding the world's governments, we teachers are all trying to accomplish the same things. Part of it is having the students understand the material. The other part is having them understand the process of understanding the material and why it is more important than the material they are learning. Our job is to push our students in a direction that will academically challenge them and get them out of their comfort zones. Our job is the same as coaches. We must push our players out of their comfort zones to get them to realize they can do more. No matter what the next level is, it is somewhere they have never been before, and it is something for them to build on. Both teachers and coaches thrive on the connections they make and the relationships they build with their students and players. Therefore, I believe that teachers and coaches both teach because they can, not because they cannot; and they have a place in the dynamics of developing young minds and bodies for the future.

Choosing to be a full-time, high-quality student-athlete is a two-fold commitment. They are committing to the academic and athletic standards/expectations set forth by their institution. Although most athletes like the physicality of the work, they know their sports will take a toll on their body in the long run. Student-athletes are also what Derrida (2000) would describe as "displaced persons," but they are displaced by choice. They see an opportunity arise because of their athletic talents and choose to step away from one group and into another, eventually realizing they must adapt to survive in both worlds. Coffino (2018) understands the importance of "the other classroom" and believes coaches have the opportunity to be creative and reach our players in ways classroom teaching cannot.

* * *

> Never look backwards or you'll fall down the stairs. –Rudyard Kipling

Athletics gives students an opportunity to impact the world in a unique way. Their talents and skills are valuable in the athletic realm. Those attributes can bring them all the social rewards imaginable along with bringing the institution they represent, whether high school or college, attention and a positive reputation. But when the athletic days are over and the desire to pursue that career is no longer present, the professional opportunities do not present themselves, or the body gives out in ways that prevent the athlete from playing further competitively, there is a time of re-entry into the "normal" world, and that can be a tough thing to accomplish quickly. At this point, student-athletes who are no longer playing begin to lose that identity or become disassociated with it. They have been used to the intensity, notoriety, attention, physical and mental development and deterioration, long days, and tough academics that go along with life, and the ceasing of all of that at one time can be life-altering.

Often, the now former student-athletes must find other ways to fill those voids in their lives, changing their daily routine. The identity of being an athlete is now gone. Some of them turn to coaching, training, recreational play within their sport, or some other type of association with athletics to be able to have an extension of their earlier identity. Some find other skills they possess to develop with the same intensity. There is a fear of losing that "athlete" identity because that is what they have dedicated themselves to being for a major part of their lives. The NCAA recognizes this problem and is working with athletic departments to help athletes in this transition. Erin Reifsteck (2014) wrote an article for the NCAA and discusses this point:

> Student-athletes may struggle with this transition and find it difficult to maintain their activity levels once they are no longer competing. Colleges and universities can fulfill their commitment to the holistic development of their student-athletes by implementing educational programming and incorporating specific strategies to promote lifelong physical activity among their student-athletes. (para. 7)

There is a wider, more educated understanding that the loss of the athletic identity is hard on the student and there must be supports and outlets in place for them to transition out of their continuously competitive role. This concept can also apply to high school student-athletes because there is a greater number of them that do not continue that identity once they graduate. This holistic approach must start at the high school level and help those that lost the athletic identity at an earlier age than the collegiate athlete. Hopefully, in both cases, they have set themselves up for the future by focusing on the academic side of their experience just as much as the athletic.

Iain Thomson's (2005) book *Heidegger on Ontotheology: Technology and the Politics of Education* discusses Heidegger's thoughts on education. Heidegger uses the word *paideia* which is a Greek term that means a system of broad cultural education. He explains, "Paideia means the turning around of the whole human being in the sense of displacing us out of the region of immediate encountering and accustoming us to another realm in which beings appear" (p. 159). This defines the situations of most student-athletes; Heidegger's idea of *paideia* is a process that students, once they make their choice to identify as an athlete, will experience multiple times as they find their niche within their groups and society (Thomson, 2005, p. 159). Once they leave their respective sport, they go through a second kind of *paideia*. In a sense, they must go through a re-entry phase and learn their footing as "every day, regular" people. In this case, I am not talking about the professional athletes. That is a different aspect entirely. This applies to the collegiate athletes who finish athletic competition, complete their degree, and graduate. Once they graduate, student-athletes must acclimate themselves to a new environment. This environment usually does not require the level of competition they are used to. They can still fill that void with other competitive activities, pick-up basketball or softball games, weightlifting or a gym routine, or a hobby that involves a specific skill. The adjustment can be tough as they progress in their professional career and familial obligations. The dedicated time to athletics and competition dwindles with the more responsibility they take on elsewhere. This can be a tough transition for them as they get used to their new way of life.

Once athletes come to terms with not playing and competing every day anymore, their second *paideia* begins. They must be able to make peace with that concept so that it does not affect the other aspects of their life. Only around 11% of collegiate student-athletes become professionals, either through the draft in their sport or through the free-agency process. That number is derived from only NCAA participants. Not included are NAIA or JUCO student-athletes. As these schools usually have a lesser enrollment than NCAA schools, their number of participants is smaller as the number of athletic programs they offer is smaller. For all the issues the NCAA has with their athletic rules and regulations, they are very proactive in the area of helping their athletes prepare for life after college once their playing days have ended. The NCAA understands that out of the 1,100 colleges and universities that support athletic programs, most of their students reach their athletic pinnacle in college. Therefore, their life after the game, the second *paideia*, is much more important.

Entering into the second *paideia* is a rediscovering of oneself. These individuals are being displaced for a second time, possibly within a span of two to four years depending on circumstances, and having to find a new direction in life fairly quickly. Leaving a familiar setting and group of people and starting over with a gaping hole in their day and feeling of purpose and drive is a tough adjustment for many student-athletes. Unfortunately, some of them unintentionally fill those gaps with substance abuse or a deterioration of their mental health. They do not recognize life without their competition, familiar surroundings, or people they depended on for a number of years. Sometimes they leave the game because of a negative circumstance, a career-ending injury, a lapse in academic eligibility, being replaced by another player, or a lack of affordability due to little or no scholarship. These are all difficult situations and contribute to the struggle student-athletes have in moving into another phase of life. Of course, it is not always bad. Many student-athletes transition through their second *paideia* and find success on the other side. They form new friendships, find purpose in their professional careers, and develop a healthy routine to stay active as they grow and mature.

Once student-athletes leave the athletic realm and begin to focus on life after sports, I believe the lessons they learn by participating in athletics influence their decisions, behaviors, family choices, and life paths. I want everyone involved in education but not involved in athletics to understand the role athletics plays in the development of the young students we are charged with fostering. The possibilities of opportunities to further their education and playing career can lead to impacts on the local societies they move to. I want other educators to see how athletics is another vehicle to help students become better people, and becoming a better athlete is a byproduct of the lessons they learn. I am also hoping for parents of these students to understand that athletics is an identity, but that it does not define their child. Time and time again, as a high school coach, I have seen where parents are so concerned about their child's possibility of playing a sport or advancing to the next level to the point that all other issues surrounding that student are ignored. When this happens, the students are usually not very successful outside of the protection of their parents. As a result, those athletic careers come to an end much quicker than anticipated. This is when I wish those students and parents would take a step back and learn from their situation.

As educators, we all want to help our students become better. We want to set them up for success in the next stages of their lives. We want them to become the "ideal citizen." I feel that student-athletes match that description. Plato got it right—a well-balanced combination of athleticism and academics is a recipe for success. We want our student-athletes to be men and women of thought and action. The key is for them to be able to think critically and apply the correct action in those special moments. It is our job as teachers and coaches to help them learn those lessons, develop the skills, and give them guidance to help them become who they are supposed to be—the ideal citizen.

References

Anderson, R. L. (2004). *Calliope's sisters: A comparative study of philosophies of art*. Pearson Education.

Barker, C., & Jane, E. A. (2016). *Cultural studies: Theory and practice*. Sage.

Bowen, D. H., & Hitt. C. (2013, October 2). High school athletics aren't killing academics. *The Atlantic*. http://www.theatlantic.com/education/archive/2013/10/high-schoolsports-arent-killing-academics/280155/

Bullough, R. V. (2001). *Uncertain lives, children of promise, teachers of hope*. Teachers College Press.

Coffino, M. J. (2018). *The other classroom: The essential importance of high school athletics*. Rowman and Littlefield.

Derrida, J. (2000). *Of hospitality*. Stanford University Press.

Foucault, M. (1995). *Discipline and punish: The birth of the prison* (A. Sheridan, Trans.). Vintage Books. (Original work published 1977)

Frost, R. (1992). The road not taken. In *Selected poems* (p. 163). Gramercy Books. (Original work published 1916)

Green, B. C. (2008). *Sport as an agent for social and personal change* (V. Girginov, Ed.). Routledge.

Hall, D. (2003). *Life work*. Beacon. (Original work published 1993)

Kant, I. (2015). *The educational theory of Immanuel Kant* (E. F. Buchner, Trans.). Forgotten Books. (Original work published 1908)

Kipling, R. (2013). *The bridge builders*. Create space PubliDeadtree [ebook edition]. A word to the wise.

Lambert, C. (1998). *Mind over matter: Lessons on life from the art of rowing*. Houghton Mifflin.

Marsh, H. W., & Kleitman, S. (2003). School athletic participation: Mostly gain with little pain. *Journal of Sport and Exercise Psychology*, 25, 205–228.

Plato. (1991). *The republic* (A. Bloom, Trans.). Basic Books. (Original work published ca. 375–380 BCE)

Reifsteck, E. (2014). Moving on: Staying physically active after college sports. NCAA. https://www.ncaa.org/sports/2014/12/10/moving-on-staying-physically-active-after-college-sports.aspx

Ryan, R. M., & Deci, E. L. (2000). Self-determination theory and the facilitation of intrinsic motivation, social development, and well-being. Retrieved May 2, 2020 from https://selfdeterminationtheory.org/SDT/documents/2000_RyanDeci_SDT.pdf.

Schubert, W. H. (2009). *Love, justice, and education: John Dewey and the utopians.* Information Age Publishing.

Serres, M. (1995) *Genesis* (G. James & J. Nielson, Trans.). The University of Michigan Press. (Original work published 1982).

Shaw, G. B. (1903). *Maxims for revolutionists* [eBook edition]. Project Gutenberg. http://www.gutenberg.org/cache/epub/26107/pg26107.html.

Tanney, M. (2017). Shaping lives. In Z. Logsdon & M. E. Miranda (Eds.), *If not for athletics: A collection of stories that demonstrate the power and impact of sports* (pp. 110–111). Black Lake Publishing Company.

Thomson, I. D. (2005). *Heidegger on ontotheology: Technology and the politics of education.* Cambridge University Press.

Wooden, J., & Tobin, J. (2004). *They call me coach.* Contemporary Books.

Yeats, W. B. (2010). *Autobiographies: The collected works of WB Yeats* (Vol. 3). Simon and Schuster.

· 13 ·

AN EDUCATOR'S PATH: JOURNEY OF AN UNEXPECTED TEACHER

Kay R. Lilly

Some people enter the field of education knowing that it is where they belong. They prepare from a young age and work their way towards the classroom knowing that they want to be an educator. I am not one of those people. I like to say that I stumbled into the field of education. At the beginning of my university education, I was unsure of what I wanted to do. I was majoring in business and quickly realized that was not the place for me. I had always loved history, so I decided I wanted to change my major but was told by my family that I would need to get a teaching certification if history was the route I wanted to take. So, I entered into education classes thinking I would never actually be in the classroom. I went through the motions attending elementary and middle school education classes. I felt very out of place. I did not feel comfortable with the age group and was not engaged at all in what was going on. Then I began my field work at the high school level and fell in love. I loved everything about the atmosphere of being at the high school level, from the students to the activities to the content. I knew that I had found my place.

After deciding that high school was where I wanted to be and graduating, I began my search to find a school to begin my career. I was hired on as a part time secondary history teacher within the same community that I had grown up in. I was familiar with the school, but once I arrived, I quickly realized that there were needs that I had not been exposed to during my time as a student within the community. The school was much more ethnically, religiously, and culturally diverse than the ones I had attended as a child. In addition, the school was home to students who came from some of the wealthiest families in the area. However, with every year that passed, the school began to serve more and more students who came from some of the most impoverished areas within the district. This created a distinct set of challenges within the school that it had not previously had to handle. I came into the school during this shift and became very vested in helping meet the needs of these learners within our school. I became a firm believer in the concept of educating the whole child and helping to meet all of their needs so that they can then learn to understand the curriculum (Miseliunaite et al., 2022). I served on various committees that were working to ensure that students had access to essentials such as food, medical care, and school supplies. In addition, I began teaching study skills and remedial classes which connected me to many diverse students who had a variety of educational, emotional, and economic concerns. Looking back now, I feel that these classes were often where I felt I made the most impact and which allowed me to be most helpful to my students.

Within my own history classes I began to realize that there were many issues preventing me from having a positive learning environment. The first major problem that I realized was that students were extremely disengaged from the history curriculum. Traditional methods of teaching history through primarily lectures were not connecting with the students. The students were bored and so was I. I began to look at alternative delivery methods that would be more engaging such as project-based learning and the use of gamification. The next major issue that I identified was that the history that was being taught was not representational of our diverse student body. The standards emphasized a primarily white, Eurocentric focus that was not a true representation of the historical framework of America. Little was mentioned about women and minoritized groups which make up a large segment of the American population. I felt that a more representative curriculum could impact overall student learning and help my students connect with the subject in a deeper way.

As a result, I began looking at how to bring other voices and perspectives into the classroom to use alongside different instruction methods in order to increase overall engagement and mastery of content within my classroom.

I quickly found myself wondering how to go about this endeavor. I was a brand new teacher, and many within the field of education were resistant to change or did not even want to acknowledge that the unique challenges our students faced existed. How would I get others who I was collaborating with to accept some of the changes that I wanted to make? I decided that going back to school at the graduate level might lend an air of legitimacy to the changes I was making in my classroom and provide me with additional ways to better serve the student body and my colleagues. I obtained my master's and specialist's degrees in quick succession. Within my programs I focused on diversity within education and project-based learning. I learned about many different pedagogies and curriculum theories that I could use to transform my classroom. I left graduate school feeling that I had a good base and could move forward making changes within my classroom.

Just as happened with entering the education field, I never planned on obtaining my doctorate degree. My plan after my specialist's degree was to get administration certification and move out of the classroom and into the administrative level. I enrolled in my district's aspiring leaders program, but while I was in the course the superintendent made the comment that going forward it would be highly encouraged that administrators have their doctorate degree. It looked like I was going back to school. I embraced this new path and decided that this would be another way that I could strengthen my own classroom pedagogy and further work towards diversifying my instructional strategies and content to meet the needs of my learners. I also felt that I had something to prove to myself and wanted answers to questions I was asking about the state of education. Could someone who had been a mediocre student at the undergraduate level and had stumbled into the field of education really rise to getting a doctorate in this field? Were others seeing the issues within the education system that I was? I was one classroom teacher, in one school—could I really affect change within this field?

When I began my course work, I learned about many new alternative curriculum models, curriculum theorists, and theories. They were all very interesting, but I kept coming back to one in particular: Culturally Sustaining Pedagogy (CSP). CSP was developed by Alim and Paris (2017) and asserted that,

> CSP seeks to perpetuate and foster—to sustain—linguistic, literate, and cultural pluralism as part of schooling for positive social transformation. CSP positions dynamic cultural dexterity as a necessary good, and sees the outcome of learning as additive rather than subtractive. (Alim & Paris, 2017, p. 1)

This introduction to CSP struck a chord with me as it summed up what I was attempting to do in the classroom but had not yet been able to achieve. I wanted to create a classroom where all students had a voice and where all perspectives and points of view were taken into account. I wanted to create a truly representational historical framework. I wanted to develop an environment that uplifted students and allowed them to see and build on their strengths.

As I researched further into CSP I began to understand that I had only scratched the surface of the use of pluralistic education in my classroom. I came to realize that engaging in this work would require an entire shift in how I viewed students and education. I required a shift in lens. So far in my teaching career I had bought into a deficit view of education and my students in particular. I was commonly using phrases such as "achievement gap" and "at risk" when discussing current issues in education. What I failed to fully realize was that in doing this I was placing blame on students rather than looking at issues within institutions of education that were continuing to fail our students. Rather than looking at what my diverse students brought into the classroom, their assets, I was looking at what I perceived that they were missing or lacking. My students all brought a unique set of skills, background knowledge, and life experiences into the classroom. Recognizing and fostering these traits alongside using asset-based thinking, employing innovative instructional strategies, and diversifying the curriculum would help me move towards what I was trying to achieve in the classroom.

But this was easier said than done. There are so many pressures within the field of education that teachers must handle, such as pacing, standards, content development, curriculum development, assessment analysis, classroom management, and common planning just to name a few. I began to understand that this would be a multistep and multiyear process. It would be a process of trial and error. In some areas I could quickly make changes, but others would take time to implement. So how did this impact "my plan"? Since I started teaching my goal was to progress forward into administration. I began to ask why. Would administration bring fulfillment? Could I enact the change that I wanted? Would I be making a more positive impact at the administrative level? I came to realize that the answer was no to all of those questions. Leaving the classroom would mean leaving most of my direct contact with students and my ability to create a diverse, pluralistic, positive learning environment.

So where does that leave me today? I fully feel and embrace that my time within the classroom is not done. I am constantly working to create a more culturally sustaining atmosphere within my classroom. I also believe that by staying in the classroom I can help other educators who are seeking to make similar changes. The research may change in the future, new theories will be developed, and new challenges will have to be faced. I understand that there may never be a finish line on this journey, but I now feel that I am no longer stumbling along. I can walk with confidence into the future with the ultimate goal of helping to effect positive change within my classroom, school, and community.

References

Alim, S., & Paris, D. (2017). What is culturally sustaining pedagogy and why does it matter? In D. Paris & H. S. Alim, *Culturally sustaining pedagogies: Teaching and learning for justice in a changing world* (pp. 1–21). Teachers College Press.

Miseliunaite, B., Kliziene, I., & Cibulskas, G. (2022). Can holistic education solve the world's problems: A systematic literature review. *Sustainability, 14*(15), 9737. https://doi.org/10.3390/su14159737

· 1 4 ·

BUILDING BRIDGES: ENSURING EVERY VOICE IS HEARD WITHIN THE SOCIAL STUDIES CLASSROOM

Kay R. Lilly

The Role of Social Studies

Inclusivity is a term that has been used by many to describe and characterize the field of social studies in the K-12 educational setting. It is the goal of most modern social studies educators to create a learning environment that is inclusive of all cultures and groups and where all individuals feel included. E. Wayne Ross (2006) describes social studies as the most inclusive of all of the school subjects and further defines it as "the study of human enterprise through space and time" (Ross, 1994, p. xi). Social studies as a contemporary curriculum was formally introduced through the National Education Association's 1916 Committee on Social Studies and has been influenced by ideas about social welfare and improvement movements that were going on at the time (Kliebard, 2004; Ross, 2006).

Over time the curriculum of social studies has changed as new time periods, perspectives, and methods of analysis have been added. The field has been modernized in order to encompass a more globally connected world. According to the National Council for the Social Studies, the modern "social studies is the study of individuals, communities, systems, and their interactions across time and place that prepares students for local, national, and global civic life" (2024). In addition, they outline the purpose of social studies by stating as "an inquiry-based approach, social studies helps students examine vast human experiences through the generation of questions, collection and analysis of evidence from credible sources, consideration of multiple perspectives, and the application of social studies knowledge and disciplinary skills" (National Council for the Social Studies, 2024). However, one could argue that within many of the social studies classrooms in the United States, we are not currently meeting all components of that definition and purpose of social studies in the modern K-12 setting.

What Is Missing?

Historically the United States education system has been dominated by a curriculum that highlights White Euro-American norms and culture (Talley-Matthews & Wiggan, 2018). In social studies specifically, this focus on White Euro-American culture has created deficits within the social studies curriculum whereby not every ethnic, cultural, and religious group is represented in a way that matches the contributions that they have made to the historical record. Often contributions are minimized or left out altogether. This chapter will focus on the Georgia Standards of Excellence specifically, and highlight how what is seen in Georgia mirrors the larger national trend. When looking at the Georgia Standards of Excellence for United States History there is minimal inclusion of diverse groups within the existing curriculum (Georgia Department of Education, 2016). Listed below are different groups included and their representation in the standards:

- Indigenous Americans: three times as a group, no one person mentioned by name
- Women: three times as a group, one person mentioned by name
- Muslim Americans: no mention as a group, no individual mentioned by name
- Asian Americans: no mention as a group, no individual mentioned by name
- Hispanic Americans: no mention as a group, one person mentioned by name
- Black Americans: inclusion surrounding slavery and Jim Crow era, one mention of civil rights, two individuals mentioned by name, little discussion of specific individuals, culture, or positive contributions
- LGBTQ+: no mention as a group, no individual mentioned by name

(Georgia Department of Education, 2016)

As a result of the lack of diversity, what has been created is a one-size-fits-all educational model that does not reflect the actual historical record or the student body that sits within our schools. This one-size-fits-all education model has created opportunity and engagement gaps amongst any groups who have been "othered" based on ethnicity, religion, or cultural characteristics (Martell & Stevens, 2019). This curriculum model often does not fully consider contributions of these diverse groups to our society culturally, historically, economically, socially, and politically. In addition, it often fails to recognize individual identities, or to consider inequities that exist within our society and their effect on the educational system and learning process (Alim & Paris, 2017). Therefore, change is needed in order to help ensure that the social studies curriculum is a true representation of the people and groups who helped to create it.

It is important that students analyze historical events from multiple perspectives, and therefore, in order to achieve this, state and national standards should be changed in order to include all groups (Eraqi, 2014). Studying history from multiple viewpoints allows students to develop a much richer and deeper understanding of those events. In addition, looking at events through multiple lenses helps students to dispel and understand any biases or stereotypes that may exist and move away from a one-sided understanding of those events (Eraqi, 2014). For example, Kruegar (2019) explains how these stereotypes exist when learning about Indigenous Americans. Often students are taught to see Indigenous Americans as one homogeneous group that all live a similar lifestyle and have the same culture rather than seeing them as many very diverse groups (Kruegar, 2019). This creates for students an incomplete and inaccurate idea of the history and culture surrounding Indigenous Americans, and this incomplete picture is created for many other groups as well.

Another issue within the current social studies curriculum model is that instruction is often based on outdated and inaccessible instructional strategies. It is important that social studies instructors work to modernize instructional strategies being used within their classrooms so that they are conducive to all learners. This will allow more students to gain the historical thinking skills needed to be successful in the classroom. Therefore, changes in pedagogy are needed in order to meet the needs of all learners in the classroom and move from a teacher-centered approach to a more student-centered approach (Alim & Paris, 2017; Ladson-Billings, 2021a).

Lastly, currently in the United States, the teaching force in the public education system does not often mirror the student bodies that they serve. Most teachers in the United States are White, female, middle-class, and monolingual English-speaking; therefore, it is common that teachers and their students do not share the same cultural and linguistic background or experiences (McKoy et al., 2017; Thomas et al., 2020). School demographics are changing, and many educators are not prepared to meet the diverse needs of their student populations (Lomeli, 2021; Warren, 2018). What is needed is a way to help teachers and schools at large connect with all of their students and create a more pluralistic learning environment where all students can succeed and thrive.

The Bridge

Currently, many teachers recognize that these issues surrounding representation, identity, and inequity exist within the K-12 social studies classroom and are working to change the way that social studies is taught in order to reflect the pluralistic society within our classrooms and as a means to combat educational inequities. The hope is to allow for the inclusion of all student identities to help all students feel valued and to assist all students to better succeed within the classroom (Matrell & Stevens, 2019). This pluralistic representation will not only allow for a more accurate historical record within social studies classes but will also seek to create increased engagement amongst diverse student populations, provide a focus on identity, and help students develop a critical consciousness surrounding our society (Charles, 2019; Torres, 2021).

Historically there has been much work done surrounding how to add culturally related material into the classroom. Gloria Ladson-Billings (1995) began this work with the introduction of Culturally Relevant Pedagogy in 1988, which sought to investigate how teachers were able to assist minority students to become more successful within the classroom. Culturally Relevant Pedagogy focuses on student learning, cultural competence, and sociopolitical/critical consciousness (Ladson-Billings, 2021b). Her work sought to identify how teachers could include content and pedagogical knowledge that was outside of the traditional education curriculum to help these students become more successful and be represented more within the education system in the United States (Ladson-Billings, 2021a; Ladson-Billings, 2021b).

Culturally Relevant Pedagogy has expanded since that time and has developed into what is now referred to as Culturally Sustaining Pedagogy. Introduced by Django Paris in 2012 and further researched by both Paris and H. Samy Alim, Culturally Sustaining Pedagogy seeks to "perpetuate and foster—to sustain—linguistic, literate, and cultural pluralism as a part of schooling for positive social transformation" (Alim & Paris, 2017, p. 1).

Culturally Sustaining Pedagogy hopes to bring to light those cultural groups that have been traditionally marginalized and ignored as well as works to counteract the educational damage that the marginalization of these groups has done (Paris, 2012).

Tenets of Culturally Sustaining Pedagogy

Culturally Sustaining Pedagogy seeks to make direct connections between students' language, literacies, and cultural identities and the curriculum. Culturally Sustaining Pedagogy acts as the bridge that allows teachers to incorporate ways to value and highlight their students' identities and backgrounds. Culturally Sustaining Pedagogy seeks to include but also move beyond the main tenets of Culturally Relevant Pedagogy (Alim & Paris, 2017; Ladson-Billings, 2014, 2021a). It moves past the position of relevancy and works to "connect culture directly to sustenance as both its target and its source" (Bucholtz & Lee, 2017, p. 55). At its core, Culturally Sustaining Pedagogy includes teachers focusing on, valuing, and practicing languages, literacies, and cultural identities (Delman et al., 2024; Alim & Paris, 2017). Culturally Sustaining Pedagogy focuses on reinforcing students' strengths instead of trying to attack their weaknesses by challenging teachers to rethink the way they present learning (Alim & Paris, 2017; Irizarry, 2017). Additionally, Alim & Paris (2017) propose that there is power in establishing and cultivating learning communities that sustain and value cultural practices and have students interact with their ever-evolving literacy, language, and culture within and around their lives. Similarly, Irizarry (2017) notes students' learning experiences enhance their educational opportunities when Culturally Sustaining Pedagogy is integrated into classrooms.

Culturally Sustaining Pedagogy hopes to include practices that value and critically engage students with their cultures and languages as well as with those of other groups (Alim & Paris, 2017). Kinloch (2017) explains "for CSP to be effective, then collaborative, collective, critical and loving environments must be fostered that support young people's cultural identities, academic investments, and critiques of White middle-class values" (p. 29). In order for Culturally Sustaining Pedagogy to be effective within the classroom, environments need to support young people's cultural identities and academic learning, while also allowing them to critique the values and norms of the dominant White Eurocentric culture (Delman et al., 2024). To achieve this aim teachers need to decenter White Eurocentric cultural norms, understand

and recognize culture as complex and constantly changing, and teach towards a socially just society by combating prejudice and discrimination (Alim et al., 2020; Borck, 2020; Doucet, 2017).

Additionally, Culturally Sustaining Pedagogy can help to foster stronger relationships which can assist teachers in helping their diverse students to be more successful in the classroom (Gay, 2000; Woodley et al., 2017). Relationships that can be strengthened through the use of Culturally Sustaining Pedagogy include teacher-student, teacher-family, and teacher-community. Through showing cultural competency, a respect for languages and literacies, and a willingness to work with stakeholders, teachers can build stronger connections with their students, their families, and the community. This can in turn assist teachers and school at large in meeting the many varied needs of their students.

Lastly, for educators to fully incorporate the tenets of Culturally Sustaining Pedagogy, they must focus on social justice and advocacy. One of the core tenets of Culturally Sustaining Pedagogy is that it seeks to "disrupt the pervasive anti-Indigeneity, anti-Blackness and related anti-Brownness and model minority myths" (Alim & Paris, 2017, p. 2). Alim and Paris (2017) state that in order to do this there needs to be a "reimagining of the purpose of education" (p. 3) and further states that, "Culturally Sustaining Pedagogy demands a critical, emancipatory vision of schooling that reframes the object of critique from our children to the oppressive systems" (p. 3). Therefore, to reimagine, reframe, and emancipate schools away from the dominant White Eurocentric cultural norms, teachers need to engage in work surrounding advocacy and social justice while also seeking to foster a pluralistic education for all students (Delman et al., 2024).

Existing Research

According to Tally-Matthews and Wiggan, to be an effective social studies teacher one must understand the social, political, cultural, and physical environments in which students live and learn (2018). 2017–2018 demographic figures show that a 51.9% majority of students are classified as nonwhite, yet the teaching field is dominated by white women (Tally-Matthews & Wiggan, 2018). Therefore, it is becoming increasingly important for teachers to understand the pluralistic nature of their classrooms and work to align their curriculum to meet the diverse needs of their learners. Braden and Gibson (2021) highlight this as an ethical responsibility that teachers have for developing a culturally responsive/sustaining curriculum. Two studies that highlight these needs are those conducted by Jeong (2020) and Cavallaro and Sembiante (2021). Both cite the need to develop a pluralistic curriculum based on the changing population within the United States. In their study, Cavallaro and Sembiante highlight the fact that "students' successful engagement in middle school reading is disconnected between curricular content and students' culturally-informed experiences" (2021, p. 2) and through their study sought to bridge that gap with the use of culturally sustaining systemic functional linguistics informed literature. In Jeong's study, they highlight how white teachers can recontextualize the curriculum to meet the needs of diverse learners in their classrooms (2020). Again, the issue is that the curriculum and student population do not match, thus harming the learner and creating a disconnect in the learning process. These studies found that there was a positive perception of Culturally Sustaining Pedagogy by teachers and students. They felt that it provided the much-needed inclusion for minority students within the classroom. Jeong (2020) highlighted how the increased use of Culturally Sustaining Pedagogy allowed teachers to develop better relationships with students and increased engagement amongst the student population, while Braden and Gibson (2021) highlighted how Culturally Sustaining Pedagogy helped to prepare preservice teachers to better meet the needs of all learners that will one day be in their classroom.

Culturally Sustaining Pedagogy expands on current student-centered approaches that seek to connect students' lives and cultures with instruction (Chen et al., 2021). Culturally Sustaining Pedagogy seeks to shift away from White, middle-class-centered norms as the basis for cultural, literacy, and academic standards in the classroom. It works to ensure that all students feel that their identity is seen and valued in the classroom. Culturally Sustaining Pedagogy works to bring groups who are often marginalized into focus to develop a more pluralistic approach to education in which all groups are valued. In addition, it seeks to undo existing educational structures which have worked against these groups in order to ensure their success within educational institutions (Schieble & Pollack, 2021). More specifically, it works to assist in current areas of concern such as discipline outcomes, attendance-related issues, low achievement scores, and dropout rates among minority students (Chen et al., 2021; Schieble & Pollack, 2021). The hope is that through the use of Culturally Sustaining Pedagogies, all students will be represented within the curriculum and be valued for their cultural contributions to the fabric of our society.

Research shows Culturally Sustaining Pedagogy links student-driven content and engagement. Nganga et al., (2021) and Irizzary (2017) studied student response to diverse content and found that it led to increased student engagement. In their study, Nganga, Kambutu, Scull, & Keonghee Tao Han interviewed students in a rural school in the Rocky Mountain region of the United States. Over 73% of students expressed a desire for a more diverse curriculum. They emphasized the importance of including their cultural groups meaningfully and showcasing their success. Students noted that increased cultural inclusion and awareness sparked more interest in the class content (Nganga et al., 2021). Similarly, Jason Irizzary (2017) studied student response to Culturally Sustaining Pedagogy in the classroom and found that historically minoritized students felt underrepresented within the curriculum. His findings highlighted the importance of diverse representation in education for diverse student success. This was evident through the words of one student who said, "we have the power in the class, to like learn stuff, hard stuff, but stuff that we are like connected to, we do the work" (2017, p. 90). Both of these studies highlight how when students feel seen and heard within the curriculum that they are more apt to do the work and become engaged in a more meaningful way.

Using Culturally Sustaining Pedagogy in Practice

There is no one way or instructional method that allows teachers to create a classroom centered around Culturally Sustaining Pedagogy. Alim and Paris assert that Culturally Sustaining Pedagogy "exists wherever education sustains the lifeways of communities who have been and continue to be damaged and erased through schooling" (2017, p. 1). Therefore, Culturally Sustaining Pedagogy can look very different from classroom to classroom in terms of what is being taught, how it is being taught, and why it is being taught, but the overall goal remains the same. While there is much flexibility to developing Culturally Sustaining Pedagogy, research shows some commonalities between instructional strategies that have been successful in the classroom. First is a curriculum that allows for the use of student identity. Ramirez and Jaffee (2016) and Journell and Castro (2011) both looked at how to use students' immigrant identity to explore civic education. Both studies used the case study model to look at the instructional practices of two secondary education teachers each. These studies found that not only did students better learn the curriculum, but all participating instructors were able to create a more open and collaborative learning environment for their students (Ramirez & Jaffee, 2016; Journell and Castro, 2011). In addition, based on the findings of Lea III et al. (2019) and Husband and Kang (2020), diversity of voice is the second commonality that can be found within the practices of those who utilize Culturally Sustaining Pedagogy. Both studies found that providing students with culturally responsive materials and opportunities to share their voice about those materials increased student engagement and achievement in the classroom (Husband & Kang, 2020; Lea et al., 2019). These instructional practices among others demonstrate how adapting curriculum can help instructors to develop a Culturally Sustaining Pedagogy.

While there are many benefits to making changes to the current state standards in order to make them more inclusive, the question becomes how to do so. One way this could be done would be to model the Advanced Placement Course and Exam Description (CED) and the International Baccalaureate History Guide. Under both the College Board and International Baccalaureate designs, teachers do have certain concepts that they have to teach, but they are given choices when it comes to what examples, events, and people to use to teach that concept. Harris and Girard (2020) highlight this idea of increased teacher choice in the state standards. In their article, they show how different states have implemented varying levels of teacher choice as it relates to standards and the questions and considerations that must be made for teachers to make those decisions (Harris & Girard, 2020). Therefore, there are still guidelines as to how information is selected for inclusion in the curriculum, but it allows for a curriculum that is much more inclusive and reflective of the United States that we live in today. This would allow teachers to choose topics that not only are more representational of the students within their classrooms, but also those topics that would be more engaging for their students.

While changing state and national standards to be more inclusive would be most beneficial to creating more inclusive standards, the process of changing standards is a long and often difficult task. That does not mean, however, that no change can be made in the classroom. There are things that teachers can do in the interim within the classroom to promote inclusivity and the inclusion of multiple perspectives. Examples of teacher actions include:

- Utilizing sources from multiple perspectives
- Supplementing areas of weakness in the standards
- The use of Project and Problem Based learning

- Including more student choice
- Emphasizing community and parent involvement

(Delman et al., 2024; Ross, 1994)

These steps allow teachers to create a more inclusive curriculum in order to ensure that all students are represented in the classroom.

Another way educators and schools can support Culturally Sustaining Pedagogy in practice is by committing to inclusive practices in the areas of community and family engagement. Students' homes and communities provide a wealth of knowledge for both the students and the education system. By working alongside families and using their knowledge, this can serve as a tool to help sustain dignity, support literacy learning in the classroom, and help with opportunities to critique dominant practices, teaching towards a pluralistic society (Alim et al., 2020; Flores & Springer, 2021; Paris, 2021).

Applying Culturally Sustaining Pedagogy to United States History

United States History is not something that can be relegated to only certain groups. U.S. History is made up of many different events, people, and cultures which come together to make it what it is. Therefore, it is vital that the standards that we use in the classroom be representative of everyone's history. Educators can work together to ensure that multiple perspectives and voices are being taught and represented. This in turn will help to increase student content knowledge, student engagement, and student's critical thinking skills (An, 2016; Normore, 2017). These changes do not have to be overwhelming, and there are different approaches that can be taken in different classrooms and at different levels in order to make curriculum more culturally sustaining.

The first step is twofold and involves improving student relationships and allowing for a stronger student voice. As Alim and Paris (2017) have highlighted, Culturally Sustaining Pedagogy is multidimensional and encompasses not only content and instruction but also strong student-teacher relationships. One way that a teacher can build those relationships can start at the beginning of the year by utilizing multi-modal ways for students to introduce themselves to the teacher. Through these introductions, students can not only help the teachers get to know them but also outline what is needed to help them be more successful academically and socially within the classroom. Woodley, Hernandez, Parra, and Negash's article *Celebrating Difference* (2017) highlights this by expressing how it is validating the experiences of students and showing them that their culture and prior experiences do matter, and that the classroom would be a welcoming space. This simple step lays the foundation for establishing Culturally Sustaining teaching practices throughout the year by providing teachers with the early connections needed for good relationships with students and families.

An additional way that teachers can use Culturally Sustaining Pedagogy in the classroom is by highlighting student voices. This can be done in many ways, but one way is by allowing students to have input on who and what is studied through the course. This will have to be done with some guidance to adhere to the standards; however, if designed in a meaningful way, it is possible to highlight different individuals and events. For example, when looking at the Industrial Revolution, there are many different inventors from diverse backgrounds which can be incorporated into the curriculum. Also, when looking at civil rights in the United States, it is possible to include a variety of different civil rights movements, such as those of African Americans, Asian Americans, Hispanic Americans, Indigenous Peoples, LGBTQIA+ Peoples, and Women.

The next step in this process involves the selection of more culturally responsive materials (Alim & Paris, 2017; Gay, 2000). Building off the standards, it is possible to add a variety of meaningful voices to enhance students' learning experience. This can be done relatively easily within a history course by adding a variety of primary and secondary sources. As it stands there are only two sources that are mentioned within the Georgia Standards of Excellence for U.S. History. Those include Martin Luther King Jr.'s "I Have a Dream" Speech and the works of Langston Hughes. There are so many more sources that can be brought in to give students a more complete idea of the contributions of different groups in U.S. History. Some possible examples of primary documents include: the use of Native poetry and songs about issues they faced and are facing, the use of differing views on civil rights by leaders such as Malcolm X and Marcus Garvey, and the use of immigrant narratives during the Industrial Revolution to fully understand the conditions faced. These small steps can play a large role in ensuring that students are introduced to multiple perspectives, cultures, and understandings related to the events covered in U.S. History. It also would allow students from diverse backgrounds to have more of a sense of ownership and authorship with the curriculum, thus helping to improve their engagement and understanding of the topics covered (Murff, 2020).

Additionally, incorporating a focus on social justice and advocacy is a key component to Culturally Sustaining Pedagogy (Alim & Paris, 2017). This can be done within the United States history curriculum by highlighting different struggles that our country has faced and ways that different groups advocated for change. In addition, it can be incorporated through having students look at current events and analyzing how history relates to those events and what can be done to amend or correct them. This will also allow the students the opportunity to look at events that are meaningful to them and use their historical analysis skills to make connections to the existing curriculum. This in turn will help students build their critical thinking skills so that they are better able to advocate for change in the future.

While the use of Culturally Sustaining Pedagogy in instruction design can improve academic outcomes, utilizing it in assessment design can also lead to higher academic achievement. Cataldo (2021) asserts that current high stakes assessment models are not an equitable and culturally relevant way in which to assess students. He asserts that when you utilize a one-size-fits-all assessment model that it does not take into account students' diverse backgrounds and needs (2021). The danger he writes is that,

> as students progress throughout their K–12 educational career, they begin to realize that the essential purpose of schooling in urban America, amid social issues such as poverty and lack of educational resources, is to teach towards the tests. This is where, unfortunately, teachers and students in urban America find themselves feeling frustrated with high-stakes assessments in schools, as it is the only official means for assessing student learning and holding teachers accountable for student learning. (Cataldo, 2021, pp. 1)

The way to fix this, Cataldo says, is to switch from a high stakes testing model and to a performance based assessment model which would more accurately represent the current generation of students in the classroom (2021). Another study which looked Culturally Sustaining Pedagogy based on holistic design and the use of project-based learning was conducted by Aghasafari et al. (2021). Within this study project-based learning provided teachers with the flexibility to allow for the use of diverse voices, multimodal learning, and the inclusion of students' background knowledge and cultures. They found that students had increased academic achievement and engagement as a result. Thus, because it could improve academic results, teachers may be encouraged to adopt Culturally Sustaining Pedagogy within their classrooms.

Because of the foundation of social studies as a subject centered around people and cultures, it is very possible to incorporate Culturally Sustaining

Pedagogy into the classroom. While some teachers may be intimidated or concerned by the thought of utilizing a new pedagogy, there are things that schools and school systems can do in order to help prepare teachers for this more diverse way of instruction. As with instructional strategies and practices, there is no one common way to assist educators in developing a more Culturally Sustaining Pedagogy. However, one tool that has helped many educators is professional development. Professional development serves to introduce both preservice and existing teachers to the topic of Culturally Sustaining Pedagogies and to assist them in putting it into practice in their classrooms. Some scholars have used the Culturally Responsive Teaching Outcome Scale (Peters et al., 2018; Thomas et al., 2020) and others have used learning communities (Lomeli, 2021) to measure the effectiveness of professional development in this area. However, all found that following professional development, teachers reported they were better able to understand the importance of and develop a Culturally Sustaining Pedagogy in their classroom. While not all scholars believe that professional development is always the most effective means for introducing educators to this topic, as discussed by Ladson-Billings (2021), research shows that when done effectively and in a sustained manner it still pushes educators to think about these topics as it relates to their classroom (Martell & Stevens, 2019). Whatever method is used by teachers to become more familiar with Culturally Sustaining Pedagogy, be it self-study, graduate school, or professional development, it has the potential to transform the social studies classroom into a more engaging and culturally sustaining environment that can benefit all students.

References

Aghasafari, S., Bivins, K., & Nordgren, B. (2021). Arts integration and culturally sustaining pedagogy: Supporting bi/multilingual high school learners in biology. *Journal of Interdisciplinary Studies in Education, 10*(1), 59–81.

Alim, H. S., & Paris, D. (2017). *Culturally sustaining pedagogies: Teaching and learning for justice in a changing world.* Teachers College Press.

Alim, H. S., Paris, D., & Wong, C. P. (2020). Culturally sustaining pedagogy: A critical framework for centering communities. In *Handbook of the cultural foundations of learning* (pp. 261–276). Routledge.

An, S. (2016). Asian Americans in American history: An AsianCrit perspective on Asian American inclusion in state U.S. history curriculum standards. *Theory & Research in Social Education, 44*(2), 244–276. https://doi.org/10.1080/00933104.2016.1170646

Borck, C. R. (2020). "I belong here.": Culturally sustaining pedagogical praxes from an alternative high school in Brooklyn emerge. *Urban Review: Issues and Ideas in Public Education, 52*(2), 376–391.

Braden, E. G., & Gibson, V. (2021). A framework for supporting preservice teachers (PSTs) in culturally sustaining nonfiction writing. *Theory Into Practice, 60*(3), 242–253. https://doi.org/10.1080/00405841.2021.1911579

Bucholtz, M., Casillas, D., & Lee, J. (2017) Language and culture as sustenance. In D. Paris & H. S. Alim (Eds.), *Culturally sustaining pedagogies: Teaching and learning for justice in a changing world* (pp. 43–59). Teachers College Press.

Cataldo, K. (2021). The need for culturally relevant performance-based assessments post-covid-19. *Perspectives on Urban Education, 19*(1), 1–5.

Cavallaro, C. J., & Sembiante, S. F. (2021). Facilitating culturally sustaining, functional literacy practices in a middle school ESOL reading program: A design-based research study. *Language & Education: An International Journal, 35*(2), 160–179. https://doi.org/10.1080/09500782.2020.1775244

Charles, M. (2019). Effective teaching and learning: Decolonizing the curriculum. *Journal of Black Studies, 50*(8), 731–766. https://doi.org/10.1177/0021934719885631

Chen, D. A., Lord, S. M., Mejia, J. A., & Hoople, G. D. (2021). A critical reflection on the challenges of implementing culturally sustaining pedagogy. *2021 IEEE Frontiers in Education Conference (FIE)*. https://doi.org/10.1109/fie49875.2021.9637339

Delman, M. F., Lilly, K. R., & List, R. J. (2024). *Culturally sustaining pedagogy in progress: Views in the K-12 classroom* [Unpublished doctoral dissertation]. Augusta University.

Doucet, F. (2017). What does a culturally sustaining learning climate look like? *Theory Into Practice, 56*(3), 195–204. https://doi.org/10.1080/00405841.2017.1354618

Eraqi, M. M. (2014). Arab-American and Muslim-American studies in secondary social studies curriculum. *Arab World English Journal, 5*(3), 45–64.

Flores, T. T., & Springer, S. (2021). Our legends and journey stories: Exploring culturally sustaining family engagement in classrooms. *Theory Into Practice, 60*(3), 312–321.

Gay, G. (2000). *Culturally responsive teaching: Theory, research, and practice*. Teachers College Press.

Georgia Department of Education. (2016, June 9). *United States History—Georgia Department of Education*. United States History. Retrieved April 11, 2022, from https://lor2.gadoe.org/gadoe/file/6d0fa279-21d4-4f08-aaa0-9f0e5f3ad6bf/1/Social-Studies-United-States-History-Georgia-Standards.pdf

Harris, L. M., & Girard, B. (2020). Evaluating the support of teacher choice in state history standards. *History Teacher, 53*(4), 613–633.

Husband, T., & Kang, G. (2020). Identifying promising literacy practices for black males in P-12 classrooms: An integrative review. *Journal of Language and Literacy Education, 16*(1), 1–34.

Irizarry, J. G. (2017). "For us, by us": A vision for culturally sustaining pedagogies forwarded by Latinx youth. In D. Paris & H. S. Alim, *Culturally sustaining pedagogies: Teaching and learning for justice in a changing world* (pp. 83–98). Teachers College Press.

Jeong, H. (2020). Agency and pedagogy in literacy education: Toward culturally sustaining pedagogy for immigrant adolescents. *Journal of Asian Pacific Communication, 31*(1), 79–99. https://doi.org/10.1075/japc.00058.jeo

Journell, W., & Castro, E. L. (2011). Culturally relevant political education: Using immigration as a catalyst for civic understanding. *Multicultural Education, 18*(4), 10–17.

Kinloch, V. (2017) "You ain't making me write": Culturally sustaining pedagogies and Black youths' performances of resistance. In D. Paris & H. S. Alim (Eds.), *Culturally sustaining pedagogies: Teaching and learning for justice in a changing world* (pp. 25–41). Teachers College Press.

Kliebard, H. (2004). *The struggle for the American curriculum.* Routledge.

Krueger, J. (2019). To challenge the settler colonial narrative of Native Americans in social studies curriculum: A new way forward for teachers. *History Teacher, 52*(2), 291–318.

Ladson-Billings, G. (1995). Toward a theory of culturally relevant pedagogy. *American Educational Research Journal, 32*(3), 465–491.

Ladson-Billings, G. (2014). Culturally relevant pedagogy 2.0: A.k.a. the remix. *Harvard Educational Review, 84*(1), 74–84. https://doi.org/10.17763/haer.84.1.p2rj131485484751

Ladson-Billings, G. (2021a). *Culturally relevant pedagogy: Asking a different question.* Teachers College Press.

Ladson-Billings, G. (2021b). Three decades of culturally relevant, responsive, & sustaining pedagogy: What lies ahead?. *The Educational Forum, 85*(4), 351–354, DOI: 10.1080/00131725.2021.1957632

Lea, C. H., 3rd, Malorni, A., & Jones, T. M. (2019). "Everybody is an artist": Arts-based education and formerly incarcerated young Black men's academic and social-emotional development in an alternative school. *American Journal of Community Psychology, 64*(3–4), 333–347. https://doi.org/10.1002/ajcp.12378

Lomelí, R. S. (2021). Critical praxis círculos: The impact of culturally responsive teacher development. *Taboo: The Journal of Culture & Education, 20*(2), 120–141.

Martell, C. C., & Stevens, K. M. (2019). Culturally sustaining social studies teachers: Understanding models of practice. *Teaching and Teacher Education, 86*, 102897.

McKoy, C. L., MacLeod, R. B., Walter, J. S., & Nolker, D. B. (2017). The impact of an in-service workshop on cooperating teachers' perceptions of culturally responsive teaching. *Journal of Music Teacher Education, 26*(2), 50–63.

Murff, D. (2020). *Culturally responsive pedagogy: Promising practices for African American male students.* Information Age Publishing.

National Council for Social Studies. (2024). Social Studies. https://www.socialstudies.org/about/definition-social-studies

Nganga, L., Kambutu, J., Scull, R. W., & Keonghee Tao Han. (2021). High school students of color in the U.S. speak about their educational experiences: Schooling, culture, and pedagogy. *Journal of Social Studies Education Research, 12*(3), 1–27.

Paris, D. (2012). Culturally sustaining pedagogy: A needed change in stance, terminology, and practice. *Educational Researcher, 41*(3), 93–97. https://doi.org/10.3102/0013189x12441244

Paris, D. (2021). Culturally sustaining pedagogies and our futures. *The Educational Forum, 85*(4), 364–376. https://doi.org/10.1080/00131725.2021.1957634

Peters, J., McMullen, B., & Peters, P. D. (2018). Professional development school experiences and culturally sustaining teaching. *Journal of Higher Education Theory & Practice, 18*(1), 32–48. https://doi.org/10.33423/jhetp.v18i1.533

Ramirez, P., & Jaffee, A. T. (2016). Culturally responsive active citizenship education for newcomer students: A cross-state case study of two teachers in Arizona and New York. *International Journal of Multicultural Education, 18*(1), 45–67.

Ross, E. W. (Ed.). (1994). *The social studies curriculum: Purposes, problems and possibilities*. [PDF file]. State University of New York Press. https://www.researchgate.net/profile/E-Wayne

Ross, E. W. (2006). The struggle for social studies curriculum. In E. W. Ross (Ed.), *The social studies curriculum: Purposes, problems and possibilities* (3rd ed., pp. 17–36). State University of New York Press.

Schieble, M., & Polleck, J. (2021). The opportunities and constraints of a virtual field experience during a global pandemic for ELA teacher candidates' learning about culturally sustaining pedagogy. *Contemporary Issues in Technology and Teacher Education, 21*(2), 231–265.

Talley-Matthews, S., & Wiggan, G. (2018). Culturally sustaining pedagogy: How teachers can teach the new majority in public schools. *Black History Bulletin, 81*(2), 24. https://doi.org/10.5323/blachistbull.81.2.0024

Thomas, C. L., Tancock, S. M., Zygmunt, E. M., & Sutter, N. (2020). Effects of a community-engaged teacher preparation program on the culturally relevant teaching self-efficacy of preservice teachers. *Journal of Negro Education, 89*(2), 122–135.

Torres, Alejandra (2021) Using digital libraries to engage the whole student: Culturally sustaining pedagogies, trauma-informed classrooms, and project-based learning *Journal of Critical Digital Librarianship, 1*(1), DOI: 10.31390/jcdl.1.1.05

Warren, C. A. (2018). Empathy, teacher dispositions, and preparation for culturally responsive pedagogy. *Journal of Teacher Education, 69*(2), 169–183.

Woodley, X., Hernandez, C., Parra, J., & Negash, B. (2017). Celebrating difference: Best practices in culturally responsive teaching online. *TechTrends: Linking Research & Practice to Improve Learning, 61*(5), 470–478. https://doi.org/10.1007/s11528-017-0207-z

· 1 5 ·

FINDING ANCHORAGE

Dawn R. May

Introduction

In analyzing oneself, it provokes the interpreter to have to relive a space of introspection and vulnerability. This process willingly (or unwillingly) forces the participant to face the perimeters of their spectral memory which can be both uncomfortable and inspirational. As this reflection has made me revisit eras of my past and origins leading to my teaching beliefs, in doing so I have revisualized junctures in my lifetime that have to some degree faded throughout the years. Through this autobiographical endeavor, I have had opportunity to reconnect with some of my roots which birthed the foundations of my educational convictions and in turn my subsequent methodologies unique to me as an educator and mentor today.

I have recently realized how the genesis of my instructional mantras and teaching beliefs have gone a bit faint or buried behind the depths of life getting in the way or simply being too busy to remember. Pinar et al. (2014) points out the "regressive" step of *currere*, which he explains as "one's 'lived' or existential experience" serving as a "data source" whereupon one acquires data from "free associating" and "recalling the past" thusly "enlarging and transforming one's memory" (p. 520). In this process, the "data" is derived from the reflective journey of connecting to links from one's pivotal life lessons as produced by personal lived experience, which in the end culminate as influential to one's behaviors, attitudes, and personal pursuits. For me, this reflective journey has been a long time coming as life challenges and the blur of overinvestment of the day-to-day have forced this cathartic process to grow stagnant. To reflect on this piece, I am appreciative, in that it has forced me to reconnect with my origin story and life's impactful moments which have been fundamentally near and dear to my personal mission and vision and subsequent roles and responsibilities as an educator.

Finding Anchorage

My personal journey in becoming an educator begins with lack of anchorage, and no, I am not referring to the mooring of a boat but speaking in other more poetic terms. In this case, I use the word "anchorage" as a secured center to which I could confide and take hold of during life's inescapable peaks and valleys. This is an intangible space, something born out of our subjectivities. In this liminal perspective, my understanding of place in the world began from the view of a life lived as a latch key kid of a single mom and in turn maneuvering through childhood surviving on inference rather than from the direct instruction of a parental figure. From this juncture, childhood evolved into adolescence fueled by introversion and a marginalized sense of living on the social periphery toward a teenagerhood which yearned for an emotional port in the storm.

Life Lesson Part 1: The Importance of Presence

So here begins pivotal moment one. My mother and father divorced when I was five, and it was in that moment I began to raise myself. Starting in the first grade, I walked myself to the bus stop with a key on a string hanging precariously around my neck. The bus stop was across a main road, and for that stop I was the only child. I can remember every morning looking out the kitchen window from the second story peering back and forth between the clock and the bus stop. Some mornings I had horrible anxiety. I hated venturing out the door knowing I was absolutely alone, and absolutely alone I would make my way back again at the end of the day. Some kids may have looked at the absence of a parent seeing you off to school as freedom or independence. For me it was an unwelcome source of angst and incertitude.

Upon reminiscing about this part of my childhood, I revisit memories of my mother and the realization she was my primary person in life. I remember so clearly how she would leave for work in the dark and in turn come home in the dark. Adrift in my childhood, my warmest memory of my mother is of her grading papers in her armchair. She would routinely fall asleep with papers in hand. My mother was an elementary school teacher of 32 years, so one could easily suggest that teaching might be in my blood. As she slept soundly, I savored those impermanent moments as they were in many ways one of the only opportunities I could enjoy spending time with her. With my mother working and raising three children on her own, I missed the singular exemplar I yearned for to help navigate the unknown.

Although my mother loved me and had no other choice but to provide for her three children, the consequence of the dynamic was a very lonely and isolated experience. In my case the central piece and most influential component of the familial common place was my mother. This juncture of life was influential to my teaching mantra in that in looking back it was the start of a life philosophy which I now describe as "making good where others could not." You will see as I divulge more that the evolution of my teaching journey is not a result of an integral teacher who changed my life or an epiphany which shaped my educationist passions. For you, my reader, the life lesson I have to offer is that there is empowerment in lessons learned from the not-so-great teachable moments or not-so-great administrators or the not-so-great faculty members acting as the fuel to refine the bad and use it to reshape or to reconstruct practices, culture, relationships, methodologies, or even the life experience of another human. Teachable moments are sometimes the most potent moments that challenge ineffectiveness and in turn make change toward the better. So, as my mother struggled to be present, my life lesson here is that presence—be it physical or mental—is an intangible source of feeding another's needs. The idea of presence for my students and even for my own children has been life lesson one. Understanding your students, forming relationships with them and getting to know them beyond just showing up has implicit power which shapes trust, support, and nurturance. Be intentional with your presence.

Life Lesson Part 2: If My Teacher Doesn't Care, Then Who Should?

In maneuvering most of my childhood from the periphery, I traveled through the social nuances of school fixed in the margin. I was not a "goth kid" who withdrew to make a point; in fact, I was just your average suburban adolescent that no one would question as feeling ostracized or uncomfortable in her skin. But my childhood isolation left more than the eye could see. Without connections like cousins, aunts or uncles, even friends of the family or neighbors, I had a tremendously hard time negotiating trust, and my self-confidence was fragile and riddled with a fractured sense of self-esteem. Life in high school offered social judgment and hierarchies and a learning environment that was more or less stern and sterile. My interactions with high school teachers were not necessarily warm, and they engaged students as if they were receptacles where the student-teacher engagement mainly necessitated an effort to fulfill obligatory daily lessons to then move on to the next one. Not to say I didn't ever have a good experience. I do remember a few teachers fondly. However, for most of my high school teaching experiences, they were seemingly matter of fact.

As my second pivotal moment entails life in high school, it was my senior year and the occurrences (or better yet, the lack of occurrences) relevant to my Advanced Placement (AP) Spanish class that sealed the deal in the formation of yet another core philosophy important to my teaching career.

My AP Spanish class was small, maybe ten students. We had a native speaker from Mexico, Señora Romero. For the sake of this story, I have given my former teacher a pseudonym as the events of the story are really the more relevant elements in need of being discussed. She was, in my opinion, the classic example of teacher burn-out. One would think that the potential in an AP Spanish course would be unmeasured. By this time students would have acquired such a level of Spanish that the social engagement and interaction could have been significantly immersive, energetic, and forever impressionable. However, that was not the case with Señora Romero. For an entire year, it was stunningly obvious that she only really shared the classroom experience with two of the ten students—a girl from Venezuela and an affluent boy who had the means to study abroad over the summer of his junior year. The rest of us were not worth much. Every session we would enter her room where she sat behind her desk—nothing more, nothing less. To further emphasize the point, I can't remember a single activity or unit we did while with her. For the first time in my Spanish acquisition journey, the content was lackluster, uninviting, and void.

In looking at the idea that teachers are an essential variable in creating meaning, then teacher attitudes and behaviors can become a self-fulfilling prophecy. William Schubert (1986) highlights this point via Joseph Schwab's four commonplaces (1973) by pointing out the potency of the teacher/student experience when he asks the questions, "In what ways does the teacher model attitudes and behavior? How does the teacher convey messages about what he or she considers important or valuable? What does he or she convey is worthwhile to students?" (p. 302). When a teacher portrays apathy, discrimination, judgment, disinterest, or disdain, the environment will tend to deprive rather than offer an encouragement to thrive. The energy produced by the teacher predetermines a student's academic and social future. The lack of awareness by teachers that their practices perpetuate exile can be both a literal and emotional exclusion. As Ming Fe He (2009) sustains, those who are aware of the impact of exile "cultivate curiosity in teaching, learning, inquiry, and life with conscious reflection on their diverse exile experience" (p. 471) with the intent to ultimately "challenge assumptions and recognize contradictions between theory and practice, and to critically examine the impact of theory on practice and practice on theory" (p. 471). When one is conscious of being exiled and the potential of exiling others, the deeper awareness of teacher interaction turns from being mundane to a deeper, more profound appreciation of teacher as facilitator. In this same light, Clandinin (2010) offers John Dewey's vision to teaching as it relates to teacher relationships and children:

> Working within a Dewey-inspired conception of curriculum, then, the teacher is not a kind of metaphoric conduit that delivers a curriculum mandated or planned elsewhere, but is an active agent in the ongoing composing and living out of the curriculum. (p. 247)

Ming Fang He (2016) further elaborates Dewey's message in pointing out, "Dewey believed that self can be cultivated through imagination which, in turn, is a gateway through which a meaningful experience is created through interaction between self and its environment" (p. 43). He (2016) leaves us with the understanding that "meaningful experience" comes to fruition as a result of the "interaction between self and its environment" (p. 43). The teacher plays a vital role in setting the tone, rigor, and allure present in a meaning-filled space. In all, the profound influence teachers had on my feelings of exile and their complacent effort at helping me as a student to find a place to fill my voids has become my fuel, integral to the drive behind my efforts as a teacher. My educator mantra holds firm that our past lived experiences, sometimes for the worse, can open gateways toward empowerment and change which have immense potential to redirect the "todays" of future students' tomorrows, hopefully making them better than our experienced yesterdays.

Lessons Learned: What Does This Mean to You?

What I thought was an open sea of water, unyielding and overwhelming as a life lived by the viewpoint of a latch key kid, turned out to be a deeply impactful venture helping to procure empathy, humility, and care for the lived experience of others. Teaching without connection or sensitivity to the students who walk in the door does not do justice to the term "teacher" or the genuine intention of learning. Good teachers teach to inspire kids to critically see the world and feel empowered to participate within it, and this caliber of teaching/learning comes from self-reflection and critical awareness of oneself first. In this capacity, my life's trials and tribulations and living in the periphery helped me to relate to students and the voids with which they might be contending. Pinar (2011) summarizes this experience best when he states:

> It is the structural noncoincidence of the alive body—the time and space of subjectivity—that invites us to experience *experience* [...] to remember what we have undergone, to forget we cannot bear to remember, and to understand what we can recall and feel compelled to comprehend. It is subjectivity wherein we begin to know ourselves and the world we inhabit and that inhabits us. (p. 8)

The experience of my hardships resulted in the refinement of my future. It is in the quest for unwavering anchorage that the quell of life encouraged me to find harbor within the landscape of teaching. Most of us can probably affirm that there is something from our past that has led us to our present, and in the case of the liminal space special to teaching, a space that is not black and white, literal or concrete, but a space that sees beyond the first impression or apparent constructs. Within this sphere, there is empowerment in embracing the dark of a tumultuous past as it might follow to the light of an enlightened tomorrow. Pinar (2011) offers the suggestion that to embrace the present "we must flee to the past" as it holds immense potential to find passage to the future (p. 41). Ultimately, some of the most potent and life-altering lessons may be caused by the moments where integral institutions or people may have historically fallen short or acted in a capacity that disenabled opportunities for support, nurturance, or growth. It is in these deficits that life lessons lie—life lessons which hold significant potency for change, reform, and the redevelopment towards the construction of something better.

References

Clandinin, J. (2010). Curriculum studies, the nature of: Essay 1. In Craig Kridel (Ed.), *Encyclopedia of curriculum studies* (p. 247). Sage Publications, Inc. DOI: https://doi.org/10.4135/9781412958806

He, M. F., & University, G. S. (2009). Exile pedagogy: Teaching in-between. *Handbook of Public Pedagogy*. Routledge. DOI: https://doi.org/10.4324/9780203863688

He, M. F. (2016). Exploring an East-West epistemological convergence of embodied democracy in education through cultural humanism in Confucius-Makiguchi-Dewey. *Journal of Curriculum Studies*, 48(1), (pp. 36–57). Routledge. DOI: 10.1080/00220272.2015.1088066

Pinar, W. (2011). *The character of curriculum studies: Bildung, currere, and the recurring question of the subject*. Palgrave Macmillan.

Pinar, W., Reynolds, W., Slattery, P., & Taubman, P. (2014). Understanding curriculum as autobiographical/biographical text. In Joe Kincheloe & Shirley Steinberg (Eds.), *Understanding curriculum: An introduction to the study of historical and contemporary curriculum discourse* (p. 520). Peter Lang Publishing, Inc.

Schubert, W. H. (1986). Paradigms in curriculum. *Curriculum: Perspective, paradigm and possibility* (pp. 169–185). Macmillan Publishing Company.

Schwab, J. (1973). *The Practical 3: Translation into curriculum* (Vol. 81). The University of Chicago Press. https://www.jstor.org/stable/1084423

· 1 6 ·

THE ONTOLOGY OF METAMODERNISM AND THE RECONSTRUCTION OF HUMAN CIVILITY

Dawn R. May

You might ask: What business does a Spanish teacher have philosophizing over the nature of society and the evolution of human civility? Although I teach Spanish, impactful instruction should maintain teacher-as-student just as much as teacher-overseeing-students. The magic of teaching and the liminal space of learning curate a curiosity beyond the mundane requirements of classroom management, lesson planning, and methodology. Good educators internalize the null forces of curriculum and its implicit effect incurred by both students and society at large. Although my teacher duties may primarily navigate bridging the gap of monolingual learners toward bilingual transformation, an educationist looks for the societal lessons learned to then permit opportunities for the same doors to open in the stretches of a student's mind. For an educationist, it is not only about curriculum, lesson planning, or management, but wonderment over the underlying that permeates the institution of education. In this light, I would like to expose the null influence of technology, the new world order that is the lived experience of students today. We can all attest that the infiltration of technology, be it a tablet, laptop, or phone, has fundamentally changed the culture of education and the nature of society in general. With that, let's take a more critical look on the null permeation of technology both in and outside the classroom and how it has impacted the current nature of teaching.

The Fall of Civility

The evolution of any one civilization and its subsequent progress can arguably be associated with the time and context in which it may have met its peak. In looking back, what happened to the Byzantines, the Egyptians, or Romans? According to history, these were all superior civilizations somehow subject to ruin even though they were historically known as once standing world powers. It is fair to say societies as a whole encounter an ebb and flow of foundational impacts through practices related to religion, education, economics, gender, disability, race relations, government rule, and overall power struggle, which then concludes with the formation of norms and practices. As a Spanish teacher, this lens on society is an omnipresent component to my classroom, especially in attempting to relay cultural norms, traditions, and customs, and should most predominantly highlight the people who spoke it.

In understanding the past, it helps to appreciate the present. For most of us we can relate to the more highly solicited, epochal influences which by curriculum scholar standards are the foundational points of reference as they pertain to educational practices to date. With that in mind, why do scholars refer to the Enlightenment, modernism, or even postmodernism in their efforts to break down educational progress, or conversely, educational subjugation? References to the Enlightenment may pay homage to human liberation via reason and rationale. As for modernism, a scholar may attribute actions of prescription and positivism to classroom practices, whereas postmodern references would do so under the ideas of deconstruction, the questioning of grand narratives, and the development of identity politics. So, in this context of historical influences and societal progression, I would like to ask you, the reader as an aspiring educator, where is society now? What are the societal struggles we face today? What is today's context that defines our current epoch to date? And what does this mean for our educational tomorrow? William Pinar (2015) points out the importance of historical awareness in that being located in a certain historical moment makes one a subject of history due to exposure to historical place, thusly enacting "the subject as historical" leading to the embodiment of "issues and injuries inherited from the past" (p. xiv). Huebner (1999) suggests history as prognosticator in that "to participate responsibly in history, one must criticize and create. To surpass the technical foundations of education, then, requires historical awareness of where we once were, sensitivity to present problems, resistances and binds, and openness to future possibilities" (p. 432). Historical awareness is not to be taken for granted, and as an educator who intends to impact the "now," it is important to know how "now" got here.

With that lens in mind while I look at my Spanish instruction today, my methodologies and philosophies have been forced to evolve, taking on different form and shape than what I might have used even ten years ago. In looking back at my "innovative" classroom engagements, where I encouraged students to work in groups, get out of their chairs, and be empowered with "alternative" forms of assessment (group presentations, song analysis, charades, storytelling through pictures, etc.), all of these "alternative" forms relied on the key quality of being social. For most classrooms, traditional settings tie their practices to seat work, lecture, paper and pencil, multiple choice exams ultimately supporting dry and dissociative activities. The "alternative" element here was the word "social." Students were invested and participatory as I unbridled my classroom with unconventional opportunities which were interactive and interpersonal while, let me remind you, still teaching them how to speak Spanish.

However, with the onset of the phone, a contemporary student's lived experience now determines social as the "foreign language," where having to interpersonally interact is unpleasant, uncomfortable, and actively evaded. Why did my practices ten years ago excite and produce firm learning but today fall flat and impotent? Because the students of today only know "social" through the comfort of voyeuristically watching other people's lived experiences via a screen rather than going out and taking initiative to create their own. Speaking to the present day, the fundamental wiring of teens is a lived experience that can be described as socially and emotionally remote, introvertedly perched behind screens motivated to consume the observable "likes" and "Snapchat" streaks of other people's lived moments.

So, again I revisit the question: Why would a Spanish teacher take the time to philosophize the nature of society and human civility? It is important as educators to take the time to develop your lens. How do you see the tangibles (your lessons, your classroom structure, etc.), but also what are your beliefs when it comes to empowerment, critical awareness, and education that is meaningful, deeply acquired, and long lasting? Let's face it: "our now" will be someone else's footprint on the past and those footprints, like the integral moment Rosa Parks refused to give up her seat on the bus as well as women's suffrage in the 18th century, constitute pivotal moments of lessons learned and a road map toward a better humanity for tomorrow. This Spanish teacher—or really, this educator—offers the reader an opportunity to see the world through epochal and historical lenses as means to analyze lived experience to better navigate educational issues of today, or even those within a prognosticated future. For instance, postmodern deconstruction was in reaction to modernism's intense and formulaic prescription. One might say we as a civilization are still in postmodern ideologies and practices; however, is it possible to portend a construction beyond the postmodern and question where is society today?

To engage this possibility, there are cultural scholars and social theorists such as Daniel Görtz, Timotheus Vermeulen, and Robin van den Akker, who project that we have been in the next epochal phase beyond postmodernism, noted as metamodernism. Such scholars suggest that metamodernism surfaced in the early 2000s, where we shifted "from postmodernism to metamodernism [. . .] just as the sixties were the defining transitional period for the shift from modernism to postmodernism" (Vermeulen & van den Akker, 2015, para. 5). According to Daniel Görtz and Emil Ejner Friis, who mutually write under the name Hanzi Freinacht (2017) in the book *The Listening Society*, metamodernism consists of a distinct array of societal movements which are observable to date. Görtz and Enjer Friis (2017) maintain that the metamodern era will embrace notable cultural development, initiate great strides significant to societal and personal growth and ultimately culminating in philosophical and sociopolitical transformations (pp. 15–213). Van den Akker et al. (2017) also highlight the metamodern as a "variant of postmodernism" (p. 4), ultimately described as a conjoined "oscillation" between the prescribed, positivism of modernism and the deconstruction and cynical skepticism of postmodernism (p. 6). In this potential new era of lived experience, the oscillation between rigid structure and the refute against any structure at all, is the mutual state of being present in the current technological world order.

Teaching in Technological Hegemony

In society today, technological advancements such as the Internet and social media platforms like Facebook, Instagram, and Snapchat have in concept constructed a boundaryless, virtual world offering unrestricted or unfettered access to human connectivity, enabling less exclusion and more liberation. As educators, is this what we are really seeing at the moment? Has access to technological resources enabled a more evolved humanity or has it just chained us further? If Vermeulen & van den Akker's conjecture of oscillation is true and the tension of both epochal philosophies present themselves in society, then where do students and teachers stand within this tug and pull? It is the opinion of this writer that those of us in the metamodern era are facing a striking crisis as it pertains to interpersonal relationships, care for one another, and overall compassion as a people. It is in many ways a retrogression of human civility. People are being reduced to online personas, perfectly worded perceptions, ameliorated and callused, only to be left with a lack of filter and an absence of empathetic regard. We are subjects of a digital, hive-minded collective which works to either spend hours scrolling the lived experiences of others, or troll the general-public inciting inflammatory responses and seeking to find joy at the expense of others. This new era is the current cultural norm which is in turn producing an unprecedented loss of introspective filter needed for healthy interpersonal connectedness and essential to the germination of empathy, kindness, and propriety. Under this lens, should we settle for this status quo? Can we develop from here and move beyond this disconnection? Is this just a growing pain that we need to undertake to get to the other side? Or will it be a contributing factor to our demise? The hope for the metamodern era is that we gain more consciousness over the Internet's ethereal manipulation so that the technology-human hybridity can co-exist for an even more refined humanity, better and more developed than before.

The Distortion of Interiority

Living with technology in the metamodern era is to hand all your senses, emotions, and rationale over to the omnipresent stimulus posed by constant connection to our beings. Technology has coalesced with the fiber of our lives. McLuhan (1994) asserts that the impact of technology on the human psyche is such that, "The effects of technology do not occur at the level of opinions or concepts but alter sense ratios or patterns of perception steadily and without any resistance" (p. 18). The bombardment of stimuli so interwoven into our everyday dependencies has created a numbness of which we are not even aware. Like Pavlov's dog, we are trained to respond and in turn yearn for more. McLuhan reiterates, "Subliminal and docile acceptance of media impact has made them prisons without walls for their human users" (p. 20). Sherry Turkle echoes this same concern. Turkle (2015) remarks, "we have learned that we get a neurochemical high from connecting. We recognize that we crave a feeling of being 'always on'" (p. 17). We are attached to the allurement of instant notifications, rapid responses, self-fulfilling affirmations, and enthralled with the voyeurism of seeing others through the lens of a phone. We are pulled like magnets lured to more content, more likes, more notifications, and more digestion of stimulus. Turkle (2015) continues, "We say we turn to our phones when we're 'bored.' And we often find ourselves bored because we have become accustomed to a constant feed of connections, information, and entertainment" (p. 4). Like the pique of an electrical charge, McLuhan describes technology as either "hot" or "cold." To better put this into context, "cold" stimuli are interactions that require the participant to interpret, be mentally present, forced to mindfully fill in the blanks to make sense of the encounter (McLuhan, 1994, pp. 22–23). Whereas "hot" stimuli are considered to affect "one single sense in 'high definition'" and leave the participant in a "state of being well filled with data" (McLuhan, 1994, p. 22). In other words, "hot mediums" provide short strokes of high stimulus, thus activating a state of sensatory or emotional gratification. In the overstimulation, there is a persistent attachment to it, which is an allurement like addiction. Developmentally, life in the metamodern era is experienced in "high definition" with intense and relentless external snaring. Notably, this persistent shock has deadened our connectedness to our interiority, and in turn our innermost solitude which can guard as an emotional and psychological refuge permitting a reboot managed by self-reflection. This experience of solace is crucial in that its outcome culminates with a stronger sense of self-awareness and, most importantly, personal self-restraint.

The Oxford English Dictionary (2023) defines interiority as "(a) The quality or state of being interior or inward. (b) Inner character or nature; an inner element." Interiority is the ability to pause within your inner being, assess and filter the world around you, be thoughtful and self-reflective. In contrast, it is not reactionary, hurried, impetuous, external, angry, numb, or removed. When we are constantly "on" and being lulled into the magnetism of technology's pull, we are subsequently never "alone." The lack of disconnect prohibits the revitalization and filter gained from having solitude in ourselves. Turkle sustains (2015), "in solitude we find ourselves; we prepare ourselves to come to conversation with something to say that is authentic, ours [...] and then in conversation with other people we become better at inner dialogue" (p. 10). Having this inner dialogue and being thoughtfully in tune with oneself is nourishing and breeds a more self-aware and empathetic being. We think before we act. We filter before we say. So, why is this important to you as the reader? Even more important to ask, why is this important to you as an educator? There is no doubt that teachers and professors are exemplars, models by which our students gauge the world. Sometimes teachers are the only real "parent figure" a student may witness in their lifetime. In knowing this level of power or impression, we should encourage a classroom that supports technological advancement but also moments to retain and refine human interaction and connection. As a teacher of a content that is immensely reliant on socialization, I have had to reflect over a more invasive and persistent struggle with students who are experiencing anxiety and refusal when it comes to working in groups or even with a partner. Additionally, once they feel the obligations of the lesson have concluded, their immediate selection is seeking refuge in the seclusion of their phone. The role of teacher and the innerworkings of the classroom setting now must entail opportunities for students to practice socialization in real time, an assertion to practice outer dialogue rather than just disassociated seclusion as posed by the social withdrawal furnished by their preferred screen. As exemplars and as places of growth, our classrooms need to acknowledge the social disconnects posed by technological withdrawal and build thoughtful practices to negate this threat to modern education.

Humans are Divided and Less Connected

In targeting the need for interiority, self-reflection, and interpersonal connectivity, we have to face the fact that humans really are significantly less connected despite having seemingly limitless access to each other. The other side of the screen is not only a self-secluded voyeurism, but the idea of "safety in numbers" and unaccountability in our anonymity. The other side of the screen is a "groupthink" collective where the thinking is done for us; it sets the tone for our engagement and all too many times concludes with targeted ridicule or bullying. What was once perhaps an isolated act of hostility, or a hateful rebuke only thought but not said, is now becoming the forefront of our social behaviors. According to Jaron Lanier (2010), "the groupthink problem [...] isn't so much in the minds of the technologists themselves, but in the minds of the users of the tools the cybernetic totalists are promoting" (p. 17). Lanier, a tech guru for Microsoft, holds the consensus that users of technological forums have constructed a "hive-minded" body which drives the bus on our current social norms. As we "login" and "follow," "like" or perpetuate a "streak," we bleed into the digital masses, becoming one of many only to be absorbed into the virtual realm of anonymous followers. Lanier (2010) goes on to explain, "emphasizing the crowd means deemphasizing individual humans in the design of society, and when you ask people not to be people, they revert to bad moblike behaviors" (p. 19). Digital participation in the metamodern is an abyss of numbers via a virtual cloud filled with impersonal online personas, artificial relationships, and an anonymity which tends to take on hostile, adversarial, or destructive engagement with onlookers. Lanier's comments ring true in that as a community we have lost the sense of value that comes with addressing concerns with civility and decorum. Online interactions have taken the bridle off regarding human relations, courtesy, and kindness. Furthermore, human contributions are now simply algorithms, and those algorithms have accumulated into desensitized bits. The perceived digital consciousness and any sense of authentic human connectivity are becoming more and more a prefabricated and synthetic experience.

Teachers everywhere contend with these frustrations no matter where they may derive. There is a love-hate relationship as far as education and technology goes. Progress in technology means progress in our advancement, but at what cost? Today's educator simply cannot ignore this "oscillation" between technology as an enriching tool as well as being a nemesis that seduces users into real-time self-ostracization. Perhaps it depends on the content or the level of technological savvy on the part of the teacher, but certainly for content that requires interpersonal reinforcement (the exchange of emotion and context in spoken language) technology is a distraction, a seducer toward self-imposed removal from the real-time space and real-time relationships classrooms were traditionally known for growing. In all it must be asked: Do we control our technology or is it the technology that controls us?

Limitless Anonymity Has Bred Widespread Amorality

Growing up we probably can all attest to having had an encounter with a bully. This is aberrant to the human predicament and most inherent to childhood. The sense of fear, belittlement, alienation, and mental despair that only a bully can illicit is a classic childhood torment. In the metamodern this childish torment has taken shape in the darker recesses of the Internet. What was once a hallway encounter or a lunchroom incident has proliferated via online platforms through the manifestation of "trolls." Whitney Phillips (2015) describes trolls as intentionally and willfully wanting to "disrupt and upset as many people as possible, using whatever linguistic or behavioral tools are available" (p. 2). Additionally, Phillips (2015) points out, "trolls incite paranoia, and paranoia sours the communal spirit that yearns to express itself online" (p. 16). Trolls scour the Internet and find points of contention out of what might be something very regular or personal to the average Joe. It is highlighted and made fun of at the cost of the person at the other end only for the troll to hope it "goes viral," sharing the ridicule superimposed on the victim striving to gain the highly coveted "lulz." Even more distasteful, trolls thrive under anonymity. The boundaryless or lawless realm of the virtual has created an "anything goes" mentality, where things are said, targets are demeaned, and the intended outcome is for the mere sake of getting a rise not only from the victimized but by how many others find joy in the other person's discomfort as well. Phillips (2015) defines that, "trolls [. . .] actively embrace amorality, and are, or at least profess to be pawns, in the service of nothing but their own amusement" (p. 10). In understanding this dynamic, one should take a moment to pause and ponder, what is amorality? Is this the same as immorality? For Phillips to declare that trolls are "amoral" strikes more fear than if she had said "immoral." Amoral is worse. It concludes apathy, indifference, nonfeeling. In good or bad, there is no emotional consequence for either. The pain of the victimization goes unnoticed and therefore rationalizes why trolls can inflict mockery at someone else's expense—and not think twice. Apathy is a sad side effect of our metamodern peak because of our mass connections and our technological existence living in the multitude. Currently, the cultural phase of development for today's society is a state of desensitization. We struggle to feel toward others, have remorse or entertain a second thought before evoking degrading "lulz." I have to say until pursing my educational doctorate and taking a class on media literacy, I had zero understanding on the concept of "lulz." To better understand this world, I posed questions to my students about this online culture and how it relates to social media and the impacts that social media entails. "Lulz" and trolls were matter-of-fact knowledge for them, with many of them shrugging off the term as outdated or passé. This nonchalance did not sit right with me, as it seems like an acceptance of a toxic online norm. Again, educationists need to provide opportunities to embrace empathy and reflection regarding human connection. Internet protocols both explicit and implicit, like amoral acts of trolling or even cyber bullying, are the null curriculum that we are competing against. Teachers today must make refuge in the classroom and bring to light the other side of humanity that the Internet tends to overshadow. Phillips (2015) defines it best in her final thought, arguing that "trolls are widely regarded as the primary obstacle to a kinder, gentler, and more equitable Internet" (p. 10), and the metamodern digital landscape needs to recognize the profound cultural norm of the digital practice of the "amoral" and attempt to counter it with practices of empathy, self-reflection, and opportunities to connect in "real-time" to others.

We Need Warning Labels

Today it is generally known and well accepted that cigarette smoking is dangerous for one's health. The general practice which used to be the accepted norm and the "in thing" to do came to light as an extremely unhealthy pastime which has historically and medically been confirmed as causing aggressive illnesses such as cancer, heart disease, and emphysema. In seeing the data related to smoking and its accompanying health problems, the government formulated the issuing of warning labels. Even today these are identifiable on each carton of cigarettes, and they are made to be very clear in soliciting the danger to one's health and well-being if the product is consumed. Over time the use of cigarettes has been societally curtailed. No smoking in restaurants, public areas, or airplanes, and even fewer families are seeing their use in day-to-day homes. Society has shown a reaction to the information that was exposed to them by those educative efforts. So in the same respect, if monopoly companies like Facebook, who may also have a hand in other social media platforms like Snapchat, Instagram, or TikTok, are knowingly targeting their audiences with algorithms that feed their visual and social addictions, then as consumers of these platforms, one would conclude we have the same right to know of the tactics both covert and overt each company institutes which infiltrate our emotions and psychological urges. Social media giants have our attention, they have our time, and they have our attachment. We are essentially their captive audience. McChesney (2008) brings to light this social dichotomy regarding the manipulation of the political economy of the media and what he considers the "digital communication revolution" which has been "exemplified by the Internet and wireless communication systems" (p. 17). McChesney (2008) makes clear:

> These technologies are in the process of blasting open the media system in a manner that is highly unusual, if not unprecedented. Much of the traditional thinking about communication—who says what to whom with what effect—has to be recalculated in an era in which communication and information are dramatically more accessible than ever before. And in which time and space have collapsed. These technologies, too, are central to the emergence of the global world order. (pp. 17–18)

McChesney (2008) argues that the new media technologies paired with economic powerhouses is a "policy matter" and the actuality of "generating effective policies of viable news media is a central dilemma of our times" (p. 20). The policy matter in this case is the need to inform the public of the hazards of online digital citizenry. Again, we are living in an unprecedented time—a time of technological explosion which has completely changed the face of our society, both tangibly and intangibly. This new era is unlike the others. As we pull this into education, I think we can all attest to the moments school librarians attempt to offer insight to students on how to navigate as a digital citizen, but from what I have observed, this has to do with items like plagiarism or capitalizing all letters being equal to shouting at someone. In these unprecedented times, digital citizenry should be more than the superficial or obvious. Course curriculum or culture-making as it relates to the online realm should include awareness around the manipulations of social media platforms. There should be policy that emphasizes the need for this type of "schooling." Part of a digital citizenry curriculum must include information around how social media works and the intentional manipulations behind algorithms and tracking mechanisms. The definition of digital citizenry should be more acutely defined as well as developed in light of the predominant human-technology hybridity to date. This process won't be easy and the demand for it will incite a struggle. It is to be expected that each movement of historical growth (women's rights, civil rights, gay and lesbian rights, immigration rights, etc.) has faced the worst before getting better. As history has pointed out, the societal struggle holds potential for developmental advancement via polemic exchanges which can ultimately provoke a learning curve hopefully leading to a better, more evolved humanity. Within the metamodern, we are incurring a significant developmental disaccord where online society is interpersonally more desensitized, abrasive, and less adept at practicing empathy. This is not the result of being incapable but is a result of the permissive online culture that has unbridled it. The metamodern phase today is at a definable growth peak in that the human-technology hybridity holds great potential to accelerate us into a more evolved humanity. However, without recognition or the wherewithal to take responsibility for the "negative side effects," the division and fragmentation of our current technological state has extreme potential to be our downfall. As Abraham Lincoln's statement resounds, "A house divided against itself cannot stand" (Lincoln, 1858 as cited by the National Park Service, n.d.). As we emerge through this new cultural phase, the human-technology hybrid phase, we need to push harder and with a more aggressive voice toward holding the political economy (Facebook, Google, Amazon, X, TikTok, etc.) more accountable and to a higher standard than what is currently held today. Limitless manhandling of our minds and time in ways that distort and manipulate both covertly and overtly should not be blindly accepted. As Matt Taibbi points out, major news networks like CNN, MSNBC, and Fox News are big game players when it comes to misleading and manipulating. Taibbi (2021) makes this dynamic clear as he states, "The relentless *now now now* grind of the twenty-four-hour cycle created in consumers a new kind of anxiety and addictive dependency, a need to know what was happening not just once or twice a day but every minute" (p. 14). He concludes this ideology in that, "As it turns out, there is a utility in keeping us divided. As people, the more separate we are, the more politically impotent we become" (Taibbi, 2021, p. 21).

The metamodern co-existence of humankind and technology does not have to be a dilemma that dismantles us. In moving forward, we must demand that power monopolies are held accountable for the tactics they use. Like cigarettes, they owe us a warning label. It should be expected that the big power players disclaim their maneuvers and assume a more visible and transparent responsibility for their tactics. Similar to the societal curtailing of cigarettes, exposing deceptive practices will breed knowledge; with knowledge comes power, and in power will come reform and change.

As we face the evolution of the metamodern and the current day technological conflicts as they relate to human-technology hybridity, it is important to glean the lessons learned. Metamodernism has the force and influence to actualize a "societal and political project" driven "by ideals of creating open, participatory processes, collective intelligence, inner work and 'embodiment,' co-development, and an experimental view on rituals as well as attempts to 'reconstruct' everyday life and social reality" (Henriques, 2020, para. 8). In this light of a "societal and political project," that is exactly what we are facing today. As a civilization to date, we are standing on a precipice at the end of which we must decide what we are willing to accept as the nature of the Internet, social media, and the major power players. Will we accept the current culture of technology as it relates to our humanistic division? Will we continue to follow its unquestionable allure similar to the hypnotic tune of the pied piper? Lanier (2010) reminds us:

> There hasn't yet been an adequate public rendering of an alternative worldview that opposes the new orthodoxy. In order to oppose orthodoxy, I have to provide more than a few jabs. I also have to realize an alternative intellectual environment that is

large enough to roam in. Someone who has been immersed in orthodoxy needs to experience a figure-ground reversal in order to gain perspective. (p. 23)

As with all great civilizations, like the Byzantine, the Egyptian, and the Roman Empires, there comes a time to face the societal pitfalls and determine if the division will help with its advancement or as a contribution to its downfall. Lanier is correct in stating we need to question the current orthodoxy. Without doing so, we can't change the trajectory. The use of technology today and its accompanying platforms have serious potential for either side of the coin. There must be a call to action that embraces the new metamodern culture which houses mankind's human-technology stage of development. The metamodern is asking that we redefine it with less unbridled human conflict and learn from this discord toward a more humanistic responsibility, thusly exposing the algorithms and political manipulations that keep us entrenched in online addictions and a deadened sense of empathy for our fellow human.

In all, this could be a distinct defining peak—the era when technology launches us into a more advanced society both technologically as well as humanistically. Lanier (2010) leaves us with this final note: "people are still able to steer the evolution of the net" and "against metahuman technological determinism" as "the net doesn't design itself. We design it" (p. 55). Let us break from the hypnotic and not be blindly led by the pied piper. It's time to change the narrative as the consumers. If we don't look out for ourselves (or our students), who will?

References

Freinacht, H. (2017). *The listening society: A metamodern guide to politics book one*. Metamodern ApS.
Henriques, G. (2020, April 17). What is modernism? *Psychology Today*. https://www.psychologytoday.com/us/blog/theory-knowledge/202004/what-is-metamodernism
Huebner, D. E., Pinar, W., & Hillis, V. (1999). *The lure of the transcendent: Collected essays by Dwayne E. Huebner*. Lawrence Erlbaum Associates.
interiority—Quick search results | Oxford English Dictionary. (n.d.). Retrieved June 13, 2024, from https://www.oed.com/search/dictionary/?scope=Entries&q=interiority&tl=true
Lanier, J. (2010). *You are not a gadget: A manifesto* (1st Vintage Books ed.). Vintage Books.
McChesney, R. W. (2008). *The political economy of media: Enduring issues, emerging dilemmas*. Monthly Review Press.
McLuhan, M. (1994). *Understanding media: The extensions of man* (1st MIT Press ed.). MIT Press.
Phillips, W. (2015). *This is why we can't have nice things: Mapping the relationship between online trolling and mainstream culture*. The MIT Press.

Pinar, W. (2011). *The character of curriculum studies: Bildung, currere, and the recurring question of the subject* (1st ed.). Palgrave Macmillan.

Springfield, M. A. 413 S. 8th S., & Us, I. 62701 P. 217 492-4241 C. (n.d.). *House divided speech—Lincoln home national historic site (U.S. National Park Service)*. Retrieved June 13, 2024, from https://www.nps.gov/liho/learn/historyculture/housedivided.htm

Taibbi, M. (2021). *Hate inc: Why today's media makes us despise one another: With a new post-election preface.* OR Books.

Turkle, S. (2015). *Reclaiming conversation: The power of talk in a digital age.* Penguin press.

Van den Akker, R., Gibbons, A., & Vermeulen, T. (2017). *Metamodernism: Historicity, affect and depth after postmodernism.* Rowman & Littlefield International

Vermeulen, T., & van den Akker, R. (2015, August 24). Misunderstandings and clarifications. *Notes on Metamodernism.* https://www.metamodernism.com/2015/06/03/misunderstandings-and-clarifications/

· 17 ·

HOW WAY LEADS ON TO WAY
David P. Owen, Jr.

"Two roads diverged in a yellow wood, and I—"

I love that dash (Frost, 1916/1992), and I love that poem, though not for the reasons lots of people love it. I love the old man's pause, his lie about "the one less traveled by," his affirmation of his choice after that dash to fight off the confusion and darkness of our wanderings, our past, by telling his audience what they want to hear. Not that I'm a big fan of lies, mind you; I just appreciate, and more every day, Frost's admission of the complexity of roads, and paths, and choices you're not sure you even made.

That dash gives the poem another layer, another voice somewhere between the words and the page, and that voice whispers "How did I get here? How did any of us get wherever it is that we are? Who among us can really stand in the dust of life's twilight and give directions to anyone?"

That voice echoes loud in my head when my students ask why I teach. As part of my answer, I teach that poem. I always say "I ended up teaching"—I didn't *choose* to teach, or *dream* to teach, or even *want* to teach so much as I *ended up teaching*—even though that doesn't quite tell it all, and my poems about my pathways would include far more dashes than Frost's. I do not mean to suggest it was accidental, or that I'm resigned to it, or that I wish I were somewhere else. I just don't think the answers are simple. I'm not sure I can trust the past; it's too reliant on ever-weakening memory, and our belief in others' storytelling, and our desires to paint a portrait of ourselves worth hanging in the hall. As Grumet puts it, the "selection of some events and the exclusion of others, the repudiation of some feelings and the acknowledgment of others, remind us that these accounts never can exactly coincide with our experience" (1980/1999, p. 25). The future, should it even exist already somehow, is at least too fuzzy for my nearsightedness, and is for me a realm of possibility I want to keep pluripotent. I am a creature of the liminal moment, between whatever has been and whatever will be, taking whatever opportunities come, and trying not to miss too many chances. And do I even know this moment? Am I here now, really living it? Do I get it, see it clearly? No wonder people have so often asked me, my whole career, if I'm coming back next year. But before I sound too much like Heinrich in *White Noise* (De Lillo, 1984), arguing with Jack Gladney about whether or not it's raining, let's start by keeping things simple. Besides, autobiography has been part of my career in curriculum theory from the beginning—I've approached it through literature and complexity theory (2011), the outdoors and Southern identity (2014), poetry (2017), and politics, religion, and popular music (not all at the same time, 2019). Shouldn't we, after all, consider all of the things we bring with us into the room in the morning? I can assure you it's not just Shakespeare and some lesson plans (even if you have a good bell ringer). Everything we say and do in a classroom comes from a *place*, and that place is inside us, and that place should not go unexamined. So, maybe I'll just try to tell it in a straight line for once, and see if that resonates with anyone thinking about this teacher-student life.

I was a young man without a vocation. I knew I would do something to earn my keep, and I trusted that I would work hard enough at it to be good at my job—I just didn't know what that job would be. I was interested in everything, it seemed, at least a little, and I still am. A wise young man once told me that you picked your major based on which books you wanted to keep at the end of the semester, and that's how it worked out for me. I just liked literature. I liked to read it, and think about it, and talk about it, and write about it. I liked the way books looked, and felt, and smelled, more than most things I could think of. I felt natural wandering shelves of books, making lists of things I'd read when I got a chance. So I studied literature, and like most things you live with for a while, I got pretty good at it.

When graduation began to loom, I considered a whole life of literature, and thought about a Ph.D. I could see myself on a leafy campus, heading from one conversation to another. I wasn't sure, though, about the specialization most fields require; one of the things I loved most about literature was the way it was a window to the world—all of it, maybe—and a way to explore and discuss everything under the sun. For example, I also found that I loved film, and I loved it more the more I studied it, and I especially liked to think about the ways those storytelling forms related to each other, and to everything else I could think of. The idea that I might need to narrow my focus to one writer, one era, one style, was not attractive to me. I've always been a generalist, more a "humanities" guy than a "literature" guy, really, and so I opted for a master's degree program to feel things out and figured I'd take stock again in two years. And my wife and I loved Athens, Georgia—I think it will always feel like a home to me—so we stayed in town, moved into a little duplex behind the baseball field, and embraced the poor graduate student life of art shows and readings and films and libraries and music.

Along the way, the university offered us both teaching positions that no poor, married graduate student could pass up. Tuition, a salary, and my own classes to teach? We pinched pennies and taught at the university, and loved it. I found that I really liked talking about things I felt were interesting and important, and trying to convince other people that those things were interesting and important, and good for them, too.

When those two years were up, I still wasn't sure about a Ph.D. in literature. I liked teaching, though, and thought I might try it somewhere else. High school seemed like the not-quite-college option to me, but I was wary. I hadn't enjoyed high school much myself, and so I really wasn't sure I would like going back to that world. We put in applications to school systems in nearby areas we might like to live in, and went with the first county to offer us both jobs. And so I found myself at the school where I still work, 24 years later, teaching literature and film classes.

That's not what I thought I was signing up for, though. I still played music a good bit, I was working on an album I believed in, and I was toying with the idea of pursuing music—or something else. I was by no means committed to a life of prom and pep rallies and lunch duty and parent emails and more awkwardly designed t-shirts than any closet could really hold. I was walking through the next open door, and keeping an eye out for a door at the end of that particular metaphorical hallway. I thought I'd try teaching until I figured out what I would *really* do with myself.

Why should you care about all of this? Because teaching snuck up on me, and I think it could sneak up on other people, too, who might not see education as a good career option.

I'll be honest, though—it was rough at first. That first year, with the door closed and a room full of students—even if they were younger than I was used to—talking about books and writing and big ideas, I actually felt pretty comfortable; that was in my wheelhouse. But outside the door I didn't quite know what to do with myself, and I felt like an alien. I got into a high school teaching position through the TAPP (Teacher Alternative Preparation Program), and I felt for a while like the rest of the building spoke an education-degree, teacher-prep-program language I didn't know, full of terms and color-coded charts I wasn't sure what to do with. I could handle analyzing literature, but it seemed like high school didn't have that much to do with analyzing literature, and that was a difficulty for me. What were you supposed to do on lunch duty? What if I had to break up a fight? What on earth were all those attendance codes? What if the students just outright refused to do the things I assigned?

But then I started to think about how I was watching a little pocket of America grow up—and I realized I might even get to have an effect on how America grew up. I started to think about the kind of surgeons, and bridge builders, and lawyers, and mechanics we all want in our communities—what did I want them to read, and know, and think about before they grew up to be the people next door? I was always most afraid as a young, vocation-less man that I would grow up to work in a cubicle and spend my life making a rich guy richer. But here, I got to help other people better understand the world, and find their own place in it. Maybe my place was to help people find theirs. Even on the worst days—and every teacher can tell you about the worst days—I realized that I got up every morning and helped people get the lives they wanted. I thought that maybe I could live with that.

I did get restless, though, about four or five years in, and I returned again to grad school. This time I chose a program in Curriculum Studies, which fit me like a glove—except that's not the right phrase, and feels too constrictive. Curriculum Studies hit me more like the rush of air from an opened door—the next open door I'd been looking for. Things felt wide open and fresh, and suddenly the whole world was even more interesting, and thoughtful, and thought-provoking, than I thought it had been. The gifted faculty of that program set me free as a teacher and curriculum theorist, and encouraged and challenged me in ways I didn't know I was looking for intellectually.

For four years, I was a full-time teacher and a full-time student. I didn't even take breaks, really; my wife and I were both in graduate programs at the same time (and therefore understood each other), so I often did marathon reading sessions even on the beach (that's fun for me, not torture, so don't read it wrong) during vacations, and I started on the next semester's reading lists as soon as my papers were sent off for my current classes. I know that's not for everyone—and no, we didn't have kids yet—but it was for me. Also, as abstract as graduate school is often assumed to be, and as philosophically-minded as that Curriculum Studies program could be, I found practical applications of my studies in every day of my teaching life. My graduate school experience helped me fill in the "why" of every decision I made as a teacher; it strengthened my backbone when times were tough, and energized me to be a more creative, imaginative teacher when times were good. I quickly became an advocate for my program and graduate studies in general, recommending books and ideas I'd come across to anyone who seemed like they might humor me for a few minutes. And sometimes when students would ask a "Why do we do this?" kind of question, boy did they ever get an answer.

And then just before I finished my dissertation, I was lucky enough to accompany some of the great professors and theorists I'd studied with to hear Mary Aswell Doll share her work on Flannery O'Connor in Savannah. At The Olde Pink House for dinner afterwards, I sat at a big round table with Dr. Doll, Marla Morris, William Reynolds, and John Weaver, trying not to get in the way of a quick-moving, deep and serious and funny and challenging conversation among people who had clearly known each other and worked together a long time. I was still considering joining a world like theirs, and that night they were very much what I had imagined years before that the "college professor life" would be like. Here it was right in front of me, just as interesting and stimulating as I'd imagined—it felt right. However, when the conversation came around to me, and what I was working on, and what I taught, things shifted for me in an interesting way. They were surprised at what my high school students would and could read and think about, and what kind of work they produced at their age. They were surprised that my teaching life sounded so good in so many ways, and so contrary to so many assumptions about the world of public school.

I told them about the books we read, and films we studied, and the questions students asked and arguments they made. Prompted by curiosity from around the table, pretty soon I was tying together these works into units, and then describing my overall vision for the courses—sometimes reminding myself, or maybe saying out loud for the first time, why I built those courses in just that way. As I would put it in my first book a year later, I was *"revising"* my work, seeing it fresh with new eyes, finding things in it that I maybe hadn't seen before. After really just a few minutes over dessert, my job started to sound like a pretty good one to me, and they agreed in a manner I think none of us was expecting before dinner. One of them said "maybe you should stay," just like an old friend sometimes points out what's right in front of you. And I did stay. I ended up teaching.

References

De Lillo, D. (1984). *White noise*. Penguin Books.

Frost, R. (1992). The road not taken. In *Robert Frost: Selected poems* (p. 163). Gramercy Books. (Original work published 1916)

Grumet, M. R. (1999). Autobiography and reconceptualization. In William F. Pinar (Ed.), *Contemporary curriculum discourses* (pp. 24–29). Peter Lang.

Owen, D. P., Jr. (2011). *The need for revision: Curriculum, literature, and the 21st century*. Sense Publishers.

Owen, D. P., Jr. (2014). *Duck dynasty* is a TV show: The Outdoors and southern identity. In William M. Reynolds (Ed.), *Critical studies of southern place: A reader* (pp. 162–170). Peter Lang.

Owen, D. P., Jr. (2017). *Fireflies: Memory, identity, and poetry*. Sense Publishers.

Owen, D. P., Jr. (2019). The possibility of a *search*. In *Field theory: Curriculum studies at work* (D. P. Owen, Jr., Ed.). DIO Press, Inc.

Owen, D. P., Jr. (2019). "To make some sense out of this mess": Popular art and Wilco. In *Field theory: Curriculum studies at work* (D. P. Owen, Jr., Ed.). DIO Press, Inc.

· 18 ·

GETTING THE BIG SCREEN THROUGH A SMALL DOOR: FILM AND THE HIGH SCHOOL CLASSROOM

David P. Owen, Jr.

Why Film?

I have been teaching film classes in a high school setting for roughly 15 years, and I have loved that experience every year. Those classes don't feel like my other classes, and I think the students would agree. For better and for worse, students (and I, I must admit) feel like we are leaving school a bit, somehow, when we come to film class. In fact, many teachers I have met give me a strange look when I tell them what I teach, like they think I've figured out how to get away with something. If what they mean is that I get to teach something in which students are actually interested, then I guess I agree with them.

Many of my film classes have been of the elective variety, full of a spectrum of students and student interests, and the goal most of the time has been appreciation and understanding of the art and nuance and difficulty of something they usually think of as weekend entertainment. Recently I have also been teaching a college-credit-earning IB film course, though, where the dedication and struggle are just as real and as stressful as any chemistry or math class. In both cases, the elective and the IB course, we have all discovered that studying film in high school is great but not always easy, for good and bad reasons. It is good for us all to discover how hard it is to make good films, and to realize that films are every bit as worthy of analysis and deep thinking as any other academic work. However, film also comes with some difficulties that other classes don't experience. For example, many districts don't allow R-rated films to be taught, which eliminates many of the form's greatest works (including one I will advocate for in this chapter), and sometimes even PG films are dangerous texts to choose, depending on local attitudes towards politics, language, sexual content, or violence. Things that will pass in a book just feel different on a screen sometimes. Access to the film itself can also be a problem these days. As more and more of our visual storytelling happens on a streaming service, classrooms struggle to find good ways to include it. No streaming service, as we all know, has everything you might want—and many districts aren't buying a subscription to those services anyway; in fact, some even ban those streaming services outright. Even teachers who decide to opt for the outdated technology of the DVD, as I often do, will discover that you can't really assign films for homework, since you're only buying one DVD; this means using an average of three days in class to screen films, and giving the kinds of assignments they can do without the film in front of them at home. Access, budgets, content issues—these are all problems that might have different solutions in different communities. I've found that the biggest struggle, though, is getting students (and parents) to treat film as a subject worth all the trouble in the first place.

In my own experience, and also based on the testimonies of students, when most secondary educators bring film into their classrooms, they treat it as supplementary material, as something *extra*. Sometimes they use it to reinforce understanding of a novel or play the class has read; sometimes they offer it as a reward for good behavior or performance; and other times they seem to use it when they simply have too many papers to grade. However, we ought not to treat film as if it could be replaced by a pizza party, and it ought not to replace us a substitute teacher, either. We ought to ask much more of film, understanding it and teaching it as the full artistic, textual learning experience it can be.

There are many reasons film should be more respected as a site for teaching and learning in today's curriculum. Not only does it seem that the "printed word tradition that initially dominated the language of cultural interfaces is becoming less important, while the part played by cinematic elements is becoming progressively stronger" (Manovich, 2001, p. 78), but Schrader (2006) also goes so far as to say that "motion pictures were the dominant art for the 20th century" (p. 35). Furthermore, while many who acknowledge film's power in our culture still exclude it from canonical discussions because of its just-over-100-year-old history, Schrader reminds us that the very idea of a canon is "only 200 years old" and based on a way of looking at art that has been "called into question in the 20th century" (p. 38). In some ways, film's relative youth as an art form even works in its favor, and not just because students enjoy it more; it can be an especially useful way to teach contemporary artistic issues, having developed in some cases alongside many of the last century's important movements. For example, Boggs (2001) notes that "creative directors like Orson Welles, Alfred Hitchcock, Fritz Lang, and Billy Wilder" (p. 355) explored many of the themes connected with postmodernism in the 1950s, and their early work often shows "cracks in [the] 'modern' edifice" (p. 355) that hint at the death of "grand narratives" (p. 37) announced by Lyotard in 1979. In short, film has not been nearly as "marginal" as the current curriculum would have students believe.

Treated with the respect and attention we routinely give works of "traditional" art and literature, film proves to be, at its best, an incredibly dense, complex art form, offering a multitude of pathways for text exploration and instruction whether it is studied in connection to conventional art and literature or not. In many ways, films can possess many of the most important and appreciated aspects of other art forms; clearly, for example, they can share the three-dimensional feel, emotion, and kinesthetic appeal of drama, among other elements. But they can also offer the breadth of plot and character development found in novels, the beautiful language of spoken poetry, the episodic intensity of short stories, and the impassioned rhetorical flourishes of great essays, all in varying combinations ripe for interpretation. Films have been sites for great (and often discussion-starting) explorations of history, and they have featured, and fostered, countless advances in science and technology. We are also often treated to the added pleasure of a sort of painting-in-motion and accompanying music, occasionally designed and directed by the day's most talented visual artists and composers. And let's not forget that our films take place on complex, nuanced, amazingly-detailed sets constructed by an army of expert men and women from a variety of trades. Films are, at their best, a meeting place for all curricular fields, the product of hundreds of different experts working together toward one goal; they are what we can make when our classrooms don't have so many walls.

The textbook we use in my own film classes argues that film studies is "part of a rich and complex history that overlaps with critical work in many other fields, such as literary studies, philosophy, and art history" (Corrigan

& White, 2009, p. 7), and I have certainly found that to be the case. For example, I have found that *Modern Times* (Chaplin, 1936) is a history lesson of pop culture, technology, and society; if you follow it with *Singin' in the Rain* (Donen & Kelly, 1952) and *Sunset Boulevard* (Wilder, 1950), you can extend that lesson and also get a chance to grapple with our relationship with celebrity culture. If you want American history, a genre study of the western would cover a surprising amount of ground; *The Searchers* (Ford, 1956), *Butch Cassidy and the Sundance Kid* (Hill, 1969), and *Dances With Wolves* (Costner, 1990) are some of my favorites for just such a purpose, and can often show us, on screen and in the stories we tell, how America has changed over the decades, even if all the films are set in nearly the same time and place. A film like *The Lord of the Rings: Fellowship of the Ring* (Jackson, 2001) is an excellent chance to study craftsmanship of all kinds, and see the way art departments can build worlds on screen, transport us to places we could not otherwise go—and so is *Casablanca* (Curtiz, 1942), set in a wartime Morocco and Paris that could obviously not be used for filming on location. *2001: A Space Odyssey* (Kubrick, 1968), *Gravity* (Cuaron, 2013), *Interstellar* (Nolan, 2014), and *Star Wars* (Lucas, 1977) are all excellent sites for a discussion of our interests in, expectations of, and desires from space exploration, whether we are in physics, astronomy, or political science class. Even a film like *O Brother, Where Art Thou?* (Cohen & Cohen, 2000), full of absurdist and often low-brow comedy, can upon closer look be an excellent text for the study of how we put a culture on screen (in this case the American south), and of what responsibilities we might have in doing so.

This list is by no means exhaustive, and I would actually love the challenge of finding films for every high school course. Despite its 100-year history, film still feels like a barely-touched resource for the public school curriculum. Even if films are only included in the language arts curriculum in the usual, more superficial ways, they can still be worthwhile. Films inspired by literary works can certainly be used, and sometimes are, to reinforce traditional print works, helping students to see in comparing the two formats devoted to the same content that even "books do not exist as unchanging, stone tablets but are meant to be interacted and transacted with" (Sweeney, 2006, p. 32). Students may begin through intertextual study to understand that books, experienced properly, are also living, moving, dynamic things that invite participation and discussion.

Film, though, should not be taught only as a supplement to literature, or history, or science, or any other field. It is as rich an artistic text as we have ever devised, and often gives us a chance to consider our most central, most difficult questions of the human condition. In fact, I offer two film texts for just such curricular consideration: *Citizen Kane* (Welles, 1941) and *Three Colors: Blue* (Kieslowski, 1993). Though these films do not at first glance belong together in very many ways, they are both excellent curricular texts that give us a chance to ask who we are, in ways both big and small, personal and abstract, and to consider how we think we know that.

Citizen Kane

Given its 1941 publication date, *Citizen Kane* might seem at first to be an unusual starting point for a more "contemporary" and relevant arts curriculum. However, not only does Welles's work explore some of the same themes that many of our most recent works in all media discuss, but we must also remember that in some fields, like the arts, 1941 *is* recent; a curriculum that often begins with *The Odyssey* or cave paintings leaves many teachers scrambling to squeeze in as much work from the last century as they can at the end of spring semester. Also, having been trained to privilege history, some arts teachers give works produced around and after World War II very little time, if any at all, trusting that the "classics" are more important. In this setting, "old" films are really more like the beginning of the "new" media we see everywhere today; to jump from T.S. Eliot directly to the digital hypermedia currently being developed would be to skip a lot of important steps along the way. One of those important steps is *Citizen Kane*, which Schrader (2006) calls "a textbook example" of a classic: "There is nothing about it—cinematography, composition, editing, performances, sound effects—that hasn't been copied and recopied" (p. 46) by the generations of artists since it appeared.

One of the most interesting arts discussions to pursue with film is that of authorship, since it is so hard to locate in the final product. In such a discussion, students quickly notice that a film seems to have a multitude of authors, including screenwriters, directors, actors, editors, and most importantly, the camera itself, which is a film's most powerful voice, despite its frequent attempts to seem inconspicuous. Among many other things, *Citizen Kane* is perfect for a lesson on authorship and storytelling, due to its complex narrative technique, numerous points of view, and clever plot devices. For example, the film is organized as a frame story about a quest to know the elusive, difficult, and recently deceased Charles Foster Kane, in particular the meaning of the now-infamous "Rosebud" (3rd minute) he uttered just before he died.

In this quest, we are taken on a news reporter's journey through Kane's life as told by those who knew him best, searching for the clues that will (we hope) explain everything.

As is the case with most landmark films, *Citizen Kane* means many things to many people. Some see Orson Welles's legendary first film as a story about innocence lost or stolen; some call it a biography of an American robber baron (or yellow journalist, depending); some read it as a tale of a man without love. Perhaps the most popular position on this film is the one which interprets the story of Charles Foster Kane as a quest for a Holy Grail of sorts, a journey into the very heart of what drives a man when all else is stripped away. This particular reading of *Citizen Kane* has inspired endless debate about the now-famous "Rosebud" and what it might have meant to a multi-millionaire newspaperman on his deathbed. However, though most interpretations of *Kane* return to the elusive meaning of "Rosebud," this is certainly not the only aspect of this film that merits attention, and in many ways it is not even the most interesting. In fact, the discussion in these pages is much less concerned with what "Rosebud" means than with what "Rosebud" does, and it is not nearly as interested in the tale as it is in the telling of it.

One of the many things Orson Welles offers his audience in *Citizen Kane* is a fascinating narrative. The director constructs a brilliant and densely layered web of rumor, myth, and hearsay through which the viewer is pulled by the mystery of an old man's last word. In terms of Welles's narrative strategy, Rosebud is merely the impetus, like a dangling carrot in the viewer's race to discover a man. The fact that the narrative, supposedly leading to the "real" story of Kane's life, is ultimately elusive in nature is part of the point, making *Citizen Kane* a film that does not lead its audience to discover the true nature of Charles Kane so much as it asks if Kane can be known at all. After all, a team of reporters could not even figure out Rosebud, much less learn anything substantial and/or reliable about the man himself.

To attempt to tell the private story of a public man, the direction of Welles's narrative moves generally from the outside in, from old to young, from business to personal, and from acquaintance to "loved" one. This method results in a set of perhaps-overlapping circles around Charles Kane, kind of like ripples in a body of water, except there seem to be multiple pebbles causing those ripples. The idea, as it works out in the film, is that if viewers start with the least familiar or helpful informant (the farthest circle), Mr. Thatcher, and go through Mr. Bernstein, Jed Leland, and Susan Alexander to the most helpful informant (the nearest circle), or the butler who actually heard Kane utter the famous word, then they will eventually reach an understanding of both "Rosebud" and the man who said it. Welles decides to reveal his title character only through a newsreel and one-on-one interviews with the people close to Kane, and this choice is especially appropriate in the case of a newspaper tycoon. Though logic seems to present a minor problem for Welles's more artistic narrative design in the beginning, since interviewing Kane's wife first would just make good sense, the director works around the problem by supplying his audience with the first attempted conversation with Susan Alexander. In this truncated interview, one can almost hear Welles speaking through Susan to his audience, as if he feels he must first officially discard conventional storytelling techniques:

THOMPSON: I thought maybe we could have a talk together.
SUSAN: Well, think again. (16th minute)

Free now to take any path he chooses, Welles sends his reporter to the outer rim of Kane's circle of "friends," Mr. Thatcher. Thatcher at this time is also dead, so Thompson visits his memorial library in order to read his diary entries concerning Kane. The information Thompson picks up from this first informant is helpful, but it only moves the reporter slightly closer to the real man than does the "News on the March" segment about his life that begins the film. The series of flashbacks taken from Thatcher's account serve as a sort of timeline of Kane's life up through the Depression, consisting primarily of the highlights of Kane's financial adventures and offering few glances into the character of the man. The information in these flashbacks is fairly broad, especially concerning Kane's adolescence, and it does fill in a few details not covered in the newsreel (leaving home, Christmases, arguments with Thatcher). However, though Thatcher does know a great deal about Kane the businessman, he knows little about the motivations for Kane's decisions or about the kind of person he is outside of work. Thatcher did adopt Kane, but he was always much more of a guardian than a father ("you were always too old" (29th minute)), and so it is no surprise that the old banker knows nothing about something as personal as "Rosebud."

The second interview is also with a business associate, Mr. Bernstein, but this one presents the audience with a different kind of information and paints a much different picture of Charles Foster Kane than does Thatcher's. The viewer is alerted to this fact almost immediately by the overly-large portrait of Kane in the accountant's office. The relationship here is also one revolving around business, but Bernstein's memories depict something akin to a boys' club, complete with devil-may-care takeovers and dancing girls after work. The flashbacks in this segment are also a little more personal, presenting Kane as a public defender at best ("declaration of principles" (39th minute)) and a harmless playboy at worst (see his return from European vacation, with countless priceless souvenirs (46th minute)). Bernstein also attributes Charles Kane with a healthy modesty, seen during his awkward wedding announcement to the Inquirer staff, that does not appear much in the first flashback. Thatcher does include the scene during the Depression in his diary, when Kane rues "I could have been a very great man," but even then, he is quick to remind the audience of Kane's more impetuous side, such as responding to Thatcher that he would like to be "everything you hate" (30th minute). Bernstein is indeed closer to the mystery of Kane than was Thatcher, but he is also puzzled by Kane's utterance of "Rosebud." His guess, just like his other comments on Kane, is a romantic one, musing that it is probably something he lost; after all, he "lost almost everything he had" (49th minute).

By the time Thompson reaches Jed Leland, the third informant, a careful viewer will notice that Welles has changed his direction on the path toward knowledge of Charles Kane or "Rosebud"; the audience is now traveling in two directions at once, moving both closer to Kane and farther from him. Welles reveals this paradox through the unusual memory of Jedidiah Leland, which seems to have the power to recall events of which he could not possibly have direct knowledge. Even if Leland has gathered some of the information from Emily or Charles himself, it has still been filtered through two sets of minds and emotions before Thompson hears it. Leland does reliably fill in some holes for the audience (scenes which actually include Jed), such as Kane's political career and the destruction of their friendship, but many of the other flashbacks are suspect. Though Leland assures Thompson of the accuracy of his memory just like Bernstein did, this segment explores Kane's relationship with his first wife through a series of breakfasts, the early stages of Kane's courtship of Susan Alexander, and the pivotal scene in Kane's political career with Jim Gettys, all of which are very private episodes which took place when Leland was not around. Leland insists on the power of his memory, but it is the detail of his imagination that is truly impressive. These are perhaps the most revealing glances into the life of Charles Kane, and yet they are certainly the least reliable. Even Kane's best friend is no help in the reporter Thompson's quest to discover the meaning of "Rosebud"; Leland's comments on this matter are as affected as his memories by a friendship gone wrong, dismissing the topic by saying, "I never believed anything I saw in the Inquirer" (52nd minute).

Finally, Thompson returns to Susan Alexander, who becomes the fourth informant. Susan is even closer to Kane and "Rosebud" than Leland, being not only his wife but also the person who knew him most intimately in his last years. However, Susan is also extremely biased and unreliable, only in different ways than was Jedidiah. For one, Susan *only* knew him late in life, which Welles has already told the audience through Susan's admission that she knows nothing about Kane in the pair's first scene together. This fact affects the information that she is able to reveal to the audience, since she only knows the man Kane had become and nothing about what brought him to that point. Her flashbacks also have a different feel than do the others, focusing more on Susan than on Kane. These memories are not insights into Kane's life by someone who knew him well, but rather insights into Susan's life and the part Kane played in it. Since these scenes depict *her* singing career, *her* struggles against Kane's will, *her* isolation in Xanadu, and *her* decision to leave, it is plain to Thompson that Susan would not understand "Rosebud" either, unless it directly impacted her life.

The last informant, Raymond, is the only character the audience meets who claims to have actually heard Kane say "Rosebud." However, he is also the least helpful, providing only an account of the events that led to the first utterance of the word, not a reason *why* he said it. Raymond is the closest character to understanding "Rosebud," but he is probably the farthest from understanding Charles Kane. Raymond has worked for Kane for ten years, but his relationship is with Xanadu, not Kane, and this fact plays a big part in making his information so anti-climactic. Indeed, in terms of the narrative, Raymond's only real function is to provide the audience with someone to relate Kane's last scene after Susan leaves. Thompson soon understands the futility of the interview, and leaves to survey the rest of the house with the other reporters. Though Welles finally reveals, in the film's last few moments, the secret of "Rosebud" despite Thompson's failure, he leaves his viewers with a symbol detached from its meaning.

The problem with the audience's quest to understand "Rosebud" and Kane through Welles's narrative is fourfold. First, and most obviously, the only real information about Kane available to the audience is secondary; Welles only gives the viewer direct access to Kane on his deathbed. Second, though Welles does provide the audience with a set of (hopefully?) concentric circles, or ripples, surrounding the recently departed Kane, following these circles through the interviews does not lead to a definite and shared center, or Kane's "true" identity. This is partly because the larger circles do not contain the smaller ones; the flashback narratives do not rely on each other and usually only overlap superficially. Since each character had his or her own relationship with Kane, each naturally has a different type of information to give about him. However, the result of hearing such varying accounts is that Thompson cannot discover the essence of the man, because each informant seems to have known a completely different Charlie Kane. Thatcher's adoption of Kane was always more like an acquisition (their conversations rarely stray far from Kane's fortune), and so their personal relationship was often tainted by bitterness. His Kane is generally an irresponsible, foolish, ungrateful brat content to squander his fortune playing the rebel to his guardian. If Thatcher's view of Kane is almost entirely negative, Bernstein counters it with an overwhelmingly positive testimony to the character of his boss. Bernstein does know more about the man than his guardian ever did, but the accountant's view is equally tainted; his version of Kane is an intelligent, idealist, modest, honorable defender of the common man. Jed Leland proves to be both the best and most biased (or most hurt) friend of the mysterious man, and he presents a Kane that differs from both Thatcher's and Bernstein's: Kane to Leland is a man who acts like a "swine," a man who loved himself before anything or anyone, a fallen hero who sold his soul and his cause for the right to do exactly as he pleased, no matter the consequences. Susan's flashbacks show the intense pressure she always felt from Kane, since these scenes often find her emotionally distraught. She portrays Kane as a maniacal, merciless dictator completely devoid of feeling or consideration for others. The final Kane, the one described by Raymond, is simply a man who "did crazy things sometimes" (108th minute), a depressed, bizarre enigma who wandered his mansion aimlessly. Each version of the mythical figure may be connected to the true Kane, but the audience will never know; the ripples on the surface remain, but the pebble has sunk to the bottom, if it is indeed one pebble, and the "true" Kane is gone.

The third problem for the audience concerns the paradox illustrated by Leland's imagination/memory, and this paradox speaks not only about the quest for posthumous knowledge of Kane, but also about the quest for knowledge about people in general. Moving as Welles does from the people who knew Kane the least to the people who knew him the most requires a trade-off: whatever Thompson gains through the increasing knowledge of his informants, he also loses in the same proportion through their various biases and emotional baggage. The more he learns about Kane, the less he can trust. Finally, the interview with Raymond shows another trade-off that Thompson discovers in his search, namely that the closer one gets to seeing one aspect of a man, or one piece of the puzzle, the harder it is to see the man as a whole; this kind of focus is the reason why "Rosebud" is such an empty symbol. These realizations about the ability of one man to know another are not limited to *Citizen Kane*, and Welles puts the ultimate question his narrative asks into the mouth of Jerry Thompson: "I wonder: if you put all this stuff together—palaces, toys, paintings, and everything—what would it spell?" (114th minute). Maybe Charles Foster Kane, maybe not, but one can never know for sure. We are left not only pondering the reliability of our various narrators but also our power to "know" each other at all. With the puzzle solved but the picture still cloudy, we are left looking at a shot of the same "No Trespassing" sign that opened the film. These competing characterizations, varied storytelling styles, and masterfully executed plot devices are only the barely-scratched surface of artistic elements in *Citizen Kane*, which offers opportunities for deep thinking and analysis that rival many works already in our various canons.

Three Colors: Blue

It is the mark of a great storyteller that he or she can sometimes tell a story without literally *telling* the story; in fact, the ideas expressed are often much more effective and profound for their lack of explicit revelation. Krzysztof Kieslowski is this kind of storyteller, and like *Citizen Kane*, *Three Colors: Blue* is more a work of modern art than the kind of "movie" most students will encounter on a weekend at the local theater. Kieslowski's film is a complex piece of a complex trilogy, focused on such abstract notions as liberty and what it means to be an artist and creator. He takes us to a place of rich color and music that is as tangible and affecting as it is subjective and completely independent of the natural laws of cause and effect. In the depiction of Kieslowski's fantastic universe, the auteur particularly uses mise-en-scene (color, especially, of course) and the soundtrack to establish Julie as an artist, a "composer," a character with the power to bend, mold, create, and destroy both the sounds and the people of her world. However, for all her power, Julie cannot orchestrate everything, and this realization is where the story begins.

In the film's first few minutes, it may seem to the audience that the amount of information available to them is significantly restricted. We see the wreck, but do not even know if Julie is the woman in the car or if the man was her husband, let alone whether or not anyone died. We do not know (and, in fact, never know) where they are going or why. We also have no idea that her dead husband was known internationally as a great composer of music, helped by the fact that for the film's first ten minutes, there is no music in the soundtrack. However, Kieslowski does not completely leave his audience in the dark; he only asks that we look to devices less obvious than dialogue or narration for our story information. For example, the film opens with the camera spending an extensive amount of time behind the tire of the car, which, if nothing else, leads us to consider the director's motivation for such a shot. Later, when the car stops on the side of the road, the camera shows the audience a more unrestricted range of information in the form of the leak in the brake line, which tells us, albeit subtly, what will happen to the car. From these first few minutes, Kieslowski has established the way in which he will tell the story by showing us both the more artistic style he will employ throughout the film (shot of brake line) and the classical see-the-car-crashed-into-a-tree method as a sort of practice run for the active spectator, allowing the audience to connect his use of film functions (particularly color and sound later on) with events in the plot.

From here, the focus shifts to Julie, and it will not often stray from her the rest of the film. We don't initially know anything about Julie, excepting her desperation and hurt in her attempt at suicide after the loss of her family, which are certainly emotions that do not set her apart from the average person. However, Julie is special, and Kieslowski leads us to understand this gradually. The film's first music is offered as diegetic sound from a band playing at Patrice and Anna's funeral, heard through the television by Julie. Here we learn not only that her husband was a composer, but we are also given a hint as to the importance of music in the film and to Julie. The film's first non-diegetic music and color come after about 12 minutes, during the scene in which a reporter approaches Julie in the hospital. The scene is certainly a puzzling one, but it firmly establishes Julie's connection both with music and the color blue. She is awakened from sleep (in a blue chair) by booming music, though its source is not identified. She is completely enveloped by a strange blue light while the music plays. When the scene returns to normal, the reporter speaks, apparently triggering the first of four blackouts in the film, where nothing is visible in the frame and only the music is heard. Kieslowski has already begun blurring the lines of subjective and objective reality in this scene. After all, the flash of color is different than a normal subjective one like those experienced by the murderer in *Rear Window* (Hitchcock, 1954); the blue is more like something seen from the camera's position as a sort of third-person observer. The director contributes to this strange connection between Julie, blue, and music with the curious question posed by the reporter: "Is it true you wrote your husband's music?" (13th minute).

When Julie returns home, this relationship is revealed a little more. First, she has asked to have "the blue room" completely cleared and visits it, a scene in which we first see the blue lamp. From here, Julie seems to follow the non-diegetic piano music down to the piano. We see that sheets of music have been lying open, and the music stops when Julie closes them. This power she now seems to have over the music is further established soon after, when the camera follows the music on the sheets while Julie plays it (or does she?) on the piano. However, when the music on the sheets stops, Julie keeps playing as if it did not, with the camera following the blank staff on the paper. As Julie suddenly slams down the top of the piano, showing her face lit by a blue light from an unknown source, we begin to wonder if the reporter was not correct.

The audience comes to a greater understanding of Julie's role in the relationship with music and the color blue through her attempted rejection of it. The audience also learns that Julie's talent for composing is not limited to music. When Julie visits the archives, she takes the music for the Unification Concert (full of corrections in Julie's blue, which are "no more than usual" (22nd minute)) and throws them in a garbage compactor, stopping the non-diegetic chorus that had begun when the sheets were opened and examined. She later shows her power to conduct lives as well in the "love" scene with Olivier. Again, her face is in blue and music begins (she begins composing?) when she begins to undress. Her rejection of the Julie that had existed before the crash has begun: she has sold all her belongings, destroyed unfinished music, tried to ruin her relationship with Olivier, and will soon start to go by her maiden name, all the while trying to convince herself and others that she is "like any other woman" (28th minute). However, she can't completely let go, as seen by the reappearance of the non-diegetic music she was writing when she looks at the glass pieces of the blue lamp (34th minute), the only thing she takes with her when she leaves her home.

Though Julie says she wants no memories, she is not able to shake her former life and her identity as an artist. The music and the color blue keep haunting her, refusing to let her forget. The music shows up everywhere, whether it is in her head as she is leaving the pool or being played by a man on the street, and it seems to be just waiting for her to close her eyes to reappear. The blue is also ever-present; it finds its way into her clothes and the clothes of those around her (the dancer, the old woman on the sidewalk), it shows up on her face, and it even appears behind her eyelids on the staircase when she is locked out. Other parts of her life follow her, too: Olivier won't obey her command not to miss her, her husband's necklace and mistress certainly interfere with her forgetting, and the episode with the extermination of the mice in her new apartment serves as a particularly painful reminder both of her daughter and her power to create and destroy. This last point is driven home by the appearance of the little girls for swimming lessons, visually solidifying the connection between Anna and the mice offspring with their swimsuits and bathing caps.

Julie can move out of her home, hide from Olivier, and hire the services of a cat to avoid the reminder of the mice, but she cannot shake the blue and music, and she finally realizes that it is because they are at the very heart of what she is. This lesson, that without these things she literally has "nothing" to do, as she frequently states, does not come easy, of course. In order to understand what she must be, she must first understand why she does not want to keep trying to forget herself and her life, which is shown by Kieslowski through two examples. The first example is her new friend, the exotic dancer in her building. Julie definitely seems fond of this woman, though it seems to be based in feeling sorry for her, both for her treatment and for her way of life. The dancer also wears blue, and when she visits to thank Julie (49th minute) she tells her that she also had a blue lamp like Julie's when she was little, and that she always dreamed of being able to reach it. However, she has forgotten about it until just then, enjoying a chance for short moment to have the blue light fall on her face. This story makes Julie uncomfortable to the point of needing to excuse herself from the room to attend to the flowers. In a plot device that draws the parallel between the dancer's story and Julie's life, both women seem disappointed that the man on the street has left his flute behind, just as Julie has tried to leave her music behind.

The second example is Julie's mother. When Julie visits her (57th minute), she tells her that she has "no home anymore," which is a strange statement, considering that her mother lives in a nursing home and has no "home" of her own, either. Through her mother's Alzheimer's disease (?), Julie also sees what it would really be like to live with no memory. She is visibly frustrated and saddened, and does not stay long. Through these two examples, Julie has finally realized, as the man on the street told her, that "You always gotta hold on to something" (48th minute).

What Julie has learned is that though she does seem to have a gift for "composing," she cannot control everything, shown by the loss of her family, the failure of her marriage life, and her unsuccessful attempt to forget it all. She has also learned that her exceptional abilities to compose are sometimes reciprocal; Julie's blue and music, her creative power or muse and her artistic expression, also have significant control over her. Through her period of rejection, specifically the blackout scenes (during which she is weakest and the music and blue are most dominant), Kieslowski has shown that we are sometimes bent to the will of our art just as much as it is bent to our own. Once Julie accepts this, she returns to Olivier and her life as an artist. In the film's most powerful scene, the camera falls out of focus and returns as Julie allows herself to be fully absorbed in the creation of her art, beginning a magical episode in which the two composers pull choruses, trumpets, strings, and percussion out of the air, writing and correcting as an invisible orchestra obeys their every command. Julie has returned to her "true" identity and her home. She is now comfortable as the "composer" of things, orchestrating the start of her husband's son's life and joyfully finishing her concert in, of course, a blue shirt and blue ink.

Through creative and extensive use of color and sound, Kieslowski has told a story about complex human emotions and issues with surprisingly few words. In weaving such a gorgeous, emotional tale, Kieslowski has drawn in his audience by appealing to the full range of senses that his medium will allow. It is no wonder that Kieslowski's depiction of the sights, sounds, feelings, and ideas associated with being an artist is so vivid, because his telling of Julie's story in *Blue* has shown that he, also, is truly a "composer."

Why Not Film?

Who are we, anyway, and what sort of lives should we lead? What do those lives "mean"? Should we ask others, or look deep inside for some core essence, maybe only knowable to us? Are we "born" to certain things, or do we become who we are through experience? Are we "meant" to live certain lives, or can we choose whatever path we like, beholden only to the rules and codes and values we set ourselves? Can fate sometimes thrust upon us a life that would not otherwise have been a result of our genes or our choices? These are questions these two films ask, and they are also questions we all ask at some point, and maybe at many points. And they are certainly questions teenagers ask—one haircut, friend group, hobby, or pop culture obsession to the next. Sometimes, if we're lucky, they even ask using words, and we get to talk about it.

Is school, maybe, the place where we discover who we are? Can it be? Anthony T. Kronman, for example, asserts in *Education's End* (2007) that "the meaning of life is a subject that can be studied in school" (p. 5), and that "the question of how to spend [our lives] is the most important question we face" (p. 9, my brackets); he even thinks that "all our lesser attachments appear at times to depend upon" the "question of what living is for" (p. 27). William F. Pinar argues that autobiography is "the task of self formation, deformation, learning, and unlearning" (1985/1994, p. 217)—that "the curriculum is not comprised of subjects, but of Subjects, of subjectivity," and "the running of the course is the building of the self, the lived experience of subjectivity" (p. 220). He adds elsewhere that "without encountering the complexity of one's life history and biographic situation, one cannot appreciate how to reposition oneself in private-and-public space" (2004, p. 200). In other words, both Kronman and Pinar insist that education is a vital and deeply personal experience, tied tightly to identity and subjective experience. Madeline R. Grumet, as well, has advocated an education full of "reflexive analysis," motivated by an "aspiration that it will enable the student to become the active interpreter of his past, as well as to heighten his capacity to be the active agent of his own interests in a present that he shares with his community" (1980/1999, p. 28).

Not everyone thinks this kind of work will be easy, though. Some, like Dennis J. Sumara, have pointed out the complexity of our classrooms, which he calls a "myriad of ever-evolving relationships: between teacher and students, students and each other, teacher and texts, students and texts"; to him, these relationships "overlap and intertwine," and "we are indeed entangled in them, and in no way can discern their beginnings and endings" (1993/1999, p. 290). Maybe, it seems, it might be hard for students—or us—to tell what belongs "completely" to who we are; when do we originate and influence, and when do we take influence from elsewhere? Where do we start or end? David Geoffrey Smith goes further, and points out that our notion of identity relies in large part on things like "the ancient Etruscan understanding of 'person,' which comes from the Latin word 'mask' (L. persona)" (1996/1999, p. 460). He later argues that our discussion, our very concept of identity, "depends on an assumption of the possibility of identity, that somehow if only I could change my circumstances the real me would have a chance to flourish, to find itself" (pp. 461–462). Maybe what we have is just a "fiction of identity" (p. 462), a kind of story we tell ourselves about who we are, or might be.

In this case, twisting his words a bit, we have two (film) "fictions of identity." *Citizen Kane* seems to give us an ever-out-of-reach identity, or the possibility of many identities—or maybe the absence of any single, core, discoverable identity at all. There are many Charles Foster Kane's, or no Charles Foster Kane, depending—and why would we be any different, gold-mine fortunes aside? *Three Colors: Blue*, on the other hand, seems to argue often for a core, undeniable essence or identity that cannot be discarded or destroyed, no matter the trauma or dedicated efforts to leave it behind. The good news there, I guess, is that the eventual embrace of that identity is fulfilling, and productive, and adds beauty to the world we live in, even if there is much pain in the process of that embrace.

I certainly don't know if either film has it right, or even if one is more on the right track than the other; being only human, and a teacher-student myself, I'm always learning (I hope) about me and everything else. I do know, though, that both films offer numerous opportunities to ask the biggest questions, to explore the most important issues, to start the kinds of conversations that any thoughtful young person should have—and that is a classroom I want to be part of.

References

Boggs, C. (2001). Postmodernism the movie. *New Political Science, 23*(3), 351–370.
Chaplin, C. (Director). (1936). *Modern times* [Film]. Charles Chaplin Productions.
Cohen, J., & Cohen, E. (Directors). (2000). *O brother, where art thou?* [Film]. Touchstone Pictures; Universal Pictures; StudioCanal.
Corrigan, T., & White, P. (2009). *The film experience: An introduction*. Bedford/St. Martin's.
Costner, K. (Director). (1990). *Dances with wolves* [Film]. Tig Productions; Majestic Films International; Allied Filmmakers.
Cuaron, A. (Director). (2013). *Gravity* [Film]. Warner Bros.; Esperanto Filmoj; Heyday Films.
Curtiz, M. (Director). (1942). *Casablanca* [Film]. Warner Bros.
Donen, S., & Kelly, G. (Directors). (1952). *Singin' in the rain* [Film]. Metro-Goldwyn-Mayer.
Ford, J. (Director). (1956). *The searchers* [Film]. C. V. Whitney Pictures.
Grumet, M. R. (1999). Autobiography and reconceptualization. In William F. Pinar (Ed.), *Contemporary curriculum discourses: Twenty years of JCT* (pp. 24–30). Peter Lang. (Original work published 1980)
Hill, G. R. (Director). (1969). *Butch Cassidy and the Sundance Kid* [Film]. Campanile Productions; George Roy Hill—Paul Monash Production; Newman-Foreman Company.
Hitchcock, A. (Director). (1954). *Rear window* [Film]. Alfred J. Hitchcock Productions.
Jackson, P. (Director). (2001). *The lord of the rings: The fellowship of the ring* [Film]. New Line Cinema; WingNut Films; The Saul Zaentz Company.

Kieslowski, K. (Director). (1993). *Trois couleurs: Bleu* [Three Colors: Blue] [Film]. MK2 Productions; CED Productions; France 3 Cinema.

Kronman, A. T. (2007). *Education's end: Why our colleges and universities have given up on the meaning of life.* Yale University Press.

Kubrick, S. (Director). (1968). *2001: A space odyssey* [Film]. Metro-Goldwyn-Mayer; Stanley Kubrick Productions.

Lucas, G. (Director). (1977). *Star wars: Episode iv—A new hope* [Film]. Lucasfilm; Twentieth Century Fox.

Lyotard, J.-F. (1984). *The postmodern condition: A report on knowledge* (G. Bennington & B. Massumi, Trans.). University of Minnesota Press. (Original work published in 1979)

Manovich, L. (2001). *The language of new media.* The MIT Press.

Nolan, C. (Director). (2014). *Interstellar* [Film]. Paramount Pictures; Warner Bros.; Legendary Entertainment.

Pinar, W. F. (1994). *Autobiography, politics, and sexuality: Essays in curriculum theory 1972–1992.* Peter Lang.

Pinar, W. F. (2004). *What is curriculum theory?* Lawrence Erlbaum Associates.

Schrader, P. (2006). Canon fodder. *Film Comment*, September–October, 33–49.

Smith, D. G. (1999). Identity, self, and other in the conduct of pedagogical action: An east/west inquiry. In William F. Pinar (Ed.), *Contemporary curriculum discourses: Twenty years of JCT* (pp. 458–473). Peter Lang. (Original work published 1996)

Sumara, D. J. (1999). Of seagulls and glass roses: Teachers' relationships with literary texts as transformational space. In William F. Pinar (Ed.), *Contemporary curriculum discourses: Twenty years of JCT* (pp. 289-311). Peter Lang. (Original work published 1993)

Sweeney, L. (2006). Ideas in practice: Theoretical bases for using movies in developmental coursework. *Journal of Developmental Education*, 29(3), 28–36.

Welles, O. (Director). (1941). *Citizen Kane* [Film]. RKO Radio Pictures; Mercury Productions.

Wilder, B. (Director). (1950). *Sunset blvd.* [Film]. Paramount Pictures.

NOTES ON CONTRIBUTORS

Jack D. Arrington is the science department chair for a school in the Augusta, Georgia area. He has taught at the same school for 24 years, where he has taught many sciences and currently teaches anatomy and IB chemistry. He holds a doctorate in Educational Leadership from Georgia Southern University and has also served as an instructional coach for the past three years. His research and writing interests include teacher preparation, teaching efficacy, reaching the unreachable, and the administrator's role in instruction.

Kathleen E. Barbara earned a doctoral degree in Curriculum Studies from Georgia Southern University. She has been a high school educator since 2012, teaching all levels of Spanish. Her primary interests are Spanish and cultural studies with an emphasis in curriculum development.

Stacey T. Brown is the Coordinator for the International Baccalaureate Diploma Programme for a school district near Augusta, Georgia, where she has been teaching high school English since 2002. She has a doctorate in Curriculum Studies from Georgia Southern University. Her research and writing focus on solitude and isolation of the individual, commodification, standardization, and monoculture in education, and the private-and-public intellectual.

John H. Cato holds a doctorate in Curriculum Studies from Georgia Southern University. He has been an educator since 1997, teaching mathematics and physics. His research interests include expertise, acquisition of knowledge, systems of logic, and identity. He has previously published "Mindset Matters" (*The Physics Teacher*, 2011) and contributed multiple chapters to *Field Theory: Curriculum Studies at Work* (DIO Press, 2019).

Mary K. Davis holds a doctorate in Curriculum Studies from Georgia Southern University. She has been an educator for eleven years teaching Cybersecurity. Her research interests include the emotional transitions of educators as they transition through different roles they hold, the identity of high school coaches, and the role of teacher leaders in the high school setting.

Thomas J. Davis is a high school English teacher and head baseball coach in Augusta, Georgia. He earned his doctorate in Curriculum Studies from Georgia Southern University. His research interests involve the concept of the student-athlete, the importance and role of athletics in school, and what the identity of being a student-athlete entails.

Kay R. Lilly is a Secondary Social Studies teacher for a school district near Augusta, Georgia, where she has been teaching since 2014. She obtained her doctorate in Educational Innovation from Augusta University in May of 2024. Her research and writing focus on Culturally Sustaining Pedagogy, Alternative Curriculum Models in Social Studies, and Educational Activism.

Dawn R. May is originally from Aurora, Colorado, where she attended Colorado State University. Since graduating college, she and her family have lived in Kansas, Germany, Pennsylvania, and Maryland. They eventually put down roots in Georgia, where she now teaches high school Spanish. She has three children, and is currently a doctoral candidate in Curriculum Studies at Georgia Southern University.

David P. Owen, Jr., teaches and writes in a variety of fields in Augusta, Georgia. He is a liminal scholar whose research interests include literature, popular music, cultural curriculum studies, film and television studies, Southern studies, complexity theory, aesthetics, technology, and philosophy. His works include *calling you home* (2021), *Field Theory: Curriculum Studies at Work* (DIO Press, 2019), *Fireflies: Memory, Identity, and Poetry* (Brill | Sense Publishers, 2017), *The Need for Revision: Curriculum, Literature, and the 21st Century* (Sense Publishers, 2011), *Once Out Loud* (2004), and *William Blake's "The Everlasting Gospel": A Hypertext Edition* (University of Georgia, 2001).

John A. Weaver is a professor of Curriculum Studies at Georgia Southern University. His most recent book is titled *Science, Democracy, and Curriculum Studies* (Springer, 2018), and his next book project will appear this coming year and is titled *Science, Democracy, and the University*.

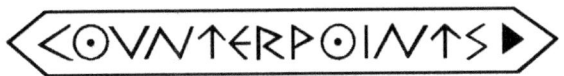

Studies in Criticality

Series Editor
Shirley R. Steinberg

Counterpoints publishes the most compelling and imaginative books being written in Education and Cultural Studies today. Grounded on the theoretical advances in critical theory, feminism, and postcolonialism in the last two decades of the twentieth century, Counterpoints engages the meaning of these innovations in various forms of educational expression. Committed to the proposition that theoretical literature should be accessible to a variety of audiences, the series insists that its authors avoid esoteric and jargonistic languages that transform educational scholarship into an elite discourse for the initiated. Scholarly work matters only to the degree it affects consciousness and practice at multiple sites. The editorial policy of *Counterpoints* is based on these principles and the ability of scholars to break new ground, to open new conversations, to go where educators have never gone before.

For additional information about this series or for the submission of manuscripts, please contact:

> Shirley R. Steinberg, Series Editor
> msgramsci@gmail.com

To order other books in this series, please contact our Customer Service Department:

> peterlang@presswarehouse.com (within the U.S.)
> orders@peterlang.com (outside the U.S.)

Or browse online by series:

> www.peterlang.com

www.ingramcontent.com/pod-product-compliance
Lightning Source LLC
Chambersburg PA
CBHW061710300426
44115CB00014B/2635